OCR

Media Studies

for GCSE

Series Editor: **Eileen Lewis**
Authors: Eileen Lewis, Michael Rodgers,
Rebecca Norris and James Goddard

DL DYNAMIC LEARNING

HODDER EDUCATION
AN HACHETTE UK COMPANY

The Publishers would like to thank the following for permission to reproduce copyright material:

Photo credits: Page 3: The Advertising Archives/Huntley & Palmer; Page 9 (top): Rex Features/David Fisher; Page 9 (centre left): Elle/Editions Internationales; Page 9 (centre right): Rex Features/Paramount/Everett; Page 9 (bottom): I'm Alan Partridge S2, 2002 © BBC; Page 12 (left): © DLT Entertainment UK Limited; Page 12 (right): Blackadder The Third 1987 © BBC; Page 13 (left): Rex Features/Lions Gate/Everett; Page 13 (right): Films of Record; Page 17, 18 and 19 (top): BBC Motion Gallery/Endeavour Productions Ltd.; Page 19 (bottom) and Page 20: Soul Purpose Productions; Page 23: Kobal Collection/Lucasfilm/20th Century Fox; Page 28 (left): Kobal Collection/Rico Torres/Dimension Films; Page 28 (right): Rex Features/Warner Bros/Everett; Page 29: Rex Features/Everett Collection; Page 30: Courtesy of Universal Studios Licensing LLLP; Page 33 (left): Top of the Pops logo 1999 © BBC; Page 33 (right): NME/IPC Syndication; Page 34 (all photos): MTV Networks Europe Inc./Viacom Networks Europe Inc.; Page 36 and 37: Stills taken from the Leftfield video "Afrika Shox" licensed courtesy of Hard Hands Limited and Sony Music Entertainment UK Limited; Page 40 (top): Alamy/David Keith Jones/Images of Africa Photobank; Page 40 (bottom): Corbis/Stephane Cardinale; Page 47: PA Images/Adam Butler; Page 48 and 49: News International Syndication; Page 50: Strictly Come Dancing, Series 6, Week 3, 2008 © BBC; Page 51 (left): News International Syndication; Page 51 (right top and bottom): Mirrorpix; Page 63 (top): Eastenders title logo/map, 1999 © BBC; Page 63 (middle images): ITV; Page 63 (bottom): Lime Pictures; Page 64 (left): Eastenders set, 2003 © BBC; Page 64 (right): ITV; Page 66: Lime Pictures; Page 69: Eastenders 2006 © BBC; Page 74: Allstar/Channel Four Films; Page 75: PA Images/Rebecca Naden; Page 77: PA Images/Sean Dempsey; Page 80 (left): PA Images/Empics Entertainment; Page 80 (middle): Rex Features; Page 80 (right): PA Images/Gavin Rodgers/AllAction.co.uk; Page 84 (top left): Strictly Come Dancing, Series 6, Week 3, 2008 © BBC; Page 84 (top right): Getty Images/Popperfoto; Page 84 (bottom left): PA Images; Page 84 (bottom right): News International Syndication; Page 86 (both images): Guardian News & Media Ltd.; Page 88: John Frost Newspapers; Page 89: Getty Images/Fox Photos/Hulton Archive; Page 90 (left): Daily Express/Northern & Shell Media Publications; Page 90 (right): News International Syndication; Page 91: Mirrorpix; Page 92: PA Images/AP/Alexander Chadwick; Page 93 (top): Janis Krums; Page 93 (bottom): News International Syndication; Page 96: The Advertising Archives; Page 97: Advert reproduced with the permission of Kellogg Company © Kellogg Company; Page 98: The Advertising Archives; Page 99 (top): The Advertising Archives; Page 99 (bottom): The Advertising Archives/Huntley & Palmer; Page 101: Barnardo's/Photographer: Nick Georghiou, Agent: Wyatt Clarke; Page 103 (left): Corbis/Christopher Farina; Page 103 (right): Rex Features/David Fisher; Page 106 and 107: © Capcom Co., Ltd. All Rights Reserved; Page 108: Eidos Interactive Limited; Page 110: Courtesy of Comedy Central; Page 114 (top left): Rex Features/Touchstone/Everett; Page 114 (top right): Elle/Editions Internationales; Page 114 (bottom left): Little Britain Series 1, 2003 © BBC; Page 114 (bottom right): Courtesy of Comedy Central; Page 116: Rex Features/Sony Pictures/Everett; Page 117: Rex Features/Everett Collection; Page 129: Rex Features/Warner Bros/Everett; Page 130: Allstar/20th Century Fox; Page 134: AKG-Images/Roadshow Film Ltd/Boland/Album; Page 146 and 147: The Conde Nast Publications Ltd.; Page 157–186: Good Housekeeping and Esquire images: © National Magazine Company, Bliss images: Panini UK Ltd; Page 188 (left): MTV Networks Europe Inc./Viacom Networks Europe Inc.; Page 188 (right): ITV; Page 190 (left): Avalon Television; Page 190 (right): Rex Features/KPA/Zuma; Page 202 (left): Rex Features/Richard Saker; Page 202 (right): PA Images/Yui Mok; Page 203: Rex Features/NBCUPhotobank; Page 216: Alamy/Ian Shaw; Page 217: Eileen Lewis; Page 222: DM Imaging/Last Resort; Page 226: Alamy/Lee Ruff; Page 228: Courtesy News Shopper; Page 230: Eileen Lewis; Page 231: Daily Express/Northern & Shell Media Publications; Page 234: Elle/Editions Internationales; Page 236: Rebecca Morris; Page 238: Eileen Lewis; Page 240: The Advertising Archives; Page 243 and 245: Eileen Lewis; Page 246, 247, 255, 256 and 262: Rebecca Morris; Page 264: Eileen Lewis; Page 278: Rebecca Morris.

Acknowledgements: Page 38: Afrika Shox, words and music by Neil Barnes, Paul Daley, Nicholas Rapaccioli and Afrika Bambaataa, © copyright 1999 Hard (UK) Hands Publishing, used by permission of Music Sales Ltd. All Rights Reserved. International Copyright Secured; Page 39: Hunting for Witches, words and music by Russell Lissack and Gordon Moakes and Kele Okerere and Matt Tong, © 2006, reproduced by permission of EMI Music Publishing Ltd, London W8 5SW; Page 55: Screenshot of BBC Radio 5 Live website, from www.bbc.co.uk/fivelive, reproduced by permission of BBC Commercial Agency, BBC Vision; Page 57: Screenshot of LBC News website, LBC 97.3, 2009-06-26, used by permission of BBC Commercial Agency, BBC Vision; Page 59: Website screenshot of BBC Radio 4, In Touch from www.bbc.co.uk/radio4/factual/intouch.shtml, reproduced by permission of BBC Commercial Agency, BBC Vision; Page 60 and 61: Screenshot of The Archers website from www.bbc.co./radio4/archers, reproduced by permission of BBC Commercial Agency, BBC Vision; Page 233: Take a Break magazine, reproduced by kind permission of H. Bauer Publishing; Page 235: Audience categories table (2000) from www.keynote.co.uk, reproduced by permission of Key Note; Page 275: Screenshot of the T4 website from www.channel4.com/t4, reproduced by permission of Channel 4.

Every effort has been made to trace all copyright holders, but if any have been inadvertently overlooked the Publishers will be pleased to make the necessary arrangements at the first opportunity.

Although every effort has been made to ensure that website addresses are correct at time of going to press, Hodder Education cannot be held responsible for the content of any website mentioned in this book. It is sometimes possible to find a relocated web page by typing in the address of the home page for a website in the URL window of your browser.

Hachette UK's policy is to use papers that are natural, renewable and recyclable products and made from wood grown in sustainable forests. The logging and manufacturing processes are expected to conform to the environmental regulations of the country of origin.

Orders: please contact Bookpoint Ltd, 130 Milton Park, Abingdon, Oxon OX14 4SB. Telephone: (44) 01235 827720. Fax: (44) 01235 400454. Lines are open 9.00–5.00, Monday to Saturday, with a 24-hour message answering service. Visit our website at www.hoddereducation.co.uk

© Lewis, Goddard, Rodgers, Morris 2009
First published in 2009 by
Hodder Education,
An Hachette UK Company
338 Euston Road
London NW1 3BH

Impression number	5 4 3
Year	2014 2013

Cover photo Magictorch/Photographer's Choice/Getty Images
Illustrations by Barking Dog
Typeset in Helvetica Neue 55 11/14pt by DC Graphic Design Ltd, Swanley Village, Kent.
Printed in Dubai

A catalogue record for this title is available from the British Library.

ISBN: 978 0340 98341 6

Contents

About the authors

Michael Rodgers teaches Film and Media and is Principal Examiner for OCR GCSE Media Studies. He lives in Wigan, home of the mighty Latics. He sings bass (the voice, not the fish) and shares an allotment.

Acknowledgements: I would like to thank my wife Patsi for her helpful comments and forbearance, my daughter Rachael for letting me monopolise the computer, Eileen our editor for her support and encouragement, and my dog Lola for lying at my feet and keeping me company.

Rebecca Morris is Joint Head of Media Studies at City and Islington Sixth Form College, London, and is an examiner for GCSE Media Studies.

Acknowledgements: City and Islington Sixth Form College, the Students' Union at City and Islington College, George Owen (otherwise I would have starved to death during the writing of my chapter!), Mary Berrisford, (for helping me out with some last minute definitions) and Tony Fahy (for letting me have some time off during term).

James Goddard teaches Media and Film at Maidstone Grammar School, has a degree in Film Studies and an active interest in the film industry and script writing.

Acknowledgements: A big thank you to my family and friends, especially Kate Tomes, who listened to my ideas frequently. I also thank my Head of Department and friend, Eileen Lewis, for all her help and support.

Eileen Lewis is Chief Examiner for OCR GCSE Media Studies and Head of Media and Film at Maidstone Grammar School. She is a freelance writer of several textbooks and resources for Media Studies.

Acknowledgements: I thank Nigel Rigby for his patience and good humour, my children and their partners for their encouragement and ideas and my students at Maidstone Grammar School for their enthusiasm and support. I also thank Steve Connolly, Laura Priest, and especially Cheryl Thomas at Hodder for managing to steer the project through.

Introduction to the course

This GCSE Media Studies course offers you a carefully planned balance between practical production and analytical, theoretical work. The exciting thing about this course is that not only do you get the opportunity to study media texts that you enjoy and find interesting, but you also get to work on two practical productions. Your practical work will help you to do well in the other parts of the course, as it will inform your knowledge and understanding of the media. Although the course asks you to cover three media areas as a whole, there is a huge amount of freedom in what you study.

Your texts can come from:

- television
- newspapers
- magazines
- video games
- advertising
- the internet
- radio
- cinema
- popular music.

For the Individual Media Portfolio, your teacher will have the opportunity to select media texts from a list of 10 engaging topics and to make choices about which medium you will work in for your practical production. For the Production Portfolio in Media Studies, you will work on a major practical production from a list of 12 set briefs. Your teacher will also select the two comedy programmes you will study in detail for your exam.

In your Media Studies course, you will learn about the key media concepts:

- media language
- genre
- representation
- audience
- institution.

You will learn new skills in the following:

- textual analysis
- practical production work – both creative and technical
- using media terminology
- recognising media techniques
- presentation
- research
- planning
- reflection.

You will produce:

- **The Individual Media Studies Portfolio. This includes:**
    - a comparative analytical assignment based on one of 10 topics
    - an accompanying production exercise (with plans/drafts)
    - an evaluation of the production exercise (written, or presented as a PowerPoint presentation, a DVD with extras, or a podcast).
- **The Production Portfolio in Media Studies. This includes:**
    - a major practical production (as an individual or in a group)
    - a production log
    - an evaluation (written, or presented as a PowerPoint presentation or a podcast).

These are both controlled assessment units. This means that most of the work will be undertaken under the supervision of your teacher. Your work will be marked by your teacher and then checked by an external moderator.

Choice of presentation

Your comparative assignment and your evaluation in the portfolio can be presented in a number of different ways – as a written essay, as a PowerPoint presentation or as a podcast. For the Production Portfolio there is also the option of producing a DVD with extras. Your teacher will choose the best format for you, and you may have the opportunity to try more than one method during the course.

How is the course weighted?

Each portfolio is worth 30% of your final GCSE grade. That means that 40% of your marks will come from the Textual Analysis and Media Topic exam.

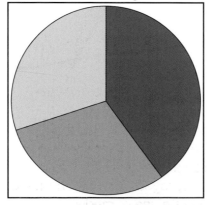

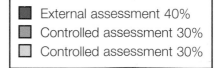

- External assessment 40%
- Controlled assessment 30%
- Controlled assessment 30%

▲ Figure 1: Your course is well balanced, with 60% of the marks awarded to your media portfolios and 40% awarded to your exam. Practical work is an important part of your portfolios, as is the ability to plan, research and evaluate.

■ Textual Analysis and Media Topic exam

There is only one exam on this course and it is split into two sections. Section A asks you to analyse an unseen action/adventure film or lifestyle magazine extract, while Section B (the Media Topic) asks you to write about institutions and audience pleasures in relation to two comedy programmes. However, the specifications may change so please remember to check the OCR website for the latest information: http://www.ocr.org.uk.

You will have picked these comedy programmes in advance and have studied them by investigating which channels they are shown on and how they appeal to their audiences. Your teacher will prepare you for the textual analysis section by asking you to watch a wide range of action/adventure films or to read a wide range of lifestyle magazines and by giving you practice in analysing them. You can see that the course can be fun, even when studying for the exam!

■ Textual analysis: denotation and connotation

Denotation means describing what you see or hear in a media text.

Connotation means working out the meanings associated with what you see or hear.

We would expect most people to be able to work out the denotation of an advertisement like this 19th century one for Huntley and Palmers biscuits.

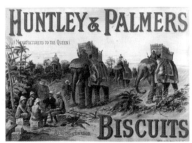

▲ *Figure 2: Huntley and Palmers biscuits*

As a media student, however, you will be able to recognise the connotations, or deeper meanings, of the advertisement and how it aims to appeal to its target audience. (See page 99 in Unit 1 for a full textual analysis of this advertisement.) This, together with an ability to recognise media techniques and the accurate use of media terminology, will gain you a top grade. There are plenty of examples of the differences between denotation and connotation later on in Unit 2.

■ Key concepts

All of your study of media will be based on the key media concepts. These underpin all media courses, from pre-GCSE level to postgraduate studies, and you will find them very useful in giving a framework to help develop your understanding and knowledge of the media.

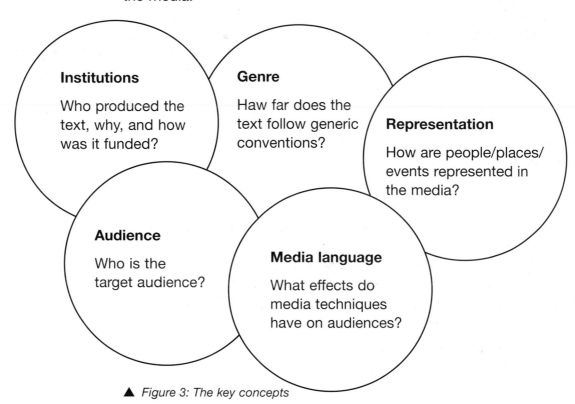

Institutions

Who produced the text, why, and how was it funded?

Genre

Haw far does the text follow generic conventions?

Representation

How are people/places/ events represented in the media?

Audience

Who is the target audience?

Media language

What effects do media techniques have on audiences?

▲ *Figure 3: The key concepts*

You will find that the concepts are all interlinked, but the course is structured so that you will focus on one or two concepts at any one time. There is a table at the end of this introduction that shows you exactly where your knowledge and understanding of each concept will be tested on the course.

■ Media language

This is a good starting point, as recognising media techniques and using the correct media terminology is a crucial part of getting a good mark in Media Studies. This concept centres on the ways that different techniques are used to create meanings for audiences. For example, camerawork is part of media language and conveys meaning to audiences just as much, if not more, than the words a character might use. The media techniques that you will focus on, particularly for the exam, are:

Moving image language
- Sound (all the elements that we hear, including music and sound effects)
- Camerawork (shots, movement, angles, framing)
- Editing (cuts, dissolves, fades, cross cutting)
- Mise-en-scène (lighting, props, costumes, sets/locations, make-up/hair, blocking or positioning of actors)

Print language
- Layout
- Typography (use of fonts and typefaces)
- Use of colour
- Use of photographs
- Mode of address (how the magazine/newspaper speaks to its target audience)
- Use of vocabulary; written style

For a full and detailed discussion of media language, please consult Unit 2 on textual analysis.

■ Genre

This is a term used for placing media texts in categories, or genres. It can be a useful tool for analysing media texts, as it helps us recognise that audiences have particular expectations of texts because of their generic conventions. These conventions are a set of elements that are repeated in texts of the same genre. For example, you would expect a sitcom to fit in with the following conventions:

- a comic drama about everyday life and relationships
- one main location (usually the home or the workplace)
- a small group of main characters
- a simple narrative that is easy to understand
- themes we can relate to, such as relationships, family, aspirations
- conventional camerawork
- continuity editing.

You can see that generic conventions include elements of narrative and style. These conventions do not always stay the same, however — there are likely to be some shifts over time. *The Office* challenges the conventions of the sitcom, for example, by not including a laughter track and by using a 'docusoap' style. Yet it can still be placed in the sitcom genre, because it does use many of the sitcom conventions.

Your work on genre will also involve looking at subgenres (a further category into which we can place texts) and hybrid genres (mixes of different genres within one text).

The term genre is used slightly differently depending on the medium you are studying, whether it be film, magazines, comedy shows, or television or radio programmes. There is detailed discussion of the term and how it relates to action/adventure films and lifestyle magazines in Unit 2, and further analysis of generic conventions in family drama films can be found in Unit 1.

You will need to have a clear idea of generic conventions before you embark on either of your practical productions, as you will be assessed partly on how well your productions fit the genre you have chosen. Once you settle into the course, you will also quickly realise that generic conventions have a significant effect on the next concept, representation.

Questions to ask about genre:
- How easily can a media text be placed in a particular category?
- How far does the text follow the codes and conventions of a particular genre?

■ Representation

You will find this concept area discussed in detail in each unit of this book. It is a part of every one of the units you will study: it is the main focus of your Individual Media Studies Portfolio, there will be a question on it in the textual analysis exam, and you will need to consider it when working on your major practical production.

The concept of representation is concerned with messages and values in media texts. You will explore how the media reflects or represents attitudes, behaviour and beliefs and how these are linked to the society we live in. You will also consider how representations vary as social attitudes change through time, or according to our cultural backgrounds.

It is helpful to think of the concept as representations of reality – how certain people/places/events/issues are mediated and presented to us by the media. We usually explore representations in the media by looking at social groups; for example, Ian Beale in *EastEnders* can be seen not just as an interesting characterisation, but also as a representative of all working-class people who have aspirations to become successful businessmen and attain material wealth (see page 69 in Unit 1 for a detailed analysis of his representation).

A study of representation is also concerned with who is excluded or included in media texts; for example, it is still (surprisingly) unusual to see black actors in the majority of television advertisements. Why do you think this is so?

You can choose to study any area of representation, although the most common ones are gender, cultural difference, nationality and age. To help you decide what to focus on, you will find detailed discussion on the following areas of representation in Unit 1:

- gender/masculinity
- old age/youth/childhood
- cultural difference/race
- social class
- national identity/Britishness
- disability
- villainy/morality
- the environment.

Questions to ask about representation:

- Who is included/excluded from the text?
- How are people/places/events represented?
- How and why do representations change according to social, cultural and historical contexts?

■ Audience

Media texts need audiences. This is the particular focus of your study for Section B of the exam on television and radio comedy. You will be looking at when and why certain programmes are scheduled on particular channels and the institutions that selected them. You will also investigate audience pleasures, such as why sitcoms like *My Family* gain higher audience ratings than *The Mighty Boosh*, for example.

Remember that there is not one single audience. This is even more obviously the case today with the fragmentation of audiences through digital broadcasting, use of iPods, mobile phones and other advances in technology. You will explore the different kinds of audiences that media producers try to appeal to and how they put those audiences into categories. For example, advertisers are increasingly reluctant to spend money on expensive advertising slots on ITV as they can no longer guarantee reaching the audiences they want.

Questions to ask about audience:

- Who is the target audience?
- How do audiences respond to and make use of the text?
- How and where is the text consumed?
- What are the audience's expectations and pleasures?

■ Institutions

The institution that produces the text will affect the meaning of the text for audiences. For example, audiences had different expectations of the 1983 James Bond film *Never Say Never Again* even though it starred Sean Connery, because it was not made by the Bond franchise EON. The 'official' Bond film *Octopussy*, which starred Roger Moore in his sixth Bond role, was released in the same year and did better at the box office.

Institutions will also affect the way that texts are constructed. Think of the way that test audiences are used by the big US studios in order to ensure box office success and how often directors are forced to change the endings of their films because the audiences did not like them.

New technology has had a significant effect on all institutions, especially British broadcasters. For Section B of the exam you will look at the background to the institutions that broadcast your two comedies and explore why they chose to do so. You will also investigate when and why they are scheduled on certain channels at particular times.

Institutions and audiences are closely linked, and many media organisations are driven by problems caused by falling audience figures. This helps to explain the increased use of celebrity stories in British magazines and newspapers and on broadcasting and internet sites.

Questions to ask about institutions:

- How was the text produced, by whom and for what purpose?
- When and where was the text produced and broadcast/ consumed?
- How was the text funded?

■ Where are the key concepts tested?

This is a handy guide for you to see at a glance where each key concept is being tested in the course. It is worth looking at this from time to time to remind yourself what exactly is being tested in each unit.

Concept	Unit	Title
Media Language Representation	Unit 1	Individual Media Studies Portfolio ■ Comparative assignment based on a topic ■ Practical exercise ■ Evaluation ▲ *Figure 4:* Call of Duty
Media Language Genre Audiences Institutions	Unit 3	Production Portfolio in Media Studies ■ Major practical production ■ Evidence of research and planning ■ Evaluation ▲ *Figure 5: Students at work on their production portfolio*
Media Language Genre Representation	Unit 2 Section A	Textual Analysis and Media Topic exam ■ Action/adventure films or lifestyle magazines ▲ *Figure 6: Example of a lifestyle magazine and an action/adventure film*
Audience Institutions	Unit 2 Section B	Textual Analysis and Media Topic exam ■ TV and/or radio comedy ▶ *Figure 7:* Alan Partridge

This book has been designed to help you learn new skills and concepts, explore a range of media texts in depth and get the most out of a very enjoyable course. And, finally, it will also help you to get the best possible result in your Media Studies GCSE!

Unit 1
The Individual Media Studies Portfolio

Introduction to Unit 1

You will probably tackle this unit fairly early on in your GCSE course. It is a good place to start, because it gives you the opportunity to learn about a media topic in depth, and then demonstrate your understanding through a practical production exercise. This unit will also help you to consider what kind of major practical production you want to work on later on in the course.

In this controlled assessment unit you will learn about:
- media language
- media techniques
- issues of representation (see page 6 for a detailed explanation of the concepts)
- a media topic, such as celebrity or popular music.

You will produce:
- a comparative analytical assignment based on one of ten topics
- an accompanying production exercise (with plans/ drafts)
- an evaluation of the production exercise (written, or presented as a PowerPoint or a podcast).

■ How is the unit assessed?
This unit is worth 30% of your final GCSE grade. Your work will be marked by your teacher according to the following weighting:
- Comparative analytical assignment: 60 marks
- Production exercise: 40 marks
- Evaluation: 20 marks.

The comparative assignment

The comparative assignment can be submitted as:
- a written essay (around 1000–1500 words long)
- a PowerPoint presentation (around 15–25 slides)
- a podcast (around 3–5 minutes long).

What topics are available?

The ten topics you can choose from are listed below. Your teacher may choose the topic for you, or you may negotiate over which topic to study. You may study more than one topic. It is important to remember that you cannot choose action/adventure films, as many of you will be studying these for the Unseen Moving Image Textual Analysis exam.

- Topic 1: Documentaries
- Topic 2: Film Genres (not action/adventure)
- Topic 3: Popular Music
- Topic 4: Celebrity
- Topic 5: Talk Radio
- Topic 6: Soap Opera
- Topic 7: Sport and the Media
- Topic 8: News
- Topic 9: Advertising
- Topic 10: Video Games

What areas of representation should I look at?

Again, this will depend very much on your teacher, but there is some room for negotiation in this unit. If your teacher has chosen to explore the representation of cultural difference in three documentaries, but you are keen to write on representations of gender, let your teacher know. It is best to focus on one area of representation, but you might find a topic where you could explore two areas, such as gender and class, successfully.

Below are some suggestions of interesting areas of representation that you might explore in this unit:
- masculinity
- age – over 60s and under 12s
- cultural difference
- villainy
- social class
- Britishness
- disability
- royalty
- the environment.

All of these areas (and more) are discussed in detailed case studies in the following pages.

■ Stereotypes

In order to explore different representations, you need to understand the term stereotype. A stereotype can be defined as a simplistic, fixed portrayal of a person, place, issue or event. They are often used as quick ways to establish character in media texts such as television comedy.

▲ *Figure 1.1: We quickly recognize that Nick in* My Family *and Baldric in* Blackadder *are based on the stereotype of the fool or 'buffoon'*

Let's discuss

■ Discuss how the following groups are often represented. Find two adjectives to describe the stereotypical representations of each of these groups in the media.

Group	Stereotype
Royalty	Out of touch, arrogant
People in their 80s	Slow, feeble
Goths	
11—12-year-old boys	
British tennis players	

■ Now identify the media texts where you are most likely to see this kind of stereotyping.
■ Why do you think this is so?

You will find detailed discussion on all of the topics in the following pages. There are also specific case studies exploring all the areas of representation listed above, with plenty of ideas on how to tackle your comparative assignment and your practical exercise.

Topic 1: Documentaries

■ What are documentaries?

Documentaries can be defined as film, radio or television programmes that are based on real people, events, or places, and are intended to record or inform.

■ Messages and values

We expect documentaries to be have some basis in 'truth', but very few actually set out to be entirely objective. By his own admission, Michael Moore set out to make a hard-hitting political documentary that attacked the Bush administration in *Fahrenheit 9/11* (see table on page 16). You could study Moore's documentary in order to analyse the techniques he uses to put his messages across. Even when documentary makers do use techniques to try to be as objective as possible, their values will inevitably affect the subject matter.

▲ *Figure 1.2: Michael Moore's political* Fahrenheit 9/11 *and Roger Graef's observational* September Mourning *are two very different types of documentary*

■ How close to 'real' can we get?

A good definition of a documentary is: 'the creative treatment of actuality' (John Grierson, 1933). The subject matter of documentaries is always going to be interpreted in a creative way by both the documentary makers and the audience. This helps us to remember that the 'truth' is a partial one, being offered from a particular point of view.

■ Points of view

Below are some useful questions to ask when analysing documentaries:

- Why has the material been selected?
- What has been left out?
- How has the documentary been ordered?

- What effect does the ordering of the events have on the representation of the subject matter?
- How are diegetic and non-diegetic sound used?
- Does the sound anchor the visual footage (pin it down with a particular interpretation) or does it contradict the visuals?
- How is lighting used? Does it encourage the audience to identify with or feel alienated from the subjects of the documentary?
- What techniques are used in the camerawork?
- Is it useful to consider the people appearing in the documentary as 'characters' who have been 'cast' by the documentary makers?
- Can you identify a 'point of view' in the documentary?

Documentary timeline

1896:	Audiences panic when watching *The arrival of a train at La Ciotat*; the Lumière Brothers refer to their films as 'documentaries'.
1899:	Méliès uses historical reconstructions in *The Dreyfus Affair*.
1922:	Robert Flaherty uses dramatised reconstructions in *Nanook of the North*, an account of a year in the life of the Inuit Eskimo.
1930s:	British documentary film movement developed by John Grierson.
1966:	*Cathy Come Home* – Ken Loach's use of ciné-vérité helps this drama documentary about a homeless family change social attitudes.
1980s–90s:	Development of video cameras leads to video diaries and 'reality TV'.
1982:	*Police* - Roger Graef's 'fly on the wall' series leads to improvements in police procedure.
2003:	Michael Moore wins an Oscar for *Bowling for Columbine*.

■ Documentary techniques

Documentaries may contain some or all of these techniques:

- voice-overs
- ciné-vérité footage
- eyewitness accounts
- interviews
- archive footage
- undercover filming
- dramatised reconstructions.

■ Categories of documentary

Documentaries can be divided into a wide range of categories or forms, including reality TV. This is partly why documentaries are often controversial, as there are so many different ways of telling the stories of 'real' people, places and events.

Documentary form	Techniques	Example
Expository	Interprets events for the audience, often using a presenter, voice-over, eye-witnesses, archive footage, 'experts' and sometimes reconstructions. This form is often referred to as a 'voice of God' documentary because of its clearly explained messages.	Simon Schama's *History of Britain* (BBC, 2000–2002)
Ciné-vérité	Attempts to give the audience a more intimate relationship with the subject matter, using hand-held cameras, 'natural' sound and lighting, and minimal editing. This suggests audiences are almost participating in the action and gaining access to private thoughts and perspectives. At times, the documentary maker will intervene in the action themselves.	Pennebaker's *Don't Look Back* (1967); Nick Broomfield's *Biggie and Tupac* (2002); Watson's *The Family* (1974); Smith's *The Family* (2008) and Dineen's *Geri* (1999)
Observational	Uses the techniques of Direct Cinema, aiming for a sense of objectivity. The documentary maker remains 'invisible', observing but not interfering with the action.	Roger Graef's *September Mourning* (ITV, 2002)
Reflexive	Draws attention to the process of constructing the documentary, refusing to offer a clear interpretation by offering a number of contradictory viewpoints instead.	Morris' *The Thin Blue Line* (1988, US)
Reality TV/docusoap	Uses ciné-vérité, but often places it within the structure of an overtly critical voice-over, interpreting the subjects' actions for the audience.	Flitcroft's *Boys Alone* (2004) and *Boys and Girls Alone* (Channel 4, 2009)
Video diary	Gives apparent control to individuals, who use direct address to the camera to construct a first-person narrative. However, footage may be edited.	*VideoNation* (BBC, 2000–present)
Undercover documentary	Has the explicit aim of exposing injustices or corruption.	*The Secret Policeman* (BBC, 2003)
Documentary drama	Mixes fact and fiction through dramatic reconstructions. This category causes the most debate, usually around issues of authenticity.	*Hillsborough* (ITV, 1996)

■ Narratives in disguise

Documentaries rarely stick rigidly to these categories, but tend to be a mixture of different documentary forms. Nevertheless, all offer a version of events and are forms of storytelling.

Let's compare

You will need to compare two or three documentaries. If you find it difficult to write a side-by-side comparison, analyse one documentary first, then mention the first one regularly as you analyse the second, arguing that it is similar or different in the directors' use of techniques and intentions.

A useful way to plan a side-by-side comparison of representations and techniques in two documentaries is to draw up a table like the one below:

Fahrenheit 9/11 (Moore, 2004)	*September Mourning* (Graef, 2002)
Produced for cinema by Miramax. Widely distributed.	Produced by small independent company Films of Record and screened on ITV1.
A political campaigning documentary with a clear message.	'An intimate portrait' of the victims of 9/11 and their families.
'Voice of God': Moore explicitly attacks the Bush administration.	Observational form: follows the families over six months, rather than actively constructing events.
Hard-hitting polemic: Moore drives his point home in every sequence.	Personal tragedy: Graef allows the subjects to speak for themselves.
Self-reflexive: Moore often appears in the documentary and is a major player.	The interviewer and crew are 'invisible' and self-effacing.
Camerawork mixes ciné-vérité style with archive footage, animation, sequences from the 60s cowboy series *Bonanza*, maps and graphs.	Camera mostly hand-held with ciné-vérité style, focusing on the subjects.
Editing keeps audience watching; many very short sequences using a variety of visual material. Juxtapositions: sequences placed next to each other to reinforce Moore's viewpoint.	Documentary moves at a slower pace, giving the subjects time to express themselves. Sequences structured through repeated long shots of the two towers of the World Trade Center before the 9/11 attacks.
Soundtrack includes non-diegetic sound FX and music from a wide range of genres, used to reinforce, mock or contradict the visual material.	Only diegetic sound used in order to keep the audience focused on the victims and the ways their families have dealt with their grief.
Imposes Moore's view on the subject matter.	Producers aim to record their subjects' views without influencing them.

Resources:

Bruce Parry's *Tribe – Journey to the clouds: Bhutan* (BBC2, 2007)

Ray Mears' *Bushcraft – Jungle Craft* (BBC, 2004)

Exemplar task: Compare the codes and conventions of two documentaries, analysing how the documentary makers use techniques to construct representations of other cultures.

Tribe is an interesting documentary series to study, as there is an underlying tension between Bruce Parry's intentions and the ways in which audiences are likely to interpret the subject matter. Accompanying the title sequence (a montage of ten shots from the episode to follow), Parry states in a voice-over: 'I believe there's only one way to really understand another culture and that's to experience it first hand – to become ... one of the tribe'. Parry and his film crew spend one month with each community they visit, exploring their way of life and the threats facing each group.

Yet despite his intention to focus on the tribal group, the main narrative centres on how well Parry can fit into the group's way of life. He is prepared to take drugs, eat bizarre foods and take part in strange rituals in order to immerse himself completely in the culture. As the audience is strongly encouraged to identify with Parry through the techniques of camerawork, editing and sound, they experience the culture through his eyes.

The audience is further encouraged to identify with Parry through his use of direct address to the audience. In the episode pictured in Figure 1.3, he travels to a remote Himalayan village in the kingdom of Bhutan to stay with the Layap

▲ Figure 1.3: Bruce Parry shares a cuppa made with yak's milk with his Layap host, Kencho

people, devout Buddhists and yak herders whose village is cut off from the rest of the world by deep snow for six months of the year. Close-up shots of Parry increase the audience's sympathy for him as he explains just how difficult the journey will be: 'four days' hard trekking'; 'It's touch and go whether I'm even going to make it'; 'higher than I've ever been in my life'. This sets up one of the main narrative threads: the personal challenge that Parry himself is facing and his determination to overcome seemingly impossible obstacles. Although it is not his explicit intention, the focus on Parry's quest deflects the audience's interest away from the cultural group that Parry is investigating.

Parry's sense of humour and willingness to take part in any aspect of the villagers' lives is endearing. In this episode the hand-held camera close-up shots of Parry wrestling with a yak in order to help the villagers feed it with salt increases the audience's sense of concern for Parry, as do the sub-titles translating the villagers' comments: 'He must hold it or it'll gore him!'

Despite this focus on Parry's survival and the audience's concerns for his safety, the documentary succeeds in representing the villagers in as positive a light as possible. As Parry drinks a potion made from yaks' butter, caterpillars and whisky, the villagers' hospitality is reinforced through the warm, red glow from the fire which is then juxtaposed with a misty, cold blue long shot of the mountains outside.

Parry has more screen time than any of the members of the tribe, although he mostly ensures that he is not framed centrally, but at the side. It could be argued that he works hard not to use or exploit the stunning scenery as a backdrop for his own adventures, but tries to allow the audience space to reflect on the villagers' customs and Buddhist beliefs.

▲ Figure 1.4: Bruce Parry is framed to the side of the stunning Himalayan mountains in Tribe

Parry acts as mediator for the audience, whether explaining how the women of Bhutan can marry more than one man at a time, or trying to develop an understanding of the principles of Buddhism and reincarnation. He uses the discussion of the Buddhist approach to suffering and desire as a central theme in this episode. Parry's interpretation helps the

audience to find a way into understanding the villagers in this remote part of the world. It also helps Parry to link the stages of his documentary together, forming a structuring device.

▲ Figure: 1.5: The Buddhist priest that Parry consults during his stay in Laya

When Parry's attempt to trek to the even more remote village of Lunana fails, he struggles with his sense of failure, but skilfully manages to link his thwarted ambitions to his understanding of Buddhism in a direct address to camera. The camera works in sympathy with Parry's disappointment; it pans across the landscape, slightly out of focus from the fading light to symbolise the fading of hope. The non-diegetic music suits the mood and acts as a lament, reinforcing Parry's struggle over giving up his ambitions. This sequence finishes with a point-of-view long shot of a disappointed Parry watching the yaks stubbornly standing still and refusing to go any further at the foot of the pass.

One of the ways in which this series compares with Ray Mears' *Bushcraft Survival* series is that Parry's stated aim is to develop knowledge and understanding of the people he visits, while Ray Mears focuses on teaching survival skills and how best to learn more skills from different cultural groups.

Tribe explores interaction between different cultures, while Ray Mears explores 'the art of living outdoors': how we can use plants, trees and natural materials to survive in the jungle, desert or wilderness. This difference in aims clearly has a big impact on the differing representations of the cultural groups visited in the two series.

▲ *Figure 1.6: Bruce Parry with his Layap hosts in the kingdom of Bhutan*

Let's compare

Using this case study as a model, compare it with one or two of the following:

Ray Mears' *Bushcraft Survival* (BBC, 2005)
Michael Palin's *Himalaya* (BBC, 2004)
Ewan McGregor and Charlie Boorman's *Long Way Down* (BBC2, 2007)
Billy Connolly's *Journey to the Edge of the World* (ITV, 2009)

■ How do the representations of the presenters differ?
■ How do the representations of the cultural groups they visit differ?
■ What are the key messages of the programmes?

Case study 2 – Representations of children and gender

Resources:
Boys Alone (Channel 4, 2002)
Girls Alone (Channel 4, 2003)
Boys and Girls Alone (Channel 4, 2009)

Boys Alone (Channel 4, 2002) was described by some critics as 'an interesting social experiment', but by others as 'trash TV'. A *Lord of the Flies* style experiment placed ten 11-year-old boys in a suburban house for a week, apparently without adult supervision. This resulted in conflict and destruction. This documentary generated a great deal of debate as it feeds into a widely held stereotype of young males as uncontrolled and aggressive without adult supervision.

▶ *Figure 1.7: Still from the Boys Alone series*

The Individual Media Studies Portfolio

UNIT 1

▲ *Figure 1.8: Michael and Sim from the* Boys Alone *series*

The documentary is constructed in an observational style to a degree, but this is quickly counteracted by a dominant male voice-over that makes the destruction seem inevitable. The idea of the programme as a social experiment that objectively examines the behaviour of a group of young males can be easily challenged by analysing the technical elements of the documentary.

The casting, or selection, of the boys to take part was obviously a very important reason for the 'success' of the experiment – the boys had very different backgrounds and experiences of independence or of being away from their homes. Michael was quickly marked out as 'difficult': there are a number of shots of Michael smashing some cameras, spreading popcorn on the floor and shouting in order to lose his voice. The editing only includes those sequences that represent Michael as the cause of chaos; he is never represented in any other way.

Other boys are given roles through the camerawork, editing and voice-over, just as though the programme is a drama. Sim is the 'loner' character, with the camera often focusing on him alone in a wide shot or slowly zooming in towards him. This

represents him as him as physically and emotionally alone. George is represented as a good, supportive character in the way that he is often shown trying to establish harmony or to help Michael.

The voice-over gives clear explanations of the boys' behaviour and reinforces these 'roles'. The sub-titles and captions also help to anchor the intended meanings or 'preferred readings' of the boys' behaviour and encourage the audience to agree with them.

The ciné-vérité camerawork encourages the audience to forget that a crew is present, following the boys around the house. Yet at one point it is stated by the voice-over that the crew has had to intervene in order to stop the boys from harming hedgehogs. A psychologist is filmed discussing the boys' behaviour with them halfway through the programme.

You would find it interesting to compare *Boys Alone* with *Girls Alone* as Channel 4 clearly intended the audience to make comparisons between the boys' and girls' behaviour. While the boys caused damage through water fights and graffiti, the representation of the girls constructed them as conforming to stereotypes. They criticised others in the group behind their backs, cried, but also comforted each other.

The more recent four-part series *Boys and Girls Alone* (Channel 4, 2009) follows two separate groups of boys and girls aged 8–11, who are left without adult supervision in isolated cottages in Cornwall. The series has again created debate, with the charity Bullying UK labelling it as 'a peep show using children as victims'.

Let's research

- *This is Spinal Tap* (Reiner, 1984, US) is one of the first spoof documentaries or rockumentaries (sometimes referred to as a mockumentary). Study the film, identifying the different techniques and forms of documentary used by Reiner to create humour.
- *Don't Look Back* (Pennebaker, 1967, US) is one of the first film documentaries to use ciné-vérité. Pennebaker worked on the film as a one-man crew. Compare this film to an expository TV documentary like Simon Schama's *History of Britain* (BBC, 2000–2002). Do you think that Pennebaker gets closer to his subject matter?
- Analyse and compare two investigative documentaries such as John Sweeney's *Panorama* investigation into Scientology (BBC, 2007) and *The Secret Policeman* (BBC, 2003).
- Try comparing Michael Moore's *Fahrenheit 9/11* (2004, US) with the Naudet Brothers' *9/11* (2002, US). The Naudet Brothers were caught up in the attack on the World Trade Center and their ciné-vérité sequences are very interesting to analyse.
- Paul Watson's series *The Family* (BBC, 1974) is often referred to as the first 'reality TV' show. The series was revived by Channel 4 in 2008, following the Hughes family. Compare the two series, analysing how far the programme makers use similar techniques.

Let's produce

The production exercise has to show the teacher and moderator that you have a good knowledge and understanding of representations in documentaries. Remember that you need to cover at least two media in this unit as a whole. So if you have chosen to study TV documentaries for your comparative assignment, then you need to work in a different medium such as print, radio or film for your production exercise.

Here are some suggestions for different exercises:
- the title sequence for a new TV documentary series aimed at 15–21 year olds
- the opening sequence of a TV documentary investigating healthy eating in schools
- a storyboard for the first minute of a Michael Moore-style documentary
- a radio script for the first two minutes of a documentary on an important issue that you think is relevant today.

Let's evaluate

Your evaluation can be in the form of a written essay, a podcast, or a PowerPoint presentation. Remember to answer these questions in your evaluation:

■ What area of representation (such as gender, cultural difference or age) did you choose to focus on in your documentary?
■ What messages were you trying to convey?
■ How did you plan and research for your documentary?
■ How did you use media techniques, such as casting, framing, sound, voice-overs and direct address to challenge or reinforce messages and values?
■ What are the strengths and weaknesses of your finished exercise?

Key terms

Ciné-vérité: hand-held footage with minimal editing – aims to get closer to the 'real'
Diegetic sound and music: part of the ambient sound and dialogue when the documentary footage was shot
Juxtaposition: sequences placed next to each other to create an effect and/or reinforce a particular point of view
Non-diegetic sound: not part of the sound when the footage was originally shot
'Voice of God': usually uses a voice-over, interpreting the subject matter for the audience

■ Useful websites

http://www.screenonline.org.uk/film/id/446186: excellent site on the history of documentaries
www.britishpathe.com: *Pathé* news website with many clips of archive newsreel footage
www.mediaguardian.co.uk: website of *Guardian* newspaper with many useful articles on documentaries
www.channel4.com/health/the-family: web pages accompanying the Channel 4 documentary series or 'docusoap' *The Family*

Topic 2: Film Genres

◼ What is genre?

The word genre comes from the French and means 'type'. It is a term used in film analysis for the purpose of grouping certain films together in a series of categories.

Some of the main genres of film are:

- horror
- action/adventure
- romance
- comedy
- musical
- science fiction
- thriller.

◼ Generic conventions

In order for a film to be categorised into a particular genre, it must share similar features with other films of that genre. These features can be defined as generic conventions, giving us a method of identifying which genre a film belongs to.

Generic conventions can fall into a number of categories. The most common of these are:

- visual conventions – those we see on the screen
- audio conventions – those we hear as part of the soundtrack
- thematic conventions – the themes we identify in the film's narrative.

Star Wars: A New Hope (Lucas, 1977, US)

Star Wars Episode IV is considered to be a part of the science fiction genre: a genre that incorporates aspects of fictitious or hypothetical science or technology.

During the opening sequence of this film we see a spaceship under attack from a much larger spaceship. We then see the smaller ship invaded by vast numbers of Stormtroopers. A fight breaks out between the two sides and the human troops are forced to retreat as the main villain, Darth Vader, boards the ship. We then see Princess Leia putting a message into a droid called R2D2. After this, Princess Leia is stunned by the Stormtroopers.

▲ *Figure 1.9:* Star Wars

In this sequence we can see a number of conventions that instantly identify the genre:

- the spaceships
- the droids
- the advanced weapons
- the future setting
- the outer space setting
- the stormtroopers
- the sounds of the gun fire
- the codes of dress.

Let's analyse

Look at a sequence from any film and see if you can identify a series of generic conventions in order to place the film in a specific genre.

Film genres timeline

Certain film genres can often be extremely successful at a particular time in history. Currently, we are seeing a huge increase in comic book adaptations, a subgenre of the action/adventure genre.

Look at the following dates:

1978: *Superman* (Donner, US)
1989: *Batman* (Burton, US)
1992: *Batman Returns* (Burton, US)
2000: *X-men* (Singer, US)
2002: *Spider-man* (Raimi, US)
2003: *X-men 2* (Singer, US)
2003: *Daredevil* (Johnson, US)
2003: *Hulk* (Ang Lee, US)
2004: *Hellboy* (Del Toro, US)

- Continue this timeline to bring it up to date. You should be able to identify the growing popularity of this genre.
- Select another genre and look at key films and their release dates to see if you can identify their moment of greatest popularity.

Subgenres and hybrid genres

After working out the genre of a film we can then classify it further through identifying a subgenre: this is another category within an overall genre.

This allows us to pinpoint the exact coding of a particular film, rather than only relying on an overall category.

For example, we can brand a film as being a part of the comedy genre, but to help us further we can subdivide this genre, looking for more specific conventions in each one of the subgenres.

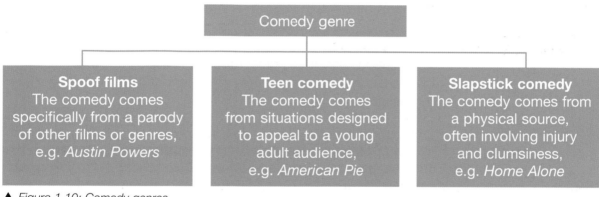

▲ *Figure 1.10: Comedy genres*

As well as subgenres we can also identify a film by referring to hybrid genres. This is where a film combines the generic conventions of more than one genre to create a new genre.

For example, one of the most common hybrid genres is the romantic comedy:

▲ *Figure 1.11: The rom–com genre*

So when we analyse a film such as *Shaun of the Dead* (Wright, 2004, UK) which incorporates zombie horror, comedy and romance, we can analyse why the film was marketed as a Rom-Zom-Com or romantic-zombie-comedy.

Let's discuss

- Is genre always easy to define?
- In both the horror genre and the comedy genre, part of the definition relies upon a certain level of audience response – a horror film should horrify and a comedy film should make us laugh.
- Does this fact change our ideas about how reliable genre is as a form of analysis?

 Representations in film genres

Different genres work in different ways, featuring different storylines and different themes. Therefore it is common for certain genres to represent different people/events/issues in similar ways depending on their generic coding. In this topic your task is to analyse the representations and ideological messages (ideas and values) within certain generic boundaries and explore the differences and/or similarities.

Case study 1 – The representation of childhood in the family drama genre

Resource: *Spirited Away* (Hayao Miyazaki, 2001, Japan)

Exemplar task: Examine the representation of childhood in two films, exploring the ideological messages which surround childhood development.

Spirited Away follows the story of Chihiro, a young girl who finds herself trapped in a spirit world after her parents are transformed into pigs by magic. During her time in this spirit world, Chihiro begins to develop and mature in her behaviour, holding down a job, helping other people, and finally rescuing her parents.

The film begins with Chihiro and her parents travelling to a new home, with her mother and father taking the front seats of the car whilst Chihiro occupies the back seat with a number of boxes and bags. The mise-en-

scène of this sequence instantly signifies Chihiro's insignificance in the family; she appears tiny in this location, dwarfed by the car seat and the props found in the car. Her parents remain facing forward throughout the sequence, never turning back to address Chihiro and in many instances Chihiro has to pull herself forward in order to address her parents directly.

The dialogue in this sequence also reinforces Chihiro's negative representation; she spends most of this sequence complaining about her situation, about the fact she has to move schools, and the fact that the only flowers she has ever received are those for a goodbye bouquet. Thus, Chihiro is represented as being a rather spoilt child, frail and insignificant, with no solid place within the family.

Later in the film Chihiro begins to develop as a character; after she gets a job at the bathhouse she begins to mature. One scene where this is particularly evident is where Chihiro must clean a stink spirit which enters the bathhouse. All other characters retreat from the spirit clutching their noses, whilst Chihiro manages to keep her composure. She clearly wants to recoil from the smell and yet in order to not offend the guest she remains strong. She is forced to wade through sludge in order to apply a herbal soak for the spirit, and yet still she keeps working. This helps to construct a strong representation of Chihiro; she is shown to be dedicated and dutiful.

During the cleaning process, Chihiro falls into the water and finds a 'thorn' sticking out of the stink spirit. At this, the whole bathhouse gets involved and pulls the 'thorn' out of the spirit. As the 'thorn' is removed it is revealed to be a bike handle and attached to this is a large amount of rubbish. It is at this point the stink spirit is revealed to be a river spirit which had become polluted with the rubbish thrown into the river in the real world. It is through Chihiro's strength of character and devotion to her job that she is able to rescue the river spirit.

If you compare the two scenes with each other, it is clear that Chihiro's representation changes within the film, as certain events cause Chihiro to transform into a more likeable character. Therefore, there is an ideological message in the film that children should be given freedom and responsibility in order to mature and develop.

Let's research

Spirited Away is also an interesting film because of its representation of Japanese culture. The film draws upon aspects of Shinto, a Japanese religion.
- Carry out some research into Shinto in order to understand what it involves and explore which aspects of the religion are portrayed in the film.
- Explore how aspects of Japanese culture are represented in the film, reflecting on what we can learn from a film text about different cultures and communities.

Other films in the family drama genre that represent childhood are:

- *Finding Nemo* (Stanton, 2003, US) – Nemo is taken away from his father who goes on a journey to rescue him, but Nemo is certainly not represented as helpless.
- *Spy Kids* (Rodriguez, 2001, US) – the children are represented as extremely strong and go off to rescue their parents, a couple of spies, from an evil TV presenter.

The Individual Media Studies Portfolio

UNIT 1

■ *Pan's Labyrinth* (Del Toro, 2006, Mexico/Spain) – whilst this is a more adult fairy tale, the representation of Ofelia throughout the film is fascinating, as she is both hero and victim and uses a fantasy world in order to escape the brutality of reality.

▲ *Figure 1.12:* Spy Kids

▲ *Figure 1.13:* Pan's Labyrinth

Case study 2 – The representation of masculinity in the western genre

Resource: *Stagecoach* (Ford, 1939, US)

Exemplar task: Explore the representations of masculinity in two films from the western genre, examining the connection to the hero role.

Stagecoach is one of the early examples of a western; it follows the story of a small group of characters who are travelling to the nearby town of Lordsburg. However, this trip is made more complicated by an Indian called Geronimo and his Apache warriors who are on the warpath. Fortunately, on their journey they pick up the Ringo Kid, 'a criminal with a heart', who helps the group make their trip safely.

The main reference point for any representation of masculinity in *Stagecoach* is John Wayne's character the Ringo Kid. His entrance to the film represents him as a very strong and powerful figure. As the stagecoach rides across the desert, the Ringo Kid stops the coach with a shout of 'Hold it!' The camera starts with a long shot of the Ringo Kid but incorporates a fast track in towards his face, ending in a close-up shot.

The Ringo Kid holds his horse's saddle in one hand and twirls his rifle in the other. He wears the conventional dress of a cowboy hero – a cowboy hat, neckerchief, shirt and trousers held up with braces. He is instantly represented as being heroic and very powerful.

▲ *Figure 1.14: The Ringo Kid*

At the end of the film, the Ringo Kid has the opportunity to get revenge on the three Plumber brothers who were responsible for the death of his own father and brother. He has only three bullets left and finds himself in a three-to-one situation and yet manages to kill all three brothers and survive. He is often shot in low angle, giving him strength. He even appears to have fate on his side as the Plumber brothers have a series of unlucky omens around them, including a black cat crossing their path and the infamous poker hand, 'the dead-man's hand'.

After this, the Ringo Kid continues to be represented in a very positive manner; for example, he is one of the few characters to show kindness towards the character of Dallas, a woman who has been driven out of the previous town by the 'law and order league'. However, it is during the gun fights where he really shows his strength and prowess.

If the Ringo Kid is identified as a representation of masculinity, then masculinity is represented as very positive and clearly powerful. His role as a criminal is justified by the fact he is seeking revenge for the murder of his family, and the fact the Plumber brothers are represented negatively, almost as if the fates want the Ringo Kid to avenge his family. Masculine traits include violent skill (which is both accepted and expected in the western genre), gallantry and strength. These are all traits that the Ringo Kid possesses.

Films in the western genre that represent masculinity in different ways:

- *Unforgiven* (Eastwood, 1992, US) – while masculinity is represented as incorporating similar features to *Stagecoach*, whether or not this is positive is highly debatable.

The Individual Media Studies Portfolio

UNIT 1

- *The Quick and the Dead* (Raimi, 1995, US) – this film makes a good comparison due to the shift in gender roles: the hero of the film is female and yet features many of the traits seen as masculine in *Stagecoach*.
- *3:10 to Yuma* (Mangold, 2007, US) – two different types of masculinity are contrasted, and audiences are likely to sympathise with the tough but charming villain, played by Russell Crowe.

Let's discuss

The western genre is commonly a male-dominated genre – the hero is usually male and there are very few female characters present. However, while the western is not as popular as it once was, the western films that have appeared recently have offered a very different representation of women.

Consider the film *Serenity* (Whedon, 2005, US). This is very much a western-science fiction hybrid and incorporates female characters in much stronger roles than is typical of the western genre.

In the film there are three main female characters:

- River Tam, who appears innocent and vulnerable and yet is actually a trained assassin with tremendous skill and strength
- Zoë Washburne, who is second in command on the ship, *Serenity*. She fought in the war of independence and is a brave and powerful warrior
- Kaylee Frye, who is the ship mechanic, which is often a male role or hobby. Kaylee, however, is clearly capable and highly knowledgeable about mechanics.

Explore what factors have led to this shift in gender roles. Is it:

- The hybridised genre?
- The time of release?
- The producers? (In this case, Joss Whedon, creator of *Buffy the Vampire Slayer*.)

What do you think?

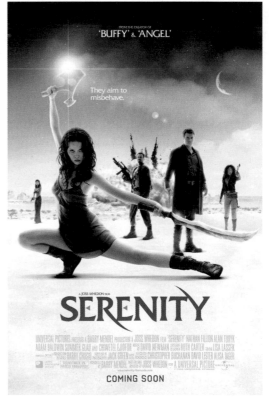

▲ *Figure 1.15: Poster for* Serenity

Let's produce

The production exercise has to show your teacher and moderator that you have a good knowledge and understanding of representations in different genres. Remember that you need to cover at least two media in this unit as a whole. This means if you have chosen to study two films for your comparative assignment, then you need to work in a different medium, such as print, radio or multimedia for your production exercise.

Here are some suggestions for different exercises:

- Produce two posters for a new family drama that challenges traditional representations of childhood.
- Put together the homepage of a website for a new film from a specific genre. The homepage should feature a character profile on the female lead, and represent her through images and text.
- Create a double-page spread for a film magazine reviewing a new British film. Look specifically at the representation of 'Britishness'.
- Design and produce two DVD covers for a new rom-com film, which represents the female character(s) in two different ways.

Let's evaluate

Your evaluation can be in the form of a written essay, a podcast, or a PowerPoint presentation. Remember to answer these questions in your evaluation:

- What area of representation (such as gender, childhood or cultural difference) did you choose to focus on in your production exercise?
- What messages were you trying to convey?
- How did you plan and research for your exercise?
- How did you use media techniques, such as casting, framing, mise-en-scène and choice of language to challenge or reinforce messages and values?
- What are the strengths and weaknesses of your finished exercise?

The Individual Media Studies Portfolio

Key terms

Cliché: (in cinematic terms) an image or storyline that has been repeated so often it has become predictable

Genre package: a film produced by a studio to fit almost perfectly into a generic category

Iconography: the representation of a character through image alone; a set of visual elements that help us to identify a genre

Narrative: the way in which the story is told to the audience. For example, the story can be recited through flashback or in a linear fashion

Parody: a copy of a film's narrative or genre for comic effect

Pastiche: a copy of a film's narrative or genre, but done more out of respect for the original source material

Spectatorship: a form of study specifically looking at how the audience reacts to a particular film

Target audience: the audience group that the product is aimed at; the film genre can affect the target audience

Theme: a central issue or idea contained within a text

Type casting: when an actor is constantly cast in the same sort of role, usually in the same genre. For example Hugh Grant commonly plays the romantic hero

■ Useful websites

www.aintitcool.com: a fan-run website that may provide a different perspective from studio-run websites

www.bbc.co.uk/film: film section of the BBC website

www.bfi.org.uk: British Film Institute website

www.channel4.com/film: links to the Film Four website

www.guardian.co.uk/film: good for film reviews and news

www.imdb.co.uk: excellent resource for finding background information on films, actors, producers and audiences

www.mediaknowall.com: useful site for students

www.nmpft.org.uk: the National Museum of Photography, Film and Television website

www.screenonline.org.uk: excellent educational website on the history of British film and television

Topic 3: Popular Music

■ What is popular music?

Popular music is a term used to describe any aspect of the music industry that can be classed as popular with audiences, either by today's standards or at the time of its original release.

As a part of this topic, you can look at a range of sources that can be classed as being part of popular music, for example:

- Chart shows, such as *Top of the Pops*
- Talent shows, such as *The X-Factor*
- Quiz shows, such as *Never Mind the Buzzcocks*
- Live music broadcasts, such as the Glastonbury festival
- Music-based chat shows, such as *Later with Jools Holland*
- Music videos, such as Michael Jackson's *Thriller*
- Music magazines, such as the *NME*
- Album covers, such as The Beatles' *Sgt Pepper's Lonely Hearts Club Band*.

▲ *Figure 1.16:* Top of the Pops *and* NME *logos*

■ Popular music and youth culture

In society there have always been subcultures. Perhaps the most famous examples of these subcultures were the mods and rockers in the mid 1960s. These were two groups in society who had contrasting ideas and opinions and clashed with each other many times throughout the 1960s. The mods often wore suits and drove scooters, whilst the rockers wore leather jackets and rode motorcycles. The two were also opposed in their music choices. Rockers were categorised by their love of rock and roll, listening to artists such as Elvis Presley, while the mods preferred rhythm and blues bands and soul music, as well as many British beat bands, such as The Who. While it is true to say that music was not the only factor that helped to define these groups, it was important.

Today, subcultures are still present in society. They fall into a wide range of categories, and music is a large factor in defining these subcultures. In today's society we have groups such as goths, emos, indie kids and new ravers. All of these groups have a number of features that help to categorise them, but of course music is one of the main influences.

 Let's research

- Research the subcultures of goths, emos, indie kids and new ravers to see if you can find out what defines each one.
- Aim to identify fashion, interests, beliefs and music tastes.

What is MTV?

MTV (Music Television) was the very first television channel devoted to music and therefore is an important part of any study of music television. It was launched in 1981 with the sole purpose of providing an avenue for the screening of music videos. *Video Killed the Radio Star* by Buggles was the first video to be screened when MTV launched in the US.

▲ *Figure 1.17: MTV logo*

However, it was not until the company was bought by media conglomerate (a large business institution that owns a number of companies) Viacom in 1986 that it began to diversify itself. After the buy-out the institution began to launch other channels, such as VH1 (Video Hits). It launched MTV Europe, MTV Asia and MTV Latin America, and eventually split itself into the genre-specific channels we know today: MTV Hits, MTV2, MTV Base and MTV Dance. This has allowed MTV itself to develop into a set of channels offering a broad range of entertainment shows.

 Let's analyse

- Look at the following logos for MTV channels.
- What do the names/logos tell us about the style of music presented on each channel?

▲ *Figure 1.18: MTV2, VH1 and MTV Hits*

What effects has the development of MTV had on the music industry?

MTV was the first of many music television channels and today there is a wide range of them available via Freeview and satellite television. This increased availability of music videos has led to a change in the way that music is consumed by an audience. Now it is much more common for people to watch their favourite band rather than just listen to them. This has placed a higher level of importance on the image of the artist. The music industry has adapted to this and uses the music video as a very effective method of marketing the artist.

Popular music timeline

1964: Launch of BBC's *Top of the Pops.*
1969: Woodstock festival held in Bethel, New York.
1971: Release of John Lennon's *Imagine.*
1975: Queen's *Bohemian Rhapsody* released with first music video.
1981: Launch of MTV.
1985: First *Live Aid* record released.
1992: First broadcast of *Later with Jools Holland.*
2001: Creation of Hear' Say, the first band manufactured through a TV reality show – *Popstars.*
2006: Final broadcast of *Top of the Pops.*
2006: Lily Allen's debut album *Alright, Still* previewed on MySpace.
2007: Radiohead 'pay what you like' digital download album released.
2008: Cheryl Cole, previous winner of reality talent show *Pop Stars: The Rivals* becomes a judge on *The X-Factor.*

Music videos

Music videos are short films or videos that accompany a piece of popular music. They have a number of features or generic conventions that help us to define them:
- the video is edited to the pace and rhythm of the song
- an element of performance is present in the video
- a lack of diegetic or ambient sound
- a connection between the narrative and themes of the video and the lyrics of the song
- the artist's presence in the video.

In the music industry the music video can have a number of purposes:

- to promote the artist, creating an image for the artist
- to promote the song the video has been constructed for
- to promote a film, if the piece has been recorded as a part of a film soundtrack
- to promote a director; many film directors began their career as music video directors, for example David Fincher, Michel Gondry, Spike Jonze and Jonathan Glazer
- to represent the ideology of the institution, and deliver a message to the audience.

■ Representations in popular music

Different forms of popular music will represent people/events/ issues in different ways. It can even be the case that a song and its music video feature different representations. Your job is to explore and compare these representations in two different media or in two texts from the same medium that fit into the topic of popular music.

Case study 1 – The representation of race in music videos

Resource: Leftfield's *Afrika Shox* (Chris Cunningham, 1999)

Exemplar task: Compare the representation of ethnicity in two music videos, exploring their ideological messages.

In the video for *Afrika Shox*, Chris Cunningham and Leftfield deliver a strong ideological message to the audience, with the representation of race as the main focus. The video uses special effects, mise-en-scène and camerawork in order to construct a particular representation and leaves a lasting effect on the viewer.

The video begins with a series of low angle panning shots, establishing the location; we see a city that towers above us. The city appears devoid of colour, the sky is very grey and the buildings themselves have very little

colour. This instantly creates a very imposing and rather depressing feel to the video, setting an oppressive tone that will be carried on throughout.

▲ *Figure 1.19: Still from Leftfield's* Afrika Shox *video*

As the camera begins to focus on the ground level of the city we are shown an alleyway filled with rubbish bins and shot in very low key lighting. Out of the darkness appears our main character for the video, an Afro-Caribbean man dressed in military green clothes with what appear to be dog tags around his neck. His eyes are glazed over and he appears disorientated and stumbles through his environment.

▲ *Figure 1.20: Main character appears*

As the video progresses, we see our main character come into contact with a series of other people, many of whom are white, middle-class males. At one point, the main character reaches out to one of these businessmen and another person walks past him, brushing against his arm. As he does this, the main character's arm falls from his body and shatters as it hits the ground. The main character looks at what is left of his arm with a silent scream on his face, while the camerawork uses shot reverse shot to cut between him and the businessman sitting and reading his newspaper. The businessman looks up briefly but soon turns back to his newspaper. The man who knocked into the main character looks down with a look of indifference on his face and then moves away. He is shown to the audience in low angle while the main character is shown in high angle, clearly demonstrating the power balance between the two characters.

▲ *Figure 1.21: The destructive result of the main character coming into contact with other people*

The video continues, with the main character losing his foot and his other arm as he moves through the city. Eventually, he is hit by a taxi and shatters into dust as the video ends.

The video represents the central character as being weak and vulnerable through the camerawork and the mise-en-scène. He seems separate from the rest of the world he inhabits; many of the other characters do not appear to notice him, even as he stumbles his way across the roads and literally falls apart.

However, while the suggestion is that the main character is weak, it is not necessarily meant in a negative way; he is the victim of the video, helpless and in need of aid. It is the other characters who do not appear to react to him, or show any desire to help him, who therefore become the negative characters in the video. This is especially the case with the businessman who knocks the arm off the main character. He causes physical damage to the main character and is one of the few other characters who notices his presence, and yet he shows no consideration or empathy. This gives the businessman a high level of negativity in his representation.

With this in mind, we can interpret the video as conveying a message that relates to the treatment of other races. It condemns any form of racism and suggests that more tolerant and helpful behaviour is required in order to aid race relations.

 Let's analyse

Afrika Shox

Afrika Bambaataa
Feel the rhythm of the Afrika Bambaataa
Are you ready for the new age?
They are setting the stage
For the renegades
To control your mind
They planned it yesterday
Fffffff-free

Zulu nation here to stay
Let's get electrofied
Pump it, rockin' it, stickin' it, funkin' it Afrika
Pump it, rockin' it, stickin' it, funkin' it Zulu nation
Z-U-L-U that's the way we say Zulu
Z-U-L-U that's the way we say Zulu

■ How can these lyrics from *Afrika Shox* be used as evidence to support the above interpretation of the ideological messages of the video?

 Let's compare

Compare Leftfield's *Afrika Shox* with other music videos that feature representations of race, such as:
■ Madonna's *Like A Prayer* – this video caused a great deal of controversy when it was originally released, as it features a black Jesus, and Madonna dancing in front of burning crosses, symbols of the racist organisation the Ku Klux Klan.
■ Michael Jackson's *Thriller* – this video has become famous for many things, perhaps mostly for the dance sequence; however, it is also interesting to explore the representation of race in the video by looking at both Jackson and his girlfriend in the video.

Case study 2 – The representation of political and environmental issues in popular music

Resources:
Band Aid's *Do They Know It's Christmas?* (2004)
Bloc Party's *Hunting for Witches* (2006)
Michael Jackson's *Earth Song* (1995)

Exemplar task: Explore how political and/or environmental issues are represented in two different forms of popular music.

Popular music has often been seen as an ideal opportunity to present messages to an audience about serious issues, as the power of music has long been considered to be more than just entertainment. Perhaps the most famous example of this is Band Aid and Bob Geldof. In 1984, Geldof recruited a large group of top music artists to record the song *Do They Know It's Christmas?* in order to raise money for famine relief. In 2004, the same song was released with a new, more up-to-date group of performers, again to raise money for charity. The song features lyrics designed to raise awareness of famine and poverty around the world and the video for the 2004 version of the song incorporates footage of famine-stricken parts of Africa.

There have been many examples of popular music that have featured the artists' messages about aspects of politics or current affairs. One such modern example is Bloc Party's *Hunting for Witches*.

Bloc Party's *Hunting for Witches*

I'm sitting on the roof of my house
With a shotgun and a six pack of beer
The newscaster says "The enemy is among us!"
As bombs explode on the 30 bus
Kill that middle class indecision
Now is not the time for liberal thought

So I go hunting for witches
Heads are going to roll
So I go hunting
1990's, optimistic as a teen
But now it's terror, airplanes crash into towers
The Daily Mail says "The enemy is among us!"
"Taking our women and taking our jobs"
All reasonable thought is being drowned out
By the non-stop baying, baying for blood
So I go hunting for witches
Heads are going to roll
So I go hunting
I was an ordinary man, with ordinary desire
I watched TV, it informed me
I was an ordinary man with ordinary desire
There must be accountability
Disparate and misinformed
Fear keeps us all in place

The lyrics of the song focus on terrorism in the modern world, with clear references to 9/11 and to the London bombings in 2005: 'As bombs explode on the 30 bus'. The song also appears to make direct comments on how the media reacted to these events, suggesting that the media created a sense of panic and encouraged people to suspect others around them. The song is a powerful piece of work that aims to do a lot more than just entertain.

Songwriter Kele Okereke said: '[That song was] written when I was just observing the reactions of the mainstream press in [the United Kingdom] and I was just amazed at how easy it'd been to whip them up into a fury.' Therefore, the message is that in the band's opinion the media's reaction to these events was extreme and scaremongering; the media is being represented in a negative way by the lyrics of the song.

▲ *Figure 1.22: An elephant who has been killed for his ivory. Jackson looks at this theme in the* Earth Song *video*

The desired effect is to show the contrast between what should be and what is, exploring the damage that hunting and pollution are doing to the environment and wildlife in certain parts of the world.

The video continues with these kinds of images, showing the audience a family walking through a war-torn village and tribesmen watching forests being pulled down. Meanwhile, Michael Jackson himself performs the song in what appears to have once been a forest, where there are tree stumps all around him and much of the location is on fire. At the end of the video the destruction and devastation we have seen throughout appears to repair itself, as the video moves into an almost rewind-like state; forests repair, animals come back to life and pollution disappears. The video carries a very clear message about the state of our planet, and Jackson uses his music video to represent his own opinions on environmental issues.

Another example of this is the music video for *Earth Song* by Michael Jackson. The song, released in 1995, deals specifically with environmental issues and animal welfare, and the accompanying video shows images of deforestation, animal cruelty and war.

One of the first images used in the video is of an elephant that has been killed for its ivory. The elephant lies in a deserted field with dead trees and plants all around it. A group from an African tribe appear and look down on the carcass of the elephant with clear looks of sadness on their faces. There is then a slow dissolve to reveal the African plains as they should be: the audience see elephants, giraffes and zebras in this new environment. The location is much greener, with trees and grass and a water source. However, soon after this the same slow dissolve effect is used to return to the previous image with the dead elephant, and the bare, colourless and lifeless African plain.

▲ *Figure 1.23: Michael Jackson performing* Earth Song

Let's research

- Björk is an artist who frequently uses her videos to comment on environmental and political issues. Look at a video such as *Declare Independence* and explore the news stories which surrounded her performance of this song in Shanghai.
- Look at the press coverage of the Live Aid concert in 1985 and the Live 8 concert in 2005. Analyse the ways in which the press represented these charity events.

Let's produce

The production exercise has to show your teacher and moderator that you have a good knowledge and understanding of representations in popular music. Remember that you need to cover at least two media in this unit as a whole. That means if you have chosen to study two music videos for your comparative assignment, then you need to work in a different medium, such as print, television or radio for your production exercise.

Here are some suggestions for different exercises:

- A CD/DVD front and back cover for a new band from a musical genre of your choice, showing the band in a dominant position.
- A script for a radio interview with a new band, talking about their latest music video and the political messages contained within it.
- A double-page spread from a music magazine, reviewing a new British girl band.
- A newspaper or magazine article about the British music scene and youth subcultures.

Let's evaluate

Your evaluation can be in the form of a written essay, a podcast, or a PowerPoint presentation. Remember to answer these questions in your evaluation:

- What area of representation (such as subcultures, race, political or environmental issues) did you choose to focus on in your production exercise?
- What messages were you trying to convey?
- How did you plan and research for your exercise?
- How did you use media techniques, such as casting, framing, mise-en-scène and mode of address to challenge or reinforce messages and values?
- What are the strengths and weaknesses of your finished exercise?

Key terms

Acoustic: music played through non-electrical means, often played live without mixing or voice alteration

Conglomerate: an institution that owns a large number of companies and outlets

Crossover: describes a movement from one medium into another. In popular music it can be used to describe a music artist breaking into the film industry or vice-versa

Diegetic sound: sound that can be heard by the characters or is part of the 'world' of the film or video

Lip-synch: often known as miming, this is when an artist mouths along to the song being performed as opposed to singing or playing live

Marketing: often considered to be the purpose of a music video, this is the process of selling a (media) product

Mass media product: a media text that is designed to appeal to a large proportion of the audience

Social networking site: a website designed to act as a social environment for the users; a way of keeping in contact and sharing ideas and opinions, for example on music

Verse/chorus: the main sections of a song – the chorus is the repeated part of a song, while the verse becomes the bridge between the choruses and is often designed to be sung solo

■ Useful websites

www.bbc.co.uk/totp: homepage for the long-running BBC music broadcast, featuring news, reviews and history features on popular music

www.guardian.co.uk/media: a good archive source for news stories relating to the release of certain songs and the music industry

www.mtv.co.uk: homepage for the first television channel devoted to music, it features news, videos and images from a variety of bands old and new

www.nme.com: webpage of the popular British music magazine the *NME* (New Musical Express)

www.qthemusic.com: website for music magazine *Q*, with some great resources on past issues and covers

http://music.aol.co.uk/: a great source for looking at music videos

Topic 4: Celebrity

What is celebrity?

A celebrity can be defined as a person who is famous during their lifetime. This fame may be due to:

- birth – royals like Prince Harry or wealthy socialites like Paris Hilton
- achievement in a particular field, such as Johnny Depp's acting achievements or David Beckham's sporting ones
- an appearance on reality TV
- an association with another celebrity.

Hierarchy of celebrities

The individual's place in our celebrity culture can be defined through a hierarchy – an ordering in terms of importance, according to how they are valued in our society. For example, Hollywood actors have for some time been listed as 'A' or 'B' class celebrities and are paid accordingly. By comparison, people who appear on reality TV shows are often referred to as 'Z list' celebrities.

Let's discuss

Working in pairs, write down the names of 10 celebrities, including actors, sportspeople, musicians, members of the royal family and statesmen. Using the table below as a model, place the celebrities into categories. What does this tell you about how much we value each type of celebrity?

Celebrity by birth – royalty, aristocracy, children of the wealthy or famous	Celebrity by achievement – artists, writers, musicians, politicians, film stars, sportspeople, models	Celebrity by association – husbands, wives and girlfriends of celebrities, reality TV stars
Prince Harry	Chris Hoy	Chelsy Davy (Prince Harry's ex-girlfriend)
Paris Hilton	Kate Moss	Jack Tweed (Jade Goody's husband)
Peaches Geldof	Daniel Craig	Coleen Rooney (Wayne Rooney's wife)

(Adapted from Chris Rojek's taxonomy of celebrity, 2001)

■ Messages and values

The celebrity culture can be seen as reflecting values in our society at a particular time and in a particular place. The exercise above will help you to think about how much you value certain celebrities and why celebrities are represented in widely varying ways by the media at different stages of their careers.

For this topic, you can study representations of celebrity in:
- magazines
- radio
- newspapers
- the internet.
- television

This topic is particularly suitable for a cross-media study, as celebrities are often represented in strongly contrasting ways in different media.

Let's research

- **Choose three news websites and identify how many of the stories on the homepage relate to celebrities.**
- **Do you see a problem with mixing 'hard' and 'soft' news in this way?**

■ Celebrity sells

Celebrity has become more important to all forms of media in Britain over the last five years for the following reasons:
- The availability of the internet and the increase in the number of radio stations and television channels has made it easier for audiences to find out about celebrities.
- The producers of radio, television, newspapers and magazines are concerned about falling audiences and losing money. Increased competition for audiences means more reporting of celebrity news, as this helps to attract audiences.
- *The Sun* is the best-selling newspaper in Britain, with circulation figures of over three million. This success owes a great deal to its coverage of celebrity stories. Other media producers follow *The Sun*'s example.
- Social networking sites like MySpace allow fans to become 'friends' with actors and singers.
- Increased tabloidisation of the news has meant that human interest and 'soft' news stories take priority.
- Interactivity – audiences can play an important part in the construction of a celebrity through voting on reality TV shows such as *Big Brother* or *Strictly Come Dancing*.

The uses and gratifications theory and celebrity

You will find the uses and gratifications theory (McQuail, Blumler and Brown, 1972) very helpful in understanding why celebrity seems so important to almost every section of the media in 21st century Britain. The theory argues that audiences use media texts for the following reasons:

- Personal identity: we want to establish who we are in relation to others – we may see celebrities as role models or we may reject their values. *The Sun* encourages approval with headlines such as 'Send brave Jade a message of support', and rejection with stories such as 'Ashley Cole tops hate poll'.

- Personal relationships: we like to have a sense of a personal relationship with celebrities, such as soap characters or pop musicians. Social networking sites like MySpace and Facebook reinforce this as ordinary people can be 'friends' with celebrities, while celebrity magazines and tabloids use first-name terms or nicknames like 'Fergie' or 'Posh'.

- Diversion: we seek entertainment, enjoyment and an escape from our everyday lives – following the details of celebrities' lives can give us a 'second life'. This helps to explain the obsession with wealthy celebrities like Paris Hilton, whose lives are very different from our own.

- Surveillance: we want to find out about what is going on in the world. Celebrities are such an important part of popular culture, despite their superficiality, that we don't want to miss any details of celebrities' lives that others know about. This helps to account for the high audience ratings of around 12 million for shows such as *Strictly Come Dancing* and *The X-Factor*.

Celebrity timeline

1792–1805:	Admiral Nelson is a popular celebrity, much admired by the public. His fame is confirmed when he dies a hero's death at Trafalgar.
1850s–present:	Newspapers gain readers by printing more human interest stories and articles on sport and fashion. Today, *The Sun* and *The Mirror* rely on celebrity stories for sales.

1911–present:	Hollywood studios construct actors as 'stars', signing exclusive deals with them. The studios circulate fan magazines and other publicity material to magazines, newspapers, radio and (eventually) television and the internet.
1960:	First British TV soap *Coronation Street* broadcast; newspapers not only review the soap but regularly print stories about the characters and the actors.
1974:	Paul Watson's reality TV series *The Family* turns the Wilkins family into celebrities.
1993:	*OK!* and *Hello!* (1998) gossip magazines develop, based on celebrity news and specialising in celebrity weddings.
1997:	BBC docusoap *Driving School* focuses on 'ordinary' people learning to drive for entertainment and makes Maureen (who has failed her test six times) into a celebrity.
2000:	*Big Brother* first broadcast on Channel 4; 12 'ordinary' people placed in a house for three months. Impressive audience ratings attract advertisers to Channel 4 and encourage the rise of the 'Z list' celebrity.
2007:	*Celebrity Big Brother 5* mixes different categories of celebrities with disastrous results and accusations of racist bullying by 'Z list' Jade Goody against 'A list' Bollywood film star Shilpa Shetty.
2009:	Reality TV star Jady Goody is diagnosed with terminal cancer. She remains in the public eye throughout her battle and dies at home on 22 March.

Case study 1 – Representations of royalty: Prince Harry

Resources:

The People (28 January 2002) –
www.people.com/people/archive/article/
0,,20136295,00.htm
The Sun (13 January 2005) –
http://en.wikipedia.org/wiki/index.html?curid
=11322710
The Sun (1 March 2008)
News of the World (10 January 2009)
Prince Harry profile –
http://news.bbc.co.uk/1/hi/uk/3763132.stm

Exemplar task: Compare the differing representations of Prince Harry at different stages of his life.

Prince Harry has been represented in a number of different ways during his life as a royal celebrity. He is often represented as the 'bad boy of royalty' in a way that suggests a certain amount of affection as well as criticism. Seen as a rebel and more complicated than his brother William, he has been given a range of roles by the media, including teenage tearaway, playboy prince, wild child and war hero.

▲ *Figure 1.24: The photojournalism and reporting of Prince William and Prince Harry at their mother's funeral in 1997 was sympathetic*

Harry was 12 and his brother William was 15 when their mother, Princess Diana, died in a car crash. Media reports constructed them as brave victims, giving them a huge amount of sympathy. This was linked to the fact that their mother had been one of the most popular royal celebrities of the 20th century. Diana was termed 'the world's most photographed woman' and stories about her in *The Sun* and *The Mirror* unfailingly helped to sell newspapers.

The relentless press coverage led to Diana complaining to the Press Complaints Commission about intrusion into her privacy by the paparazzi (photographers of celebrities), and some believe the car crash happened because she was being chased by the paparazzi. This background helps us to understand the tensions between the media and Prince Harry and the changing representations of Harry, particularly in the tabloid press.

■ In 2002, a close-up of Prince Harry in *The People* (see URL on page 46) from 28 January 2002 represents him as a 'teenage tearaway'.

■ The alliteration in 'Drinks, Drugs and Prince Harry' is intended to double the audience's shock and concern.

■ The headline is constructed to sound like the title of the 'next chapter' in the Prince's story.

■ The inset image of Prince Charles, Prince William and Prince Harry has been selected to remind audiences that there is no mother figure to help.

■ 'Charles and William try to rein in the rowdy 17-year-old' represents Harry as a wild animal that needs taming.

■ The story focuses on Harry's admissions of underage drinking and cannabis smoking. Although this front page evokes some sympathy for Harry, this is the beginning of his representation as the 'party prince'.

Look at the front cover of *The Sun* from the 13 January 2005 on Wikipedia: http://en.wikipedia.org/wiki/index.html?curid=11322710.

■ The headline 'Harry the Nazi' is in very large font, exaggerating the importance and scale of the story.

■ The photograph shows the swastika – the official emblem of the Nazi party – centre right of shot and draws the audience's attention to the symbol, with its extremely negative connotations. The photograph is blurred and taken in low lighting, but the swastika stands out clearly on the bright red armband.

■ *The Sun* ran this story as an exclusive to help the newspaper sell.

■ There is no sympathy for Harry in this front page.

The Individual Media Studies Portfolio

UNIT 1

Following *The Sun*'s lead, the story of Prince Harry's Nazi costume was widely reported in other media, although it was generally toned down. The story was made even more significant by the fact that it broke just before the 60th anniversary of the liberation of Auschwitz, and Harry's use of the swastika was seen as insensitive to the survivors of the concentration camps and their families. Harry had to make a formal apology because the article was seen as damaging to Harry's reputation and, by extension, to the royal family as a whole.

Harry's subsequent army career and willingness to be deployed in dangerous conditions in Afghanistan alongside his fellow soldiers helped him to improve his image in the media. When it was revealed in 2008 that Harry had served a tour of 10 weeks in Afghanistan, a completely different representation was constructed of him. Headlines such as 'From wild child to war hero' began to appear (Reuters, 1 March, 2008). *The Sun*, which had previously attacked Harry, now encouraged audiences to view him as a role model and to download the photograph of him serving in Afghanistan.

▲ *Figure 1.25:* The Sun, *1 March 2008 – Harry as war hero*

In the image above, Harry is now affectionately referred to as 'one of our boys'. The audience is expected to accept this new representation of Harry as a hero without question: 'Our army of readers salutes you, Harry'. The image in Figure 1.25 shows Harry in battle gear in a war zone by himself, giving the impression that he is single-handedly overcoming the Taliban. Articles in other newspapers and on internet sites repeated this image, with some arguing that he was carrying on the fighting tradition of his namesake, Henry V, who won the Battle of Agincourt against seemingly impossible odds. This was particularly appropriate as Henry V had also behaved as a 'wild child' before becoming King in 1413. This new representation of Harry celebrates the values of patriotism, courage, honour, tradition and Britishness.

▲ *Figure 1.26:* News of the World, *January 2009*

The 'hero' role only lasted until January 2009, when the *News of the World* revealed that Harry had used racist terms in a video he had made in 2006. The video was made available on the *News of the World*'s website, where Harry's voice-over can be heard saying, 'our little Paki friend ... Ahmed' as he zooms towards an Asian cadet while waiting at an airport to fly to Cyprus. Other comments in the voice-over reinforce the negative representation.

This front page uses a medium close-up of Harry in his army uniform with a grim, humourless expression on his face. The representation aims to lessen the respect Harry may have gained from his 'war hero' role. The story is all the more damaging because it has links to *The Sun's* 2005 'Harry the Nazi' story.

The new negative representation was widely reported and discussed. Harry apologised again, while Prime Minister Gordon Brown supported him, saying that he had been a role model for young people since he had made the comment and that the public would forgive him.

The press and celebrity magazines have labelled Prince Harry as victim, teenage tearaway, wild child, bad boy of royalty, war hero, role model and upper-class buffoon. It could be argued that these representations have little to do with the 'truth' and everything to do with the fact that their main purpose has been to attract audiences to television, radio and news internet sites and to sell celebrity magazines and newspapers.

Let's research

Using Case study 1 as a model, compare the changing representations of two celebrities over their careers.

Case study 2 – Representations of age: John Sergeant

Resources:
Strictly Come Dancing Episode 9 (BBC1, 22 November 2008)
The Guardian (22 November 2008)
www.bbc.co.uk/strictlycomedancing

You would find any series of *Strictly Come Dancing* useful for analysing celebrity because the programme illustrates the power of the audience and their role in the construction of celebrities.

This case study focuses on John Sergeant, because of the variety of media representations of his performances in the 2008 *Strictly Come Dancing* series. It is also a good study for exploring the tension between the audience's relationship with celebrity culture and the expectations of the 'experts' in a talent show.

This study questions how we define celebrity and what we most value in our culture. In this case it was not so much the dancing skills of John Sergeant that made him so popular, but his self-deprecating wit and his ability to entertain the audience. It could be argued that the negative representations of John Sergeant in the press, together with the judges' harsh comments, helped to build him up as a popular figure.

Why is *Strictly Come Dancing* so popular?

- Long narrative arc – audiences follow the celebrities over a period of 12 weeks.
- Celebrities are learning a new skill – we admire their ability to adapt and cope with tough training schedules.
- 'Beauty contest' element – we know that there will be disappointments and triumphs.

- Interactivity – the audience is given power over both celebrities and judges.
- Emotional involvement of audience.
- Hierarchy of celebrities – professional dancers become celebrities in their own right and are sometimes more interesting than the 'established' celebrities.
- Tabloid coverage increases audience interest.
- Comforting return to talent shows of the past.
- Unpredictability of live TV – our need for surveillance (see the uses and gratifications theory on page 45).

▲ Figure 1.27: John Sergeant performs his signature *pasa doble with partner Kristina Rihanoff in* Strictly Come Dancing *2008*

John Sergeant, 64-year-old political journalist, was one of 16 celebrity competitors on *Strictly Come Dancing* from September to November 2008. Sergeant's main claim to fame was the 1990 incident when Margaret Thatcher's press secretary Bernard Ingham pushed him out of the way when he was reporting on the leadership election. He had also appeared on shows such as *Have I Got News For You, QI* and *Countdown*.

Sergeant regularly received the lowest marks from the judges, but comments such as: 'She does the dancing, I do the jokes' and his obvious enjoyment of the dancing endeared him to audiences. The voting system gives 50% of the votes to the judges and the other 50% to the audience, and this meant that the judges' attempts to vote him off came to nothing. Audiences voted him and his partner Kristina Rihanoff back in week after week.

The audience's support for Sergeant was fuelled by the negative criticism of the judges and by similarly unpleasant articles in the tabloid press. Even Len Goodman, one of the kinder judges, said 'This isn't Help the Aged. I'm very impressed with your sparkly dicky bow, but that's about it!' The construction of Sergeant as 'too old to dance' and 'a dancing pig in Cuban heels' backfired, because audiences refused to accept this judgement on Sergeant and exercised their right to see him differently, by saving him from being voted off every week.

Sergeant was also represented in the tabloids as smug, lacking in skill and as a troublemaker who did not follow the usual rules of *Strictly Come*

Dancing. Descriptions ranged from 'clodhopping Mr Toad' and 'leaden-footed ballroom chancer' (*The Mirror*), to 'portly journalist' and 'the lumbering broadcaster' (*The Sun*).

The Sun article below appears to condemn Sergeant, but selects a photograph that represents Phillips in a negative light, while the photograph of Sergeant represents him as smart and humorous.

However, since the tabloids did not want to be out of step with their audiences, the representations of Sergeant began to shift. *The Sun* columnist Kelvin MacKenzie urged the audience to vote for 'this bullied senior citizen'. Facebook groups were set up to support him.

Gentleman John's had enough of the bullies

By Fiona McIntosh 22/11/2008

Strictly dumb judging!

By Kevin O'Sullivan 22/11/2008

▲ *Figure 1.28:* The Sun *article about* Strictly Come Dancing

▲ *Figure 1.29:* The Mirror *(22 November 2008) represents John as bullied victim (top) and the judges as out of touch with the values of the programme (bottom)*

The clash between the way the audience viewed John Sergeant and the way they viewed the judges can be seen as a set of opposing values:

John Sergeant	The judges
Gentleman with old-fashioned values like humility	Arrogant abuse of power
Polite at all times	Rude name-calling seen as humour
Respect for others, especially Kristina	Mockery of other people
Self-deprecating	Self-important
Personality is more important than skill	Expertise is all that matters
Trying is more important than succeeding	Success is all

Sergeant eventually announced that he was leaving the show himself in Episode 9 because he feared he might win, thanking the judges for the 'extraordinary' way they had whipped up public support in his favour, showing that he had understood the values of the programme better than the judges.

The BBC received more than 2,000 complaints when he left. The broadsheets covered the story of his departure and prominent political figures supported him. He was represented in some articles as a bullied victim, although this is not a role he himself would accept.

Let's research

■ Research media representations of the Beatles and compare them with contemporary representations of Amy Winehouse.

■ Compare the representations of the celebrities involved in the Red Nose Day Climb (March 2009) in different media texts.

■ Research and analyse the representations of Cheryl Cole when 'discovered' on talent competition show *Popstars: the Rivals* (ITV, 2002) and compare them with the ways she has been represented since she became a judge on *The X-Factor*.

■ Investigate the term 'national treasure' by researching the career of Barbara Windsor, Paul Merton or another celebrity who is categorised in this way. How do people achieve this status of celebrity?

■ Find out about the work of the Press Complaints Commission, looking closely at the Code of Practice sections on privacy and the public interest. Choose two cases where celebrities have claimed that their privacy has been invaded. Analyse the representations.

Let's produce

The production exercise has to show the teacher and moderator that you have a good knowledge and understanding of representations of celebrity. Remember that you need to cover at least two media in this unit as a whole. This means if you have chosen to study celebrities in a TV programme for your comparative assignment, then you need to produce a radio, internet or print article on celebrity for your production exercise. However, it is likely that with this topic you will have looked at celebrities in a range of media, so you will have plenty of choice for your production exercise.

Here are some suggestions for different exercises:

■ A front page and editorial for a new celebrity magazine.
■ A storyboard for a new celebrity reality TV show aimed at 15–25-year-olds.
■ Two pages of a new website that focuses on celebrity.

Let's evaluate

Your evaluation can be in the form of a written essay, a podcast, or a PowerPoint presentation. Remember to answer these questions in your evaluation:

■ What area of representation (such as age, social class or gender) did you choose to focus on in your exercise?
■ What messages were you trying to convey?
■ How did you plan and research for your exercise?
■ How did you use media techniques to challenge or reinforce messages and values?
■ What are the strengths and weaknesses of your finished exercise?

Key terms

Docusoap: a reality TV series that mixes the conventions of a documentary with the conventions of a TV soap
Hierarchy: order according to how powerful a person or institution is perceived to be
Mode of address: how a media text speaks to its audience
Paparazzi: photographers of celebrities
Reality TV: focuses on the 'real lives' of individuals or groups
Tabloidisation: increased focus on celebrity and human interest stories in serious news programmes, newspapers and websites

■ Useful websites

www.bbc.co.uk/strictlycomedancing/: *Strictly Come Dancing* website
www.ok.co.uk/: *OK!* magazine website
www.pcc.org.uk/: website of the Press Complaints Commission
xfactor.itv.com: The *X-Factor* website

Topic 5: Talk Radio

■ What is talk radio?

Talk radio can be defined as a radio format based on speech, with a variety of programmes introduced by a range of different presenters. Talk radio is likely to include some or all of the following:

- news
- interviews
- discussion
- audience interaction (such as phone-ins)
- drama

- comedy
- advertisements (commercial talk radio)
- music
- sport
- documentaries.

■ Points of view

Here are some useful questions to ask when analysing talk radio programmes:

- Who has made the programme?
- How is the station's brand identity reinforced through the programme?
- How does the presenter aim to establish his or her identity?
- What is the programme's mode of address?
- How is the programme structured?
- What effect does the structure of the items have on the representation of the subject matter?
- How are music and jingles used?
- Who is the target audience? If it is a commercial station, use the advertisements to help you to identify the psychographics (values, interests, beliefs) of the audience.
- What are the values of the station?
- Do these values vary at different times of the day?

Let's research

- Research local and regional radio stations in your area.
- Find out about their target audiences, how they are funded and their audience figures.
- Why do you think the BBC is still the main provider of national and local radio stations in Britain?

BBC talk radio	Commercial talk radio stations
Radio 4	LBC
Radio 5 Live	LBC News

BBC talk radio	Commercial talk radio stations
BBC World Service	City Talk (Liverpool)
BBC Asian Network – Radio 7	Talk Sport
BBC Radio Kent and other local stations	Real Radio
BBC Radio Scotland and other regional stations	

The most successful talk radio stations have traditionally been those provided by the BBC, such as Radio 4 and Radio 2. BBC radio is funded by the licence fee, while commercial radio is funded through sponsorship and advertising.

In 2007 BBC radio as a whole commanded more than half the total radio audience, while commercial radio reached around 43% (listening figures from RAJAR). Although LBC is successfully increasing its audience, it is a London-based station and its weekly reach is only 637,000 people compared to the 9.48 million of BBC Radio 4, which is national.

Messages and values

Radio stations have to work hard to survive and attract audiences in today's competitive media world. Commercial radio has to attract the audiences that their advertisers want to reach. It is therefore essential that radio producers construct a distinctive, specific brand identity for their station. This brand identity speaks to their target audiences and offers values that their audiences can identify with.

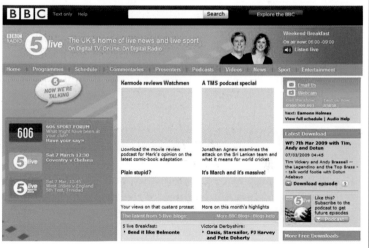

▲ Figure 1.30: The homepage of BBC Radio 5 Live. What does this tell you about the station's target audience?

Radio 5 Live website homepage (6 March 2009)	What the website homepage tells us about its target audience
Medium close-up of two presenters, Rachel Burden and Phil Williams with informal codes of dress	Lively, energetic presenters appeal to target audiences of 25–44-year-olds on average. Appeals to both male and female
Colloquial mode of address: 'Tim Vickery and Andy Brassell – the Legendino and the Top Brass – talk world footie with Dotun Adebayo"	Encourages audience to feel part of a friendly group that speaks their language

Radio 5 Live website homepage (6 March 2009)	What the website homepage tells us about its target audience
Sport panel on the left-hand side – key football and cricket matches highlighted	Football and cricket fans
Mark Kermode's podcast of his film review	Experienced and knowledgeable film critic appeals to audience, primarily 18–35-year-olds
News story on the attack on the Sri Lankan cricket team in March 2009	This links world news with sports news. Will appeal to all members of the audience
Encourages interactivity through inviting views on the custard attack on Peter Mandelson	Target audience feels involved and that their views are valued
Four different ways for audience to contact the channel displayed on right-hand panel	Recognises that the audience wants choices
Light blue colour design connotes cutting edge technology	Audience feels station is up to date and 'on the ball'
Live blogs on sports games	Audience demands up-to-date information
Option to listen live	Assumes audience listens on the internet

Let's compare

- Using the table above as a model, compare the websites of BBC Radio 7 and LBC.
- What are the brand identities of the two radio stations?
- How do they target their audiences?

■ Ways of listening

Radio listening is increasing, despite fierce competition from television and the internet. Radio can fit in with your life more easily than television; it is easily portable and personal. Today you can listen to radio in the following ways:

- digital audio broadcasting radio
- analogue radio
- satellite, cable or Freeview television
- the internet
- mobile phones
- downloaded podcasts.

Radio timeline

1918: First successful radio transmission in Britain.

1922: BBC begins radio transmissions.

1925: Lord Reith's memo to the Crawford Committee states that public service broadcasting should 'inform, educate, and entertain'.

1939: BBC radio networks merged into the Home Service.

1939–45: Radio is a powerful form of communication for military and propaganda campaigns during World War II.

1967: BBC launches Radio 1, 2, 3 and 4.

1970: BBC local radio launched.

1973: First commercial radio stations broadcast locally.

1990: Broadcasting Act makes it easier for smaller stations to get licences; rules on public service broadcasting relaxed; Radio Authority set up.

1992: First national commercial station – Classic FM.

2002: BBC stations 6 and 7 set up.

2005 onwards: Radio stations streamed on the internet.

Let's compare

Different stations not only have different brand identities, but assume different things about their audiences. Audiences are strongly encouraged to support the values of the radio station. The commercial radio station LBC (London's Biggest Conversation) broadcasts its programmes on two different wavelengths: AM and FM. It runs a rolling 30-minute news and information service during the day on AM and a mixture of phone-in, entertainment and discussion programmes on FM. In the evening and night time the FM content is broadcast on both stations (known as simulcasting). This is to ensure that audience figures are high enough to attract advertisers.

▲ Figure 1.31: The LBC news website covers celebrity stories as well as international news

- Spend some time listening to news programmes on both Radio 4 and LBC News.
- Identify the different approaches to presenting the news (look at their websites, presenters, jingles, etc.).
- How much time is spent on each news story?
- How many international news stories are covered?

Values in Radio 4 News	Values in LBC News
Public service broadcasting approach is to educate, inform and entertain	Informs in an entertaining way; no PSB remit
Hard news dominates, although it is balanced by some soft news stories, especially on the *Today* programme Sport and weather given brief slots	Hard news stories, including business news, share space with celebrity stories; extended coverage of sport, news and weather
Emphasis on news	Emphasis on presenters
Presenters are well-educated and well-informed; constructed as 'expert' interviewers	Presenters emphasise importance of audience: regular interaction with audience through phone-ins and texts
Formal mode of address; often confrontational with politicians	Colloquial, friendly mode of address with interviewees and audience
News programmes are carefully paced to give audiences time to consider issues	Fast-paced structure with 15-minute segments intercut by advertisements
Continuity announcers remind audiences of station's brand identity; music rarely used	Regular jingles to remind audiences of station's brand identity
Target audience 45+ ABC1 – professional and management workers	Target audience 35–54-year-olds ABC – professional, management and manual workers

Case study 1 – Representations of disability on Radio 4

Resources:
In Touch – Peter White (Radio 4, 3 March 2009)
http://www.bbc.co.uk/radio4/factual/intouch.shtml - *In Touch* website
Spoonface Steinberg by Lee Hall (first broadcast on Radio 4, 1997, available as an audiobook)

It could be argued that radio is particularly well suited to explore positive representations of disability, in comparison to other media. This may be linked to the fact that it is a more personal, intimate medium, which seems to speak directly to the individual listener.

The series *In Touch* is broadcast weekly on Tuesdays on Radio 4 at 8.40 pm. It specifically targets blind and partially-sighted audiences, but is constructed to interest sighted audiences as well.

The presenter, Peter White, is the BBC Disability Affairs Correspondent. He has been blind since birth and has presented *In Touch* since 1974. He is also involved in presenting other programmes for Radio 4 that are not related to disability, including *Pick of the Week* and *You and Yours*. He himself is a successful role model who is represented in a positive way on the BBC *In Touch* website and in the programmes he presents.

The mode of address of *In Touch* is relaxed and conversational, with a lightness of tone, which is constructed by Peter White's gentle pace and friendly approach to his guests. Despite this, there is a strong campaigning element to the programme. Some of the serious issues that the programme has recently confronted include improved health care and education for the visually impaired, stem cell surgery, and better treatment from airlines, hotels and banks for people with disabilities.

In Touch (Radio 4, 3 March 2009)

The *In Touch* programme broadcast on 3 March 2009 deals with three stories: what a visually-impaired person from another culture finds when they come to Britain, the experiences of paralympic champion Anthony Kappes, and how visually-impaired people could enjoy playing Wii games.

The programme begins on a positive note, with White trailing the item on the Australian student in Britain, who describes her experience in Britain as 'liberating'. This sets the tone for the whole programme and implies that representations of disability in this series are on the whole positive.

White then introduces Anthony Kappes: 'not that he needs much of a boost, he's already a two-time Paralympic champion'.

The Australian Lee Kumutat's presentation ends on a positive note, complimenting the workers on London Underground.

White's ability to laugh at himself and his disability determines the mode of address of *In Touch* and reinforces the positive representations of guests with disabilities and, by extension, audiences with disabilities. It also makes the programme accessible to those outside the core target audience and helps to explain why the programme has lasted since 1974.

Disability is far more frequently represented on Radio 4 than it is on BBC television. Radio diaries and dramas lend themselves particularly well to explorations of different kinds of disability. One of the most outstanding radio dramas that deals with disability is *Spoonface Steinberg*, first broadcast in 1997. Written by

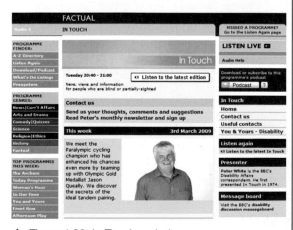

▲ *Figure 1.32:* In Touch *website*

Lee Hall, this is a dramatic monologue spoken by a seven-year-old autistic girl who is dying from cancer. Despite the serious subject matter, the drama takes a humorous, uplifting approach to disability. Although the drama has since been adapted for television and the theatre, it is the award-winning radio production that is remembered as exceptional.

Case study 2 – Representations of young people on Radio 4

Resources:
The Archers (Radio 4, 2009)
www.bbc.co.uk/radio4/archers/: *The Archers* official website

Radio 4 has broadcast *The Archers*, Britain's longest running soap, since 1951. *The Archers* is important to Radio 4, as it helps it to maintain its weekly audience reach of around 9.8 million. Broadcast in 13-minute slots six evenings a week, with lunchtime repeats, *The Archers* traditionally appeals to Radio 4's core target audience of 45s and over, but it also appeals to younger audiences. Recent plotlines include:

- the civil ceremony of gay farmer Adam and chef Ian; the racist reaction to the wedding of Church of England vicar Alan to the Hindu Usha.
- Ruth's 'affair' with cowhand Sam; the love triangle between Ed and Will Grundy and Emma Carter. This story was marketed on *The Archers* official website as `Love. Passion. Lust. Envy. Betrayal. The love triangle between Emma and the Grundy boys has it all.'

There are a number of young actors in the cast. Their storylines include: the relationship between 20-year-olds Alice and Chris; 16-year-old Pip's campaign for the environment; 23-year-old Fallon's success in the music business; 24-year-olds Ed and Emma's love triangle with 26-year-old Will.

The Archers was the first BBC drama series to be made available as a podcast in 2007.

The website is constructed like a TV soap website, with quizzes, message boards, podcasts, picture galleries, timelines, family trees and a map of Ambridge, the fictional village in which the soap is set.

Other recent storylines have been based on eating disorders, gambling addictions and the difficulties of young single mothers. The younger characters in *The Archers* are represented as obsessed by relationships, but generally law-abiding and responsible.

▲ Figure 1.33: The love triangle between the Grundy brothers and Emma Carter is represented on The Archers *website as a cartoon*

The Archers is the most popular programme on the BBC iPlayer, beating Chris Moyles' Radio 1 breakfast show. As well as appealing to young audiences, the programme has held on to its core audience.

Nearly 12 million people now listen to radio through DAB, digital TV or the internet. Around 4.4 million listen on their mobile phones, while 2.7 million listen to podcasts. These changes have given Radio 4 the opportunity to increase the audience for *The Archers*.

▲ *Figure 1.34: The colourful* Archers *website offers visitors gossip, quizzes and message boards*

Let's research

- Listen to 15 minutes of Radio 4's *Today* programme over a period of a week. How are politicians represented?
- In January 2009 the BBC refused to broadcast an appeal by the Disasters Emergency Committee for the people caught up in the conflict in Gaza. Research the reasons for this refusal, investigating how closely it is linked to the BBC's policy of impartiality.
- Listen to an omnibus edition of *The Archers*. How are elderly people represented?
- List the advertisements broadcast in a three-hour period on LBC. What does this tell you about their target audience?
- Analyse and compare the representations of young people in two radio dramas, one broadcast on Radio 4 and one on Radio 7.

Let's produce

The production exercise has to show your teacher and moderator that you have a good knowledge and understanding of representations in talk radio. Remember that you need to cover at least two media in this unit as a whole. You will probably compare representation on two radio stations for your comparative assignment, so you need to choose a production exercise in a different medium, such as a website for a radio soap.

Here are some suggestions for different exercises:

- Devise a name, logo and a print advertisement for a new commercial talk radio station.
- Produce two pages for a website to support a new 10-minute soap series for Radio 7.
- Produce a listings magazine article that promotes a new radio programme for children.
- Produce the homepage of a website to support a new local talk radio station.
- Produce a magazine review of a fictional new breakfast show for LBC.

Let's evaluate

Your evaluation can be in the form of a written essay, a podcast, or a PowerPoint presentation. Remember to answer these questions in your evaluation:

■ What area of representation (such as cultural difference, disability, or age) did you choose to focus on in your radio exercise?
■ What messages were you trying to convey?
■ How did you plan and research for your exercise?
■ How did you use media techniques, such as choice of presenters, music, jingles and mode of address to challenge or reinforce messages and values?
■ What are the strengths and weaknesses of your finished exercise?

Key terms

Format: a particular style and structure of a radio station or programme
Ident: the short jingle that identifies a radio station
Mode of address: the way in which a programme and/or radio station speaks to its audience
Psychographics: ways of defining audiences, such as lifestyle, values and interests
Public service broadcasting: broadcasting to educate, inform and entertain; broadcasting in the public interest
RAJAR: Radio Joint Audience Research – measures radio audience figures, jointly owned by the BBC and commercial radio
Remit: the terms that set out what a radio station must deliver
Simulcast: programmes that are broadcast across more than one medium or wavelength at the same time
Soundbite: a clip taken from a longer interview or speech
Vox pop: 'voice of the people' – unrehearsed interviews with members of the public

■ Useful websites

www.bbc.co.uk/fivelive/: website of Radio 5 Live
www.bbc.co.uk/radio4/archers/: *The Archers*' official website
www.bbc.co.uk/radio7/: website of Radio 7
www.lbc.co.uk/: website of LBC radio
www.mediaguardian.co.uk: *Guardian* website with useful articles on radio
www.ofcom.org.uk/radio/: a useful section of the official Ofcom site that focuses on radio
www.radiocentre.org/: commercial radio website
www.rajar.co.uk: website of the Radio Joint Audience Research

Topic 6: Soap Opera

■ What is a soap opera?

A soap opera is an ongoing serial drama produced for television or radio. The name comes from the fact that the original soap operas on US radio in the 1930s were sponsored by soap manufacturers. Soap operas have been a popular part of British television for many years; they enjoy a prime time slot on most major British television channels and receive some of the highest viewing figures on terrestrial television.

Some of the best known soap operas are:

■ *EastEnders* – a BBC production that was first broadcast in 1985. It is set in the fictitious London borough of Albert Square. It currently has four screenings per week during prime time. It is one of the most watched programmes on BBC1 and receives average viewing figures of between 6 and 9 million. (BARB, 26 January–1 February 2009)

■ *Coronation Street* – a Granada production as part of ITV, it was first broadcast in 1960 and is set in the fictional town of Weatherfield in Greater Manchester. It currently has five screenings a week with two episodes on Mondays and Fridays and one episode on a Wednesday. It achieves average viewing figures of 9 to 10 million. (BARB, 26 January–1 February 2009)

■ *Emmerdale* (formerly *Emmerdale Farm*) – a Yorkshire Television production as part of ITV, it was first broadcast in 1972 and is set in the fictional village of Emmerdale in West Yorkshire. It currently has five screenings a week, every weekday at 7 pm for 30 minutes, except Tuesdays, where it has a full hour. It has viewing figures on average of 7 million. (BARB, 6 January–1 February 2009)

■ *Hollyoaks* – produced by Lime Pictures as part of Channel 4, it was first broadcast in 1995 and is set in the fictional Hollyoaks village in Chester. It currently has five screenings a week, every weekday at 6.30 pm, but has also had a number of late night episodes in its history. It has viewing figures on average of 1.8 million. (BARB 26 January–1 February 2009)

Let's analyse

Look at these two images:

▲ *Figure 1.35: The Queen Vic and the Rovers Return*

■ The first is the setting for *EastEnders*, including the central meeting place, The Queen Victoria Pub. The second image is the setting for *Coronation Street*, including their central meeting place, The Rovers Return Inn.

■ What connotations can you draw about the two soaps based on the locations?

■ Soap opera conventions

Soap operas are considered to be a subgenre of television drama, and therefore they share many similar conventions with this genre.

However, there are some conventions unique to the soap opera:

■ a large ensemble cast of characters of different ages, genders and backgrounds

■ long-running storylines, sometimes over a number of episodes and sometimes over a number of months or even years

■ storylines that involve problems the audience or society in general may be experiencing

■ an attempted reflection of society and realism

■ time passes in the same way as in 'reality'

■ a lack of narrative closure at the end of each episode; instead there are constant cliffhangers.

Many hybrid genres have been developed where soap opera is used as a key generic feature. The docusoap – a combination of documentary and soap opera – has become very popular in recent years.

■ Watch *Ramsay's Kitchen Nightmares* (Channel 4, 2004–present).

■ What soap opera conventions has this programme incorporated in order to become successful?

UK soap opera timeline

1951: First broadcast of *The Archers'* on Radio 4.

1960: First broadcast of *Coronation Street* on ITV.

1964: First broadcast of *Crossroads* on ITV.

1972: First broadcast of *Emmerdale Farm* on ITV.

1982: Channel 4 begins broadcasting, including new soap *Brookside*.

1985: First broadcast of *EastEnders* on BBC1.

1986: Australian soap *Neighbours* is screened on BBC1.

1988: *Crossroads* is cancelled.

1989: *Emmerdale Farm* changes its name to *Emmerdale*.

1989: Australian soap *Home and Away* is broadcast on ITV.

1992: BBC launches new soap *Eldorado*.

1993: *Eldorado* is cancelled.

1995: Channel 4 launches *Hollyoaks*.

1997: FIVE is launched and brings its own soap, *Family Affairs*.

2001: A new version of *Crossroads* is launched on ITV.

2001: *Home and Away* is broadcast on FIVE.

2003: Final episode of *Brookside*.

2003: The new version of *Crossroads* is cancelled.

2005: *Family Affairs* is cancelled.

2008: *Neighbours* is screened on FIVE, after intense negotiations with production company Fremantle Media.

■ Representations in soap operas

In soap operas there is a considerable range of different representations, largely due to the variety of characters and storylines. Your task is to explore how a particular group/event/issue is represented in two different soaps. You can study two television soap operas or you may wish to include a radio soap in your analysis, such as *The Archers* (see page 60 in Topic 5: Talk Radio).

The Individual Media Studies Portfolio

UNIT 1

Resources: *Hollyoaks* (Channel 4, 2005–2007)

CLARE DEVINE IN *HOLLYOAKS*

Clare Devine is a character from the Channel 4 soap opera *Hollyoaks*. From her first appearance in 2005, through to her exit in 2007, Clare became a true soap opera villain. During her time on the show Clare has cheated on, blackmailed, threatened, lied to and even tried to murder her husband, Max. When she eventually left the soap it involved her kidnapping another character called Katie Fox, and driving off a cliff with her held hostage in the back.

Another villain in the show, Warren Fox, managed to save Katie, but Clare was seen sinking out of sight into the water. However, this was not the end of Clare, as at the end of this episode she was seen at an airport, dressed provocatively and looking fit and well, while seemingly locating her next 'victim'.

Clare Devine is a classic example of a soap opera villain. She is callous, selfish and lacks any moral values, and is the kind of character the audience can unite over in their hatred of her. At no point does she repent for the crimes she has committed and right up until her last moment on the soap she continues to 'break the rules'. Her villainy is largely represented through her actions, her crimes, her inhumane treatment of others and the other characters' reactions to her.

However, it is also due to the audiences' responses to her that she achieves the status of villain. Because Clare continues to go against audience expectations of acceptable behaviour, she remains a villain in our eyes as well as in the eyes of the other characters.

In contrast to many other soap villains, Clare is also a glamorous character; she is young, attractive and usually wearing high fashion codes of dress. She uses her looks and her femininity to manipulate her husband, Max Cunningham. However, one of the few characters who initially suspects her villainy is Max's best friend, OB. A possible reason for OB's dislike of Clare could be jealousy, because he desired her himself when she first appeared on the soap, before she became involved with Max. This suggests that OB is almost immune to Clare's charms and visual appeal because of his previously spurned advances, and this therefore shows that her power lies in her looks and sexuality.

Clare is a character who revels in her power and villainy, but also in her visual appeal and the power this holds over men. What makes her such an interesting character to explore is the way she is represented in comparison to other villainous characters. The fact that Clare is female seems to add to her villainy: the way she uses her sexuality to get what she wants is unacceptable in the eyes of the audience, which for the soap opera genre tends to consist mainly of females.

▲ *Figure 1.36: Clare and Warren Fox come to blows*

However, Clare is not the only villain in *Hollyoaks*. Warren Fox is also a very unpleasant character, who has committed murder and been involved in drug dealing and adultery, and yet during Clare's final storyline his villainy is not represented as being as bad as Clare's, and until 2009 he remains unpunished for his crimes. In fact, during Clare's departure from the soap it was Warren who became the hero of the storyline as he sought to rescue his sister Katie whom Clare had kidnapped.

Close analysis

During Clare's 'final' episode after her supposed death, she appears at an airport, revealing that she is alive and well and back to her old tricks. Her entrance shows a pair of legs coming towards the screen; she is shot in long shot and appears in the background of the frame, moving towards the camera. She wears a bright red dress, matching high-heeled shoes and is pulling a red holdall behind her. She stops with her feet now in the foreground of the shot and it is revealed that she is also wearing red striped tights.

The camera now cuts to a chest-height shot of Clare, as she takes the right-hand side of the frame, and on the left-hand side of the frame a number of older male characters are looking at her, clearly attracted to the pretty young woman. Finally, Clare finds a seat next to another male character, a wealthy-looking businessman called Miles. This is the first moment the character is revealed to be Clare as her face is finally in frame. After a short conversation with Miles, Clare looks directly forward at the camera and seemingly straight at the audience, with a very self-confident look on her face and certainly showing no sense of remorse.

The constant use of the colour red in Clare's codes of dress represents her passion and her danger. The fact that we see shots of her legs and chest before we see her face allows her visual appearance and obvious sexuality to become the focus of the sequence. And finally, the 'knowing' look to the audience at the end seems to be a final insult over the fact she remains unpunished for her villainy.

The ideology suggests that villainy is acceptable if the culprit is male, but if the character is female, the behaviour becomes unacceptable. A female character who acts out of the boundaries of acceptable behaviour is usually going to be punished; she will (almost always) receive her comeuppance.

Soaps need to use stereotypes and when a character breaks out of those stereotypical boundaries they become a villain. When a female character like Clare Devine commits acts of cruelty and violence it is seen as worse than if a male character like Warren Fox does so. Clare is not acting in a 'lady-like' fashion. Therefore, in this particular case it is clear that the gender of the characters is closely linked to their villainous representation.

Let's discuss

In *EastEnders*, the character Janine Butcher was involved in the death of another character, Barry Evans, in 2003. Although the death could have been seen as accidental, Janine did nothing to help him and instead watched him die. For this crime Janine went unpunished, as Barry's death was seen as accidental. However, in 2004 Janine had a feud with another character, Laura, and was seen arguing with Laura just before her accidental death. Even though Janine was innocent of this crime, she was convicted of Laura's murder after another character testified against her, knowing she was innocent of this crime and yet guilty of Barry's murder.

- Look at this storyline. Do you believe Janine's conviction for Laura's death was justified?
- Do you think Janine's gender has anything to do with her villainy?
- Research other female soap villains in *EastEnders*.

Let's compare

Other soap characters that make interesting comparisons in their representation of villainy:

- *EastEnders*, Stella Crawford – a character who appeared as part of the soap's cast in 2006; she began a relationship with long-running *EastEnder* villain Phil Mitchell. During her relationship she became a villain through her emotional abuse of Phil's son, Ben. Her representation makes for an interesting study, especially in comparison to Phil Mitchell, who becomes the hero of the storyline.
- *Coronation Street*, David Platt – a character whose villainous representations have climbed steadily over the past five years. He has lied, manipulated, vandalised and even pushed his mother down the stairs. What makes him an interesting character is his age (he is a teenager) and his unhappy childhood.

Resources: *EastEnders* (1985–present)

IAN BEALE IN *EASTENDERS*

Ian Beale has been a character in *EastEnders* since it first aired in 1985. During his time on the soap he has become most famous for his desire to elevate himself financially and develop the Beale business 'empire'. He considers himself above the majority of the other characters in the programme and will stop at nothing to propel himself forward financially and 'better himself'. Ian Beale owns the local café, the fish and chip shop, the fruit and veg market stall and property on the square. The Beale empire has been a lot bigger in the past, but Ian had to declare himself bankrupt after the fall of the Beale empire during 2000–2003.

Ian Beale is a successful businessman, the entrepreneur of Walford, and yet he is far from being represented as a positive character on the soap. Ian's desire to excel, both for himself and his family, is often represented as being very negative. His ambition often clouds his moral values and he becomes ruthless and selfish. In Albert Square he is seen as a bit of a joke, as the characters who work for him dislike him and even his own family seem to have a problem with the way he acts. Ian Beale should be a positive character because he wishes to provide for his family and wants to elevate himself above his origins. These are positive character traits and should allow Ian Beale to have a positive representation in *EastEnders*. However, Ian's general appearance, behaviour and the way he goes about expanding his empire and bettering himself lead to him having a negative representation.

Ian is a smart and professional character, often one of the only characters to wear a suit, making him stand out instantly from the rest of the cast. Yet this is not positive as he does not fit in with his surroundings. He is also made an object of fun by the other characters in the soap.

▲ *Figure 1.37: Phil Mitchell threatening Ian Beale*

In February 2009, during Ian's 40th birthday celebrations the rest of the pub found out about his tattoo of a devil on his back. In the middle of a serious speech about bringing Walford through troubled times (economically), he is heckled by other residents, chanting to see his tattoo. Ian eventually shows the tattoo and runs from the pub, clearly upset. This all works together to represent Ian as a rather foolish character who is not really respected by the other residents of Walford. Everyone seems to have their problems with the man, and the majority of these problems tend to stem from the fact he considers himself above others.

The Individual Media Studies Portfolio

UNIT 1

What becomes most interesting in this example, is that Ian Beale is one of the few characters in the soap who does want to elevate his social status, while other characters seem to be content with their lives, or wish to hold onto their upbringing and social class, in spite of success. However, this is not the case with Ian. Due to the negative representation constructed through his image, behaviour and the other characters' reactions to him, we can deduce that the soap suggests a negativity about forgetting your origins. It also conveys the message that there is nothing wrong with being aware of your own background, and being aware of your social class. In this context, the suggestion is that Ian is a negative charcter due to the fact he is not capable of ackowledging his working-class background, which in itself holds a very positive status.

Let's discuss

Discuss the following questions and try to reach a group response:
- Why do you think the majority of soap operas are based in more working-class settings and around more working-class characters?
- Why are there so few positive representations of wealthy characters in British soaps?

Let's compare

Compare the representation of Ian Beale with one of the following characters, focusing on social class:
- *Hollyoaks*, Jessica Harris – coming from St Albans in Hertfordshire, Jessica attended Hollyoaks community college. She came from a rich family and was often considered to be rather 'snobby' by other characters around her. When her father had to declare himself bankrupt, Jessica had to adjust her lifestyle, and resorted to conning people and gambling.
- *EastEnders*, Billy Mitchell – a member of the infamous Mitchell family, Billy is often considered the weak link of the family. He works hard to earn money for his family in a similar way to Ian Beale. However, he is often unsuccessful in business and seems to earn just enough to keep afloat. His representation is much more positive than Ian's, and he makes a good comparison.

Let's produce

The production exercise has to show your teacher and moderator that you have a good knowledge and understanding of representations in soap operas. Remember that you need to cover at least two media in this unit as a whole. This means after having studied two soap operas for your comparative assignment, you now need to work in a different medium, such as print, radio or multimedia for your production exercise.

Here are some suggestions for different exercises:

■ A script for a two-minute segment from a new radio soap opera involving characters from two different regions of Britain.

■ A storyboarded sequence for a moving image advertisement that focuses on the introduction of a new villain in a soap opera.

■ An online diary for a young character in a television soap opera, providing an insight into their reaction to a current storyline.

■ A newspaper or magazine article on a female character from a soap, exploring her background on the programme.

Let's evaluate

Your evaluation can be in the form of a written essay, a podcast, or a PowerPoint presentation. Remember to answer these questions in your evaluation:

■ What area of representation (such as villainy, social class or gender) did you choose to focus on in your production exercise?

■ What messages were you trying to convey?

■ How did you plan and research for your exercise?

■ How did you use media techniques, such as casting, framing, mise-en-scène and scripting to challenge or reinforce messages and values?

■ What are the strengths and weaknesses of your finished exercise?

Key terms

Arc plot: a long-running storyline that appears in most episodes, sometimes in the background, and at other times as the main storyline

Cliffhanger: an incomplete storyline, left at the end of the episode in order to ensure the audience will tune in to the next episode to see the conclusion

Docusoap: a 'reality TV' show which combines documentary and soap opera

Ensemble cast: a large cast where all characters have an equal level of importance

Primetime: the timeslot on television in the early evening when it is considered the majority of audience members will be watching

Scheduling: placing a television programme or radio broadcast into a particular time slot for audience viewing

Social class: a hierarchy in society based on education, occupation, income, background, etc.

Social realism: an expression of what is deemed to be a realistic representation of society

Terrestrial television: television available to everyone with access to a TV, due to the fact that it does not require satellite or cable transmission

Watershed: programmes and advertisements broadcast before 9 pm on UK television channels are not permitted to show material deemed unsuitable for younger viewers

■ Useful websites

www.bbc.co.uk/eastenders: homepage for the BBC soap opera *Eastenders*, which features news, videos, character biographies and quizzes

www.channel4.com/entertainment/tv/microsites/H/hollyoaks/: homepage for the Channel 4 soap opera *Hollyoaks*, which features news, videos, character biographies and episode synopses

www.itv.com/coronationstreet: homepage for the ITV soap opera *Coronation Street*, which features news, videos and character biographies

www.itv.com/emmerdale: homepage for the ITV soap opera *Emmerdale*, which features news, videos and character biographies

www.thesoapshow.com: a website offering information on British, Australian and American soaps

www.mediaknowall.com: useful site for students

www.guardian.co.uk/media: a good archive source for media stories relating to soaps

www.radiotimes.com: features scheduling information and reviews for current soap opera episodes

Topic 7: Sport and the Media

■ Why study sport and the media?

Sport is a very popular pastime in Britain and across the world. The variety of sports, the facilities and clubs available allow us to gain enjoyment and exercise from sporting activities. Many people also like to follow the progress of their favourite football team or sports star, even though they may not practise the sport themselves. Competitive sports have been reported since the first Olympic Games in Ancient Greece in 776 BC. Sport is an interesting topic to choose for exploring representations, particularly those of masculinity and nationality.

Sport and the media timeline

19th century:	Reports on cricket, rugby and athletics appear regularly in the press.

19th century: Reports on cricket, rugby and athletics appear regularly in the press.
1903: Tour de France established by French newspaper *L'Auto*.
1908: London Olympics widely reported – popular interest in sport increases.
June 1937: First televised Wimbledon championships.
1948: Sports Journalists' Association founded.
1966: England wins World Cup – watched on television by 32.3 million people, the biggest television audience of all time.
1974: Muhammed Ali's boxing match against George Foreman becomes headline news.
1992: *Fever Pitch* by Nick Hornby published.
2001: Hawk-Eye first used at cricket Test match at Lord's.

To investigate sport in the media you can explore a range of texts from:

- film
- radio
- newspapers
- magazines
- television
- advertising.

Sport is seen as one of the most popular subjects in the media; it is valuable to media producers as it helps to sell media texts. Many newspapers have separate sports supplements, there are sports-centred magazines and there are countless television programmes and television channels dedicated to sporting events. There have also been a number of films produced that draw the majority of their subject material from sport.

Fever Pitch (Evans, 1997, UK) is one example of this. It focuses on Paul Ashworth, who is dedicated to his favourite football team, Arsenal. After he meets and falls in love with Sarah, the story follows the development of their relationship as Arsenal progress through the football league. Sarah is initially alienated by Paul's dedication to his team and Paul must convince her that football is 'more than just a game'.

The film represents football in two ways: firstly as an extremely important part of British culture and secondly, as a principally male-dominated pastime. The film's success led to an American remake in 2005, where football was replaced with baseball and Arsenal with the Boston Red Sox. You could analyse this film as part of an investigation into football and masculinity (see more on this later in this Topic).

▲ *Figure 1.38:* Fever Pitch

Due to the popularity of sport in the media, and the vast amounts of money involved, a number of technological devices have been specifically designed to aid sport reporting. Football pitches are built with a press pit to allow photographers to take the photos they need for newspapers and tracks are often set up along the side of pitches, running tracks and other arenas to allow the camera to follow the action. Perhaps the most revolutionary form of technology developed for sport reporting is the system known as Hawk-Eye.

■ Hawk-Eye

Hawk-Eye is a computer system developed to aid adjudication in certain sports, most commonly used in tennis and cricket. The huge financial rewards available in professional sport have made it necessary to take human error out of decision making. The system has the ability to track the path of an object, such as the ball in a tennis match, and place the exact position of that object at a certain point in time. It works by using a series of high speed cameras positioned around the pitch/court. These cameras work together to triangulate the path of the ball and its position in the playing field. This has been used to great effect to analyse whether a ball is out of bounds during sporting events such as Wimbledon. Players have the opportunity to consult Hawk-Eye if they believe a ball to be out and wish to challenge the umpire's call.

◀ Figure 1.39: The Federer—Nadal Wimbledon men's final in 2007 used Hawk-Eye to make calls on points

'I think the data that Hawk-Eye is able to capture and process in user-friendly form is invaluable in helping us all gain a unique insight into how the best players in the world are able to achieve all they do. Not only are we able to sit back and enjoy watching the world's best compete with one another, now with the help of Hawk-Eye we can also learn from them too.' (TV commentator and Hawk-Eye analyst Jason Goodall)

This clearly suggests that Hawk-Eye is more than just useful for the players, but also helps us as an audience to learn from the match we are watching. These kinds of technological advances change the way the audience watches sport, and allow the act of watching to become more active.

 Let's discuss

- Consider whether certain technological advances such as Hawk-Eye would have been developed if had not been for the televised nature of these sporting events.
- Based on your discussions on this topic, weigh up the positives and negatives for televising sporting activities.

◼ Audiences for sport

All media texts are designed for audience consumption. The producers expect the audience to watch, listen, read or buy the text in order for it to become successful. However, different media texts provoke a different consumption habit in audiences. For example, you are more likely to read a newspaper or a magazine on your own than in a group. Watching sport on the television, however, is very different, as it can be more of a group activity, often with large groups of people congregating to watch a specific sporting event on TV. Major sporting events are often screened in pubs or other public places, making the experience of watching sport on television a group activity.

Audiences who go to see sporting events live find themselves in large groups; for example, Wembley stadium seats up to 90,000 spectators. When watching sport on television many audience members attempt to recreate the atmosphere at a live match by watching the programme in large groups. You can see that there are differences between the reasons for watching sport on television and the reasons for watching other forms of broadcasting. The act of watching sport instantly becomes more sociable; it becomes an event for groups to share.

Uses and gratifications theory and sport

This theory suggests that individual audience members consume media texts for different reasons, and use them in different ways in order to gain gratification. McQuail, Blumler and Brown identified these four uses in 1972:

- ◼ diversion and entertainment – an escape from our everyday lives
- ◼ surveillance – gathering information about what is going on in the world
- ◼ personal identity – we want to establish who we are in relation to others
- ◼ personal relationships – conversation and social interaction with others.

It is easy to see why sport in the media is so popular as it fulfils all these needs for audiences. The social act of watching sport as a group can be seen as more desirable, due to the entertainment gained from the group atmosphere and the sense of personal identity that is reinforced by this activity, which is an extremely gratifying experience in today's busy society.

Let's research

Research the viewing habits of audiences watching sport. Here are some questions to start.

- What sports are you most interested in?
- How often do you watch sport on television?
- Do you watch sport with a group of people?
- What reasons do you have for watching sport in a group?

Using these research findings, consider the positives and negatives for watching sport on television, as opposed to being at the live game.

Case study 1 – The representation of Britishness in the media

Exemplar task: Analyse the representations of British identity through an exploration of the press coverage of Wimbledon.

Wimbledon is the main British tennis competition. Played out over two weeks, it incorporates the men's singles, women's singles and men's, women's and mixed doubles tournaments. It usually takes place in the last week of June and first week in July and currently enjoys live coverage on the BBC as well as a great deal of newspaper coverage.

▲ *Figure 1.40: Wimbledon*

When tennis first appeared it was considered to be a sport of the 'upper classes', and it retains a certain level of that background to this day. Audiences at tennis matches are expected to remain quiet, and the officials, linesmen and players are expected to remain well-mannered and can even be fined for bad language or rude behaviour.

However, televised tennis has led to a decline in this reputation. We have seen many examples of 'bad behaviour' in tennis games, most famously John McEnroe in 1981 swearing at the umpire and shouting his famous line 'You cannot be serious' after disagreeing with the calls. More recently in 1997, the US Open saw Venus Williams bump into Irina Spîrlea as they changed ends. This small incident led to a number of negative comments, coming first from Venus' father and then from Irina herself.

The British press regularly reports on the action at Wimbledon. In newspapers, sport is usually confined to the back pages, and yet when the event is big enough the press will often place it towards the front of the paper or even on the front page. This is especially likely if the player featuring in a match is British. We have seen a number of British players at Wimbledon in recent years, including Greg Rusedski, Andy Murray and Tim Henman. When one of these players is involved the reporting moves from being a part of the sports pages to being front page news.

However, when we reach the US Open, the French Open or the Australian Open, tennis is relegated to the back pages again. It seems that a British player alone is not enough to earn a spot on the front page, but a British player in a British tournament is required for tennis to take a higher place in the news agenda.

Therefore, it is clear that a sense of British identity is extremely important to the British press and its audience. The 'soft' news story of a British sports personality winning on his/her own territory takes precedence over 'hard' news such as politics. Many of the tabloid newspapers place a high level of importance on certain players.

Look below at these headlines from Wimbledon 2008. In each headline it is Andy Murray who becomes the focal point, and each headline uses hyperbole (exaggeration to create emphasis).

Britons pin hopes on Andy Murray

The Sun website
24 June 2008

- 'Britons pin hopes on Andy Murray' suggests that everyone in Britain is behind Murray.
- The headline implies that everyone in Britain has hopes of someone British winning Wimbledon.
- The headline seeks to unite all the people of Britain under the single hope of a British champion.

Andy win sparks 'Murray mania'

The Sun website
25 June 2008

- The use of alliteration in 'Murray mania' is designed to construct a catchy and memorable phrase.
- The phrase references previous tabloid term 'Henmania' and reminds the audience of former successes.
- The headline suggests that Britain has been gripped by a strong desire – some might say close to madness – to support Andy Murray.

Andy Murray pulls off one of sport's greatest comebacks

The Mirror
1 January 2008

- The hyperbole in this headline is designed to suggest Murray's strength and extraordinary ability.
- It reinforces the idea that Murray is deserving of our praise and is what Britain needs.
- Murray is represented as the underdog who snatches victory from the jaws of failure. British people love the underdog and the 'Dunkirk spirit'.

The interpretation here is that the press is attempting to whip up a frenzy in its audience, to provide information to those who are already watching Wimbledon and to entice those who are not, to begin watching. There is a sense of British pride present in the articles – the sports personality is British and therefore we as a nation should be supporting him.

The national pride constructed in the press coverage can be seen as a sense of 'Britishness', and this is being represented as a very positive thing. The sportsmen and women on television and in newspapers are British and not only should we feel proud of them but the suggestion is that we should feel proud of ourselves because of them.

Let's research

- Research a major sporting event that is currently taking place.
- Look at newspaper and television reporting on this event and consider what it says about British identity in sport.

Let's compare

- Look at the press coverage of the England v Germany football matches throughout World Cup history, considering how the press represents national identity.
- Look at the coverage of the 2007 Rugby World Cup, focusing on England v South Africa in the first round and the same two teams in the final round.
- Look at the press coverage during the 2008 Beijing Olympics, focusing on some of the lesser-known sports where gold medals were won.

Case study 2 – The representation of masculinity in sport

Exemplar task: Compare the representations of masculinity in sport through an analysis of two football players and the press coverage that surrounds them.

AN EXPLORATION OF DAVID BECKHAM

David Beckham is a famous British football player, who has played for Manchester United, Real Madrid, Los Angeles Galaxy and AC Milan. He has also been a regular in the England football team since 1996 and was team captain from 2000–2006. In 2006 he stepped down as captain, but remained a member of the England squad.

However, while he is a talented sportsman, he has had a rather varied representation in the British media. In the 1998 Fifa World Cup, Beckham received a red card during England's second round match against Argentina. He was seen kicking the Argentinean player Diego Simeone while lying on the floor. The team went through to draw this match and lost on penalties, sending them out of the tournament. The press, particularly the tabloids (*The Mirror*, for instance, published a picture of Beckham on a dartboard), blamed Beckham for this situation and for a while afterwards Beckham was heckled and taunted. However, it has been rare for the press to criticise his sporting ability. Beckham is arguably more famous as a celebrity than as a sportsman.

Aside from his football career, Beckham has been involved in advertising campaigns for brands such as Coca-Cola, IBM, Armani and Police sunglasses, among many others. He has become a famous fashion icon for men, frequently photographed sporting a variety of different hairstyles and wearing high fashion clothing. His marriage to Victoria Beckham increased his reputation and fame. Beckham has come under attack in the press on many occasions for new hairstyles, certain outfits and his rather exuberant wedding, which was parodied in the television drama series *Footballers' Wives*.

What do you think the reasons for these different representations are? You will find Topic 4 on page 43 useful when analysing Beckham's celebrity status.

Let's analyse

Hairstyles
Over the years, Beckham has become famous for sporting different hairstyles. With each new cut comes a high level of press attention. Look at these hairstyles Beckham has adopted on the right:

Analyse these images and consider how each hairstyle represents Beckham in a different way.

▲ Figure 1.41: Beckham with a mohawk (or mohican), reminiscent of Travis Bickle from the film Taxi Driver; an 'out of bed' highlighted quiff; and a longer blond style

A NEW FORM OF MASCULINITY?

Sport has always been considered a predominantly male-orientated part of the media. Television broadcasts, press reports and even radio broadcasts on sport have a tendency to be stereotypically targeted at male audiences. David Beckham represents something different in the sporting field. There is no denying his sporting ability, he is clearly a talented man, and yet he represents a very different form of masculinity.

He has often been described as 'metrosexual', a term used to describe a heterosexual man who becomes increasingly image conscious and works hard on his appearance and look. In 2002, journalist Mark Simpson, who originally coined the phrase, wrote an article describing Beckham as the 'poster boy for metrosexuality'. This movement away from the stereotypical representation of masculinity is refreshing for a sports personality.

'[Beckham] as a man, carried a certain amount of timely association: he came to embody new mannishness and not, as is commonly supposed, just by having a high voice and wearing a sari on his hols. He has been captain of the England team since 2000, and yet has never seemed to lead by machismo, or any of the bullish qualities that are commonly thought of as 'leaderly'. He captained because he was the best at it: he captained through a process of stringent meritocracy. So his time in office ... made football a different place.' (Zoe Williams, *The Guardian*, 4 July 2006)

This offers a strong interpretation of Beckham's values: he is a representation of masculinity, but in a different way to other football players of the past. Beckham has never been seen attacking photographers or getting into fights in the middle of town centres, he is not seen frequently drinking and is often photographed with his family. He represents a different form of masculinity from the traditional form we are used to in the sporting world:

- Beckham cares about his appearance and has become a fashion icon
- he is dedicated to his family
- he is not aggressive
- he is not involved in 'macho' displays
- his reputation is based on professionalism.

Yet at the same time Beckham is a man who is clearly 'masculine' in many of the traditional ways. It is this deviation from what is considered to be more stereotypical 'masculine' footballer behaviour that leads to the rather mixed receptions in the media.

Let's compare

- Look at reports on Wayne Rooney in the British press and compare the representations of his masculinity to those of David Beckham.
- Look at the press reports on Jonny Wilkinson and compare the representations of his masculinity to those of David Beckham. Do you think the different sporting backgrounds have an effect on these representations?

Let's produce

The production exercise has to show your teacher and moderator that you have a good knowledge and understanding of representations of sport and sporting personalities in the media. Remember that you need to cover at least two media in this unit as a whole. This means if you have chosen to study two newspaper stories for your comparative assignment, then you need to work in a different medium, such as radio or television for your production exercise.

Here are some suggestions for different exercises:
- A double-page spread from a new sports magazine reviewing a local sporting event.
- A script for a radio broadcast discussing the development of British sport in recent years.
- A webpage for a local sports team, profiling the players and giving details of recent matches or events.
- A storyboard (photographed or hand drawn) for a new sports chat show incorporating female presenters.

Let's evaluate

Your evaluation can be in the form of a written essay, a podcast, or a PowerPoint presentation. Remember to answer these questions in your evaluation:
- What area of representation (such as masculinity, Britishness or regionality) did you choose to focus on in your production exercise?
- What messages were you trying to convey?
- How did you plan and research for your exercise?
- How did you use media techniques, such as casting, framing, mise-en-scène and mode of address to challenge or reinforce messages and values?
- What are the strengths and weaknesses of your finished exercise?

Key terms

Global recognition: a term used to describe a sports personality who has escalated beyond fame in his/her own country to worldwide recognition

Metrosexual: a heterosexual man who becomes increasingly image conscious and works hard on his appearance

'New' man: a recent trend in sociology where the man is seen to differ from the stereotypical representation of masculinity. The 'new' man is often more in touch with emotions and concerned with his image

Pay per view: a new form of television largely evolving from satellite broadcasting. The viewer pays for the individual programme they wish to watch; sporting events have become one of the main forms of pay per view television

Role model: a person who becomes a figure that members of the audience can look up to and relate to. Sporting stars are some of the most common types of role model

Sponsorship: a company will often invest money in a sports team, providing the team with money to buy facilities, equipment etc., and the company's name will often appear in some way on the team's kit, stadium or vehicle, as a form of advertising

Sports star: a sports personality who has evolved beyond the realms of fame for their sporting ability alone; instead these stars are often famous for their style, image, advertising connections, etc.

■ Useful websites

http://news.bbc.co.uk/sport: the BBC site for sport stories
www.guardian.co.uk/sport: a good archive source for sport stories
www.matchmag.co.uk: homepage for the British football magazine
www.skysports.com: homepage for the sport satellite channel
www.wimbledon.org: homepage for the Wimbledon tournament

The Individual Media Studies Portfolio

UNIT 1

Topic 8: News

■ What is news?

Although the answer to the question above may seem obvious, it is becoming increasingly difficult to define or categorise the term 'news'. The multichannel culture, together with other technological changes, such as the increased use of social networking sites and text messaging on mobile phones, mean that news is undergoing a rapid period of change. These changes are present in the ways that news is gathered, presented and accessed by audiences.

▲ *Figure 1.42: Hard news or soft news? John Sergeant in* Strictly Come Dancing *(2008); BBC newsreader John Snagge (1944); Jonathan Ross and Russell Brand disgraced (2008); Barack Obama elected (2008)*

Hard news	Soft news
Business news	Human interest stories
War	Entertainment
Politics	Sport
Foreign affairs	Celebrity
Disasters	Fashion

One of the key changes is in the increased mixing of soft news and hard news (see table on previous page). Traditionally, a news programme like the BBC *10 O'clock News* would have focused on hard news, with only the occasional references to soft news. Yet because of the increased competition between channels for audiences ('the ratings battle'), the BBC *10 O'clock News* broadcasts many more items of celebrity news, such as coverage of film award ceremonies, than it did five years ago.

Celebrity status

In the second half of 2008, news providers balanced the depressing news stories on the economic slump with celebrity soft news stories, such as John Sergeant's resignation from *Strictly Come Dancing* and the row over Russell Brand and Jonathan Ross's Radio 2 telephone calls to Andrew Sachs. This demonstrates a change in news values, representing the 'celebrities' as having significant status, equal to that of the politicians and world leaders in the hard news stories.

Messages and values

News texts can be seen as reflecting our society's values, although we also need to bear in mind the huge impact of changes in technology when analysing newspapers, news programmes or news on the internet.

It is interesting to compare news reporting from an earlier time period with news reporting today, in order to track changes in representations and to recognise changing messages and values.

For this topic, you can study news produced for:

- television
- newspapers
- the internet
- radio
- cinema (Pathé newsreels, for example)
- podcasts
- 24-hour rolling news channels
- mobile phones.

Let's analyse

- Compare early front pages of *The Guardian* with more recent ones (see next page).
- How has the mode of address changed?
- To what extent have the values of the news changed?
- What does this change tell you about newspaper producers and audiences?

▲ *Figure 1.43: Front pages of* The Guardian *from 5 May 1821 (left) and 12 September 2001 (right). You can compare more pages by researching them on http://www.guardian.co.uk/news/gallery*

News timeline

1922: First radio news broadcasts; presenters have upper-class accents and wear full evening dress.

1925: Lord Reith's memo to the Crawford Committee states that public service broadcasting should 'inform, educate, and entertain'.

1936–1955: BBC television news has no competition as the BBC has a monopoly.

1955: ITV begins broadcasting, with ITN providing the news bulletins and outside broadcast reports.

1967: ITV launches *News at Ten*.

1980: BBC2 launches *Newsnight*.

1982: *Channel 4 News* launched (supported by ITN).

1984: Murdoch sets up Sky satellite television.

1996: *Channel 5 News* launched; Kirsty Young presents news sitting on a desk; this informal style influences other channels' news presentation style.

1998: Launch of digital broadcasting.

2001: Internet rivals radio as news source for attacks on World Trade Center.

2008: Internet on mobiles used to break and report news on Mumbai attacks.

■ Controls

It is important to remember that all terrestrial TV and radio channels are subject to public service broadcasting requirements, with the BBC and Channel 4 being the most tightly controlled by Ofcom. This obviously has an important effect on representation, as the BBC is still committed to being 'independent, resisting pressure and influence from any source'. A recent controversial example of this is the 2009 decision by Director General Mark Thompson not to broadcast an appeal to help the victims of conflict in Gaza.

In contrast, there are no specific laws controlling newspapers, although British newspapers agree to conform to a code of practice that is supervised by the Press Complaints Commission. The internet has no formal controls and many argue that it could not and should not be regulated by the Government.

When you are analysing the representations of people, places or events in the news, your knowledge of how tightly the news producers are controlled will help to inform your analysis.

 Let's research

- Find out how Ofcom controls broadcasting (look at www.ofcom.org.uk).
- Look at the BBC's statement on impartiality on www.bbc.co.uk/bbctrust.
- Investigate the code of practice for British newspapers on www.pcc.org.uk/cop/practice.html.

 Case study 1 – Representations of war

Resources:
The Daily Sketch (3 June 1940)
The Bristol Evening Post (31 May 1940)
Dunkirk: The Soldiers' Story (BBC, 2003)
Dunkirk: The Propaganda War by Nick Higham
(http://news.bbc.co.uk)
Al-Jazeera Exclusive (BBC2, 2004)
The Mirror, Daily Express and *The Sun*
(20 March 2003)

Exemplar task: Compare the representation of the soldiers and the event of the evacuation of Dunkirk in 1940 with the representation of the soldiers and the onset of the Iraq War in March 2003.

In times of war, governments always want to increase their control over the media. This is in order to control the ways in which key events and those who are fighting in the war and conducting the war are represented. However, technological changes have made this increasingly difficult for politicians (see table on next page).

Available sources of news	
1940 – Dunkirk	**2003 – Iraq War**
■ **Newsreels** (especially Pathé News). Produced as part of the war effort, with uplifting music and authoritative reassuring male 'voice of God' style voice-over ■ **BBC radio** – only two stations, the Home Service and the Forces Programme. Television was not transmitted during the war for fear of lights at Alexandra Palace attracting enemy planes. Tightly controlled by Director General Lord Reith and the principles of Public Service Broadcasting ■ **Newspapers** that all supported the war effort	■ **Rolling 24-hour news channels** like Sky News and BBC News 24. This meant a demand for constant updating of news, with the result that there were some inaccuracies ■ **A wide range of satellite, cable and digital television news channels** ■ **The internet** with many online newspapers and TV news websites from all over the world, weblogs and other sites on news. Little or no control of the material ■ **Newspapers**, which are self-regulated, so not tightly controlled by the Government. *The Mirror* was critical of the Iraq War from the outset, while *The Guardian* and *The Independent* reported the huge opposition to the war ■ **A wide range of national, regional and local radio stations**, mostly privately owned

DUNKIRK 1940

From the table above you can see why the Government found it so difficult to control representations of the soldiers and the events of the Iraq War. Audiences had a huge range of news sources to choose from in 2003 in comparison to audiences in 1940.

Technological advances, together with the fact that there was huge opposition to the Iraq War, meant that representations of the events in the news were often negative.

In contrast, in 1940 the media helped Churchill's government to represent the defeat at Dunkirk in a positive way, turning it into a triumph.

The Dunkirk soldiers were represented as heroic figures, despite the fact that many of them did not see themselves in that way.

▲ *Figure 1.44: Turning a disaster into a triumph – the* Daily Sketch *reports Dunkirk*

Headlines read 'Heroes of Flanders Safely Home' and 'Their Spirit was an Inspiration to the Nation' (*Bristol Evening Post*, 31 May 1940). Over 330,000 soldiers had been saved, but the evacuation left over 68,000 allied soldiers dead or taken prisoner. Churchill openly referred to the event as 'a colossal military disaster', but this is not how it is remembered.

The strong use of alliteration in the headline of the *Daily Sketch* suggests triumph rather than disaster: 'Dunkirk Defence Defies 300,000'. The image almost fills the front page with a high-angle long shot of troops arriving home – at a distance so audiences cannot see the wounded soldiers or how tired and dishevelled the troops are.

NEWSREELS

The newsreels (*Dunkirk: The Soldiers' Story*, BBC, 2003) offer a very positive representation of the returning soldiers. The footage focuses on smiling, cheerful looking men, drinking tea and eating sandwiches. The non-diegetic music is upbeat, stirring and patriotic. The authoritative male voice-over is brisk and strongly persuasive that audiences should agree with its messages.

▲ *Figure 1.45: Dunkirk survivors return to a heroes' welcome at Ramsgate*

However, when the newsreel is juxtaposed with the eyewitness accounts of the veterans, a very different representation of events is constructed. The newsreel voice-over states: 'The BEF. Their discipline has been superb'. This is cut together with a close-up of the veteran guardsman Desmond Thorogood, who comments, 'We were a rabble ... People cheered us as if we were victors. But what had we done? Held them off for a little while ...'.

CENSORSHIP

When a troopship was bombed in France a few days after Dunkirk, killing thousands of British soldiers and sailors, the story was not reported. This shows how tightly controlled the representations were.

IRAQ WAR 2003

In contrast, it was impossible for the Blair government to control all the sources of news so tightly during the Iraq War in 2003. Yet the Government still tried to control the ways in which journalists represented the war. After the BBC reported on the opposition to the war, BBC reporters were banned from the aircraft carrier *Ark Royal*. BBC1's Rageh Omaar, who reported from Baghdad, was accused by the Government of representing the Iraqis in too positive a light.

The Government encouraged journalists to be embedded with the army – to be attached to them and to limit their reporting of the conflict. This meant a certain amount of censorship could take place, although journalists could use videophones, satellites and laptops to file their reports instantly and apparently without intervention.

Let's compare

If you look at the front pages of the *Daily Express*, *The Sun* and the *Daily Mirror* from 20 March 2003, the first day of the Iraq War, you can see very different approaches to representing the soldiers and the conflict. Look at the comments below to give you some ideas on how to compare the representations in the three pages.

▲ *Figure 1.46:* The Daily Express

▲ *Figure 1.47:* The Sun

The *Daily Express* tries to capture some of the patriotism of the 1940 *Daily Sketch* in World War II: 'Our troops go into battle'; 'Britons told to stockpile food and water'.

The out-of-focus long shot constructs an image of heroic troops battling against the natural world – a sandstorm – as well as the Iraqis as they land in Kuwait. The headline 'In for the Kill' is aggressive and uses assonance to emphasise the determination of 'our troops'.

The top right-hand 'ear' commands the readers to 'Back our Heroes in Iraq'.

You can see that a definite attempt has been made to construct the soldiers as heroes and to suggest a unity of purpose and commitment that did not exist in 2003.

The *Sun* front page takes a very aggressive, jingoistic stance with <u>'Show them no pity… they have stains on their souls'</u>, underlined for emphasis. This was a quotation from Lt. Col. Tim Collins' speech to the troops before the conflict began. Collins is framed against a black background, demonstrating his serious purpose. His combat gear, together with his dark glasses and cigar, construct him as a tough action adventure hero. This helps to personalise the story.

The 'Iraqis Surrender' story (top right) represents the Iraqis as cowards, desperate to give up before the war has even begun.

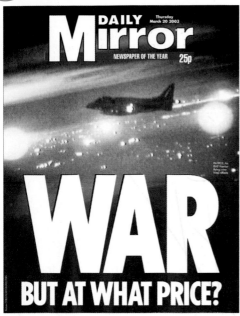

The *Daily Mirror's* headline: 'War But At What Price?' takes an anti-war stance. The full-page long shot of a dark, threatening RAF Harrier flying over Iraqi airfields, suggests it is not part of the 'real' world.

This depersonalises the war and distances us from it. It offers a very strong criticism of everyone involved in the war, including those in the RAF Harrier.

This is an interesting illustration of a very different representation to the other newspapers' representations of the onset of war and those fighting in it.

▲ *Figure 1.48:* The Mirror

BLOGGING

One of the most important developments was the use of weblogs on the internet. The BBC ran a rolling weblog of their correspondents in the Gulf. The *Baghdad Blogger* gave everyday information on how ordinary Iraqis were trying to prepare for the invasion of Baghdad. His blog became an important source of information for audiences, as they felt the blog would offer a truer representation of the Iraqi people than other news sources controlled by the governments of the coalition.

AL-JAZEERA

This popular Arabic 24-hour rolling news channel offered its viewers a very different set of representations of the war from that seen on terrestrial British television news. The station caused outrage by showing footage of captured American soldiers being interrogated and of dead British soldiers. This was a negative representation of the American and British forces. However, images of dead and captured Iraqis were also displayed in American and British newspapers and on television.

The huge range of news sources meant that audiences could compare the representation of the invasion of Iraq on the BBC *Ten O'clock News* with *Channel 4 News*, *Al-Jazeera* or the *Daily Mirror* and gain a far broader perspective of the events and those involved than audiences could gain over the Dunkirk evacuation in 1940.

The Individual Media Studies Portfolio

Let's compare

- Using Case study 1 as a model, compare the representations of the 'enemy' in the Vietnam War (1959–75) and the Iraq War (2003).
- How far do you think such representations in the news have changed?

Case study 2 – Representations of the audience: the 'citizen reporter' and Twitter

Resources: *Channel 4 News* (7 July 2005)
http://twitter.com/

Some journalists say that newsgathering changed forever with the London bombings on 7 July 2005. Within minutes of the disaster, newsrooms were deluged with mobile phone photographs, moving image clips, text messages and first-hand reports. Those who are normally part of the audience, but were caught up in the disaster, ended up as newsgatherers themselves.

The BBC *10 O'clock News* used two mobile phone sequences for its television programme and one more for its online service. Some of the rolling news channels used mobile phone footage 20 minutes after the disaster. The clips were available on internet sites, and blogs and message boards were set up. You can see a still shot from one of those mobile phone sequences in Figure 1.49.

You may see this as a positive move, encouraging fairer representations in the media. However, some of the internet reports were conflicting and misleading. There were also issues of privacy, as some of the footage and the written accounts could be seen as an invasion into the lives of those who had been injured.

TWITTER AND MUMBAI

Twitter is a news/social networking site where people leave regular short messages (up to 140 characters). Since 2008, it has been used to report and break news. During the 2008 attacks on Mumbai, Twitter may have saved a number of people's lives, as those who were trapped could gain a better understanding of what was happening, through text messaging. Twitter, blogs and internet updates could keep up with development faster than conventional news reporting through television. For example, when some radio and TV reports said the fighting was over, those caught up in the events were able to contradict this and let others know the information was incorrect. However, it is also possible that the attackers were able to use the information too.

▲ *Figure 1.49: Do citizen reporters offer different kinds of representations? The London bombings, 7 July 2005*

CALM IN A CRISIS

Janis Krums took a mobile phone photograph of the airbus that crash-landed in the Hudson River in January 2009 and posted it on *Twitpic*. It was seen by many 'followers' around the world some time before the big news agencies managed to obtain any images of the crashed plane.

▲ *Figure 1.50: Picture from Twitpic*

Let's research

■ Collect source material from TV, radio, newspapers and the internet on the election of Barack Obama on 5 November 2008. This was a very unusual news story as it was reported all over the world with an almost entirely positive representation of the event, and of Obama himself and his family. Analyse **three** of the news texts in detail, focusing on representations of race. Have news providers had to adapt the ways in which they represent racial and cultural difference?

▲ *Figure 1.51: Barack Obama*

Let's produce

The production exercise has to show the teacher and moderator that you have a good knowledge and understanding of representations in news. Remember that you need to cover at least two media in this unit as a whole. This means if you have chosen to study newspapers for your comparative assignment you need to produce a radio, internet or TV production exercise on news.

Here are some suggestions for different exercises:
■ A storyboard for the opening of a TV news programme aimed at teenagers.
■ A 30-second news bulletin for a new local radio station.
■ An internet news website aimed at a youth audience.
■ A front page of a new national newspaper with conservative values.

Case study 1 – Representations of women in advertising

Resources:
1920s Listerine advertisement
Washes Whiter 1: Women (BBC2, 1990)
Options TV advertisement (2006)

Exemplar task: Compare the changing representations of women in advertising from the 1920s, 1950s and the 2000s, using print and television advertisements.

Looking back at advertising over the 20th century helps us to see how attitudes and ideas about the roles of women have changed dramatically. The 1920s print advertisement for Listerine constructs the young woman, Edna, as 'pathetic' as she is 'often a bridesmaid but never a bride'. Her sense of self esteem and identity rely entirely on her ability (or in this case, lack of ability), to attract a husband. Edna's fear of failure is increased by the fact that she cannot expect to find a husband after the age of thirty: 'that tragic thirty-mark'. This places her in the role of the tragic heroine.

Edna is posed in a subservient, kneeling position, turning away despairingly from her 'bottom drawer', which traditionally represents the space where women would store their 'trousseau' of fine fabrics and objects that they would provide for their marriage. This drawer is almost empty, symbolising the emptiness of Edna's life without a potential husband.

Although Edna is dressed fashionably and represented as a well-off young woman through her necklace, hairstyle and make-up, the slumped shoulders and slanted pose of her head, together with her averted gaze,

▲ *Figure 1.52: Listerine – 'Often a Bridesmaid, But Never a Bride'*

construct her as powerless, unhappy, weak and helpless.

The written text reinforces this through the comparison between Edna and other 'girls of her set', who are more successful than her because they have achieved marriage. Edna's shame is increased by the unpleasant breath that is the true cause of her unmarried status – but the product, Listerine, will of course cure this problem and therefore make her a bride.

This advertisement plays on women's fear of failure, loss of youthful beauty and potential social exclusion through never marrying.

Let's analyse

Imagine that you see exactly the same advertisement, with the model dressed in contemporary clothes in a modern magazine. How would you react to the advertisement? Would the advertisement appeal to audiences?

WASHES WHITER 1: WOMEN

The methods of persuasion used in the Listerine advertisement continue to be used in the TV advertisements for domestic products in the 1950s–60s. But rather than focusing on women's fears of never getting married, these advertisements play on women's fears of failure as wives and mothers.

In the *Washes Whiter* series, early Persil advertisements represent wives and mothers as supporters of husbands and children, rather than as people in their own right (www.express.co.uk/galleries/view/464/7086). The camerawork in the TV advert reinforces the fact that they are trapped in the domestic space.

The authoritative, male 'expert' voice-over, combined with the mise-en-scène and the camerawork, construct the myth of the perfect mother on whom the family depends.

This is even more clearly demonstrated by the Kellogg's advertisement from 1959, where the wife is strongly criticised, even though she is not actually seen in the advertisement: 'His wife's fault, really ... no proper breakfast'. The message is explicit – it is *her* fault if her husband fails in his job. The female secretary

in the first advert is standing, giving her a suggestion of power. In the second office sequence, after Mrs Jones has provided Mr Jones with his Kellogg's, the secretary is sitting down and far more subservient, while Mr Jones juggles successfully with two important telephone calls (see Figure 1.53).

His previously inadequate wife has now found success – by ensuring that her husband has eaten a 'proper' breakfast.

Like the Listerine advertisement, these advertisements play on women's fears of inadequacy.

▲ *Figure 1.53: Mr Jones is ahead of the game now his wife has provided him with his Kellogg's (1959)*

As the women's movement developed in the 1980s, advertising reflected the tension between the traditional 'housewife' role and the new roles and identities claimed by women. A 1987 Flora advertisement shows a mother doing DIY, while the 1988 Princes Food range series was even more explicit in demonstrating the mother's resentment and rebellion against her role as provider.

The 2003 Options advertisement (go to www.advertisingarchives.co.uk and search for Options 2003) reflects the fact that many young women in the 21st century (like the fictional Bridget Jones) choose to live alone, rejecting the messages of the 1920s Listerine advertisement. The Options advertisement suggests that women don't need men, or at least can choose to be without them; this is reinforced by the wipe edit that almost knocks the men off their feet and the way the female voice-over interrupts the temptation of the male voice-over. The golden lighting of the kitchen contrasts with the blue of the fantasy world and constructs the kitchen as a private space of pleasure for the woman, rather than a space where she must slave for others.

However, this advertisement is polysemic – it can be read in a number of different ways. It still uses the idea of romance and fantasy to sell the product, and the fact that 'only 40 calories' is a strong selling point may suggest that this woman does regret being without a man.

▲ Figure 1.54: The rise of the independent young woman, or 'singleton', is also reflected in this Galaxy advert

Let's compare

- Find one contemporary advertisement that represents women as strong and independent.
- Find one contemporary advertisement that represents women as weak and/or dependent on boyfriends or husbands.
- Compare these advertisements with some of the earlier ones from the case study above.
- How far do you think representations of women in advertising have changed?

Resources:
Pears' Soap early 19th century advertisement
Huntley and Palmers late 19th century advertisement
Intel advertisement 2007

Exemplar task: Compare the changing representations of race in advertising from the 19th, 20th and 21st centuries.

An even clearer picture of changing attitudes and values is conveyed when we examine advertisements with different representations of race. The early 19th century advertisement for Pears' Soap (see Figure 1.55) plays on the assumption that white skin signifies childhood innocence, morality and purity. The top 'before' half of the advertisement shows a white boy wearing a white apron, with a bar of Pears' Soap in his hand, while a black child sits in the bath, waiting to be 'improved' through the use of the soap. The 'after' half shows the white child holding a up a mirror to demonstrate the cleansing power of Pears' Soap, which has made the black boy white, apart from his head. The black boy looks delighted and eager to become as white as the white boy and remove his blackness.

The association between blackness and dirt reinforces the idea that white is physically and spiritually cleaner and black skin is to be rejected if possible.

The Huntley and Palmers' biscuits advertisement shown in Figure 1.56 was produced in the late 19th century when India was part of the British Empire. The idea that whites are superior is established through the way the group of white hunters is framed in the foreground, dominating the exotic landscape. Although the elephants are large in

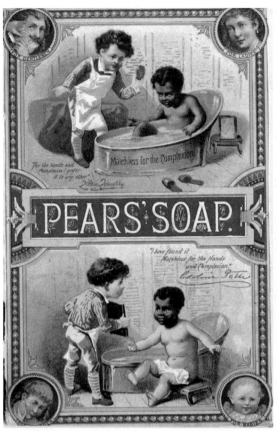

▲ Figure 1.55: This early 19th century advertisement for Pears' Soap reinforces 19th century views that white skin is superior to black. Today it would be seen as openly racist

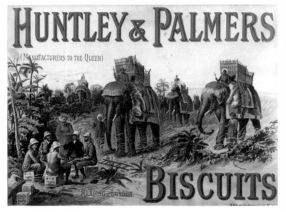

▲ Figure 1.56: Huntley and Palmers' biscuits 'civilise' the British Empire in this late 19th century advertisement

comparison, their size and power is being exploited to serve the white imperialists. All the Indians are placed in subservient still poses, waiting passively for orders from the white group, while the only Indian near the white group is constructed as servile: he stands with head bowed, partially hidden by the group.

The importance of the white group is reinforced by the sign 'Manufacturers to the Queen'. Huntley and Palmers use the assumption that whites are superior, even in a beautiful landscape with exotic creatures, to sell their product. While there is a humorous element to the advertisement in the incongruity of a 'civilised tea-time in the jungle', nevertheless the advertisement reinforces ideas about white superiority.

RACIST STEREOTYPES

British advertisements continued to reinforce racist stereotypes throughout the 20th century. One of the most notorious examples of this was the use of the 'Golly' symbol to market Robertson's jam from 1910 to 1988.

HOW FAR HAVE REPRESENTATIONS CHANGED?

As the above case study demonstrates, British companies and advertising agencies have had to adapt the ways in which they represent racial and cultural differences. Despite this, the majority of advertisements still feature white characters and those that reflect cultural diversity are difficult to find, particularly on British television. Although there are some advertisements that offer positive representations that do not rely on stereotypes, such as defining black characters by their success in sport or music, there are still some controversial advertisements, such as the 2007 Intel advertisement, which can be found at http://www.mahalo.com/'Racist' Intel Ad.

Let's compare

- Compare this 2007 Intel advertisement with the Huntley and Palmers advertisement from the late 19th century.
- Do you think they rely on similar stereotypes?
- What messages are conveyed to the audience by the Intel advertisement?

Let's research

- The Dove 'campaign for real beauty' provides an excellent case study. How far, if at all, does this campaign challenge traditional representations of female beauty?
- Investigate the Malibu 'seriously easy-going' advertisements. How far would you argue that these adverts stereotype Caribbean people in a negative way?
- Analyse some early and current channel idents from www.tvark.co.uk or http://idents.tv/blog. What do these idents tell you about the channels' values? (This task will also help you to prepare for the Media Topic exam on Television and Radio Comedy.)
- Advertisers today have to follow a code of practice. Explore these guidelines on www.asa.org.uk (the website of the Advertising Standards Authority). Advertisers must be careful not to play too obviously on fears of inadequacy and must therefore find new ways of attracting their target audiences.

- Research a range of advertisements for Levi's jeans from 1985 to the present day. What do they tell you about changing attitudes towards men?
- The Barnardo's 'Giving children back their future' advertisements of 1999–2000 (see right) depicted children in adult situations, dying or dead through drug abuse and violent crime (http//:www.barnardos.org.uk/resources). These caused a great deal of debate, with complaints made to the ASA that they were distressing and offensive. How do you think they represented victims of child abuse and neglect? Do you think the advertisements were offensive?

Let's produce

The production exercise has to show the teacher and moderator that you have a good knowledge and understanding of representations in advertising. Remember that you need to cover at least two media in this unit as a whole. This means if you have chosen to study TV advertisements for your comparative assignment you need to produce a radio, internet or print advertisement for your production exercise.

Here are some suggestions for different exercises:
- A billboard poster for a new kitchen roll aimed at men.
- A storyboard for a 30-second TV advertisement for mobile phones that features a Caribbean family and challenges stereotypes.
- A 30-second radio advertisement for a charity that supports young drug addicts.
- An internet advertising campaign for sunglasses that uses social networking sites.

Let's evaluate

Your evaluation can be in the form of a written essay, a podcast, or a PowerPoint presentation. Remember to answer these questions in your evaluation:

■ What area of representation (such as gender, race, or age) did you choose to focus on?
■ What messages were you trying to convey?
■ How did you plan and research for your advertisement?
■ How did you use media techniques, such as casting, framing, mise-en-scène and choice of slogan to challenge or reinforce messages and values?
■ What are the strengths and weaknesses of your finished exercise?

Key terms

Advertorial: looks like an article but is actually a paid-for advertisement for a product
Advertising agency: organisation that produces the advertising campaign for its clients
Demographics: information on the characteristics of an audience, such as age, salary or gender
Ident: a short sequence with music that aims to identify a channel, establishing its brand identity
Product placement: payment for a branded product to be openly used in a TV programme or film
Psychographics: ways of defining an audience according to lifestyle, attitudes and interests
Slogan: line of written text on an advertisement that sums up the message of the advertising campaign

■ Useful websites

www.absolutelyandy.com/tvadverts/: popular adverts archive
www.advertisingarchives.co.uk: archive of advertisements
www.asa.org.uk: Advertising Standards Authority's website
www.bfi.org.uk: the British Film Institute's website
www.cap.org.uk: the advertisers' code of practice
www.clearcast.co.uk/: organisation that clears TV advertisements
www.coca-cola.co.uk: interesting website to analyse
www.guinness.org.uk: useful website with clips from TV advertising
www.guardian.co.uk/media/advertising: web pages on advertising
www.nmpft.org.uk: the National Museum of Photography, Film and Television's website
www.ofcom.org.uk: the regulatory body for advertising in Britain
www.tellyads.com and www.oaa.org.uk: advertising research
www.tv-ark.org.uk: useful archive clips, from news to channel idents

Topic 10: Video Games

◼ What are video games?

Video games are entertainment-based products played on a computer or console. Initially only found in arcades, the first home entertainment systems appeared in the 1970s. Since this early appearance the consoles have become more advanced and the games more complex. It is interesting to note that many video games have found uses other than just entertainment – they have become educational tools and even exercise devices.

Video games have a number of different genres, including:
- fighting games
- first person shooters
- third person shooters
- platform games
- survival horror
- role playing games (RPG)
- sports games
- strategy games.

While each of these genres has specific generic conventions that allow us to identify them, they all share one feature: addictive game play.

▲ *Figure 1.57: An image from* Fight Night Round Three *for the XBox 360*[R]

▲ *Figure 1.58: An image from* Call of Duty: World at War *for the XBox 360*[R]

Let's identify – Genres

Look at the images on the previous page and try to identify which genre each of these video games falls into.

In each image are a number of visual conventions that allow us to identify what type of game they come from.

■ Can you identify these visual conventions and interpret the genre?

Video games timeline (European)

1978: *Space Invaders* – first of the 'Golden Age' arcade games.
1980s: Online gaming begins with bulletin boards.
1986: Nintendo Entertainment System (NES)[R] released.
1990: Sega Mega Drive; handheld Nintendo Game Boy[R].
1992: Super Nintendo Entertainment System (SNES)[R].
1995: Sega Saturn[R]; Sony PlayStation[R].
1999: *Doom* blamed for inspiring Columbine killers.
2002: Microsoft's Xbox[R] (first Microsoft console); Nintendo Gamecube[R].
2004: *World of Warcraft* – increased debate about game addiction.
2004: Nintendo DS[R] developed with more interaction and educational games.
2005: Microsoft's Xbox 360[R]; Playstation Portable (PSP)[R].
2006: Nintendo Wii[R] promises exercise and education as well as entertainment.
2007: Sony PlayStation 3[R].

■ Fresh innovations in video games

Ever since the home entertainment consoles hit the market, the major producers have been competing with each other to dominate the market by coming up with the most powerful and innovative console system. These innovations have most commonly concerned updates in graphics abilities, but have also led to a change in game formats, from the cartridge video game to the CD video game. However, it has been the Japanese company Nintendo who has really revolutionised the home entertainment systems in the past few years.

The Nintendo DS(R)

The Nintendo DS(R) is a portable games system that incorporates a touch-screen system as part of the console. Not only does this make for a more interactive experience for the game player, but it also opens the market for younger game players. However, it is not just in the game play that the DS has changed the video game market; the DS also incorporates a large number of education-based video games. There are still plenty of entertainment games for players to enjoy, but the DS seems to have become synonymous with the learning side of games. Their educational games include:

- *Dr Kawashima's Brain Training*
- *My Language Coach*
- *Driving Theory Training*
- *Cooking Guide: Can't Decide What To Eat*
- *Professor Kageyama's Maths Training*
- *My Word Coach.*

Nintendo Wii(R)

By far the biggest innovation to appear in the world of video games recently is the Nintendo Wii(R). The system offers an entirely new method of game play. Rather than the conventional button pushing and joy stick/joy pad movement, the Wii remote acts as a pointer device and monitors the movements of the player holding the remote. This allows the player to control the actions of the characters through their own physical movements as well as the buttons on the remote. To add to this, the player can use the Wii nunchuk for dual control (meaning you can play/control with both handsets) or the Wii wheel, offering driving simulation control.

These new forms of control have allowed Nintendo to appeal to a much wider target audience. The Wii has become a very sociable form of game play, and with the introduction of the video game *Wii Fit* it has also become an opportunity to exercise.

Representations in video games

Different video games represent groups/events/issues in different ways. This often depends on the genre of the game, but is also based on the technology involved in the game's production. In this topic you will need to explore and compare the representations in two different video games. As video games provoke heated debate, particularly in relation to violence and addiction, the second case study looks at the representations of video games in other media texts.

Case study 1 – The representation of women in video games

Resources:
resident evil™ 4 (2005)
Tomb Raider (1996–present)

Exemplar task: Compare the representations of gender in at least two different genres of video game.

The representation of women in *resident evil™ 4*

Video game characters usually come in a variety of different forms, ages, nationalities and even species. Frequently, video games will incorporate female characters in the lead role and in almost all games a female character features as part of the game's narrative.

Resident Evil™ is a long-running series of video games coming from video game publishers Capcom (Japan). It is part of the survival horror genre and has had numerous female characters throughout the series. *resident evil™ 4* was originally released on the Nintendo GAMECUBE[(R)] in 2005 and then later that year on the Sony Computer Entertainment – PlayStation 2[(R)] and PC. It follows the story of Leon S. Kennedy, who has been employed to rescue the President's daughter, Ashley Graham.

Ashley is very much the victim in the game, in constant need of rescue from the enemies of the game. Ashley has no means of protecting herself from the enemies and relies entirely on Leon S. Kennedy to protect her. As the player, you can instruct Ashley to wait or to follow you, placing Leon, the male character, in a position of dominance over her. There are a number of instances where the player gets the opportunity to play as Ashley in the game; however, even in

these moments the character has no attack power and the player is given the task of running around enemies and avoiding danger, rather than facing it head on. Ashley is even incapable of climbing down ladders and instead the player must wait at the bottom of the ledge and catch her in order to allow her to follow. Ashley is represented as being a weak character with no real means of looking after herself. Instead, she is entirely dependent on the male character of the game to defend her.

▲ *Figure 1.59: Ashley Graham* (© Capcom)

If we look at Ashley's image, there is a certain level of objectification of the character. She is dressed in a sleeveless orange sweater, short pleated plaid skirt and knee-high boots. Her code of dress is revealing and allows her to become objectified in the game, emphasising her vulnerability.

In *resident evil™ 4* there is a second female character, Ada Wong. Ada has appeared in previous *Resident Evil™* games and serves as a love interest/rival for Leon S. Kennedy. Ada is a much stronger character than Ashley. She appears only a few times in the game and when she does she either saves Leon or communicates with him.

During one cut scene in the game, Ada fights with Leon and the two come to blows after Ada pulls a gun on him. Ada is more than capable of taking care of herself and matches Leon in ability and outwits him by setting off a flash bomb, disguised as a pair of sunglasses. In the game, the player has the opportunity of controlling Ada Wong, but not as part of the main storyline. Instead, Ada is given her own sub-missions in the game. These sub-missions work in the same way as Leon's game: Ada attacks and fights her way through the enemies rather than running away. These sub-missions also involve Ada having to save Leon from various enemies in his own game.

▲ *Figure 1.60: Ada Wong* (© Capcom)

Visually, there is far more objectification present with Ada than there is with Ashley. In order to fight her way through a large number of monsters, possessed villagers and mutants, Ada has opted to wear a cocktail dress. This long red dress with a slit up the right side allows her right leg to be on display, while she also wears a pair of high heels and a gun strap on her right leg. Not only is this clearly less than ideal clothing for a secret agent to wear during a dangerous mission in a rural village, but it also clearly focuses on the sexuality of the character.

The two female characters in this game offer strongly contrasting representations of women. Ashley is physically weak, in constant need of a male rescuer, with no ability to defend herself. While there is some objectification of her image and codes of dress, it is not extreme. Ada, on the other hand, is a physically strong character, capable of handling herself and defending herself. However, her physical appearance is much more objectified than Ashley's, and on numerous occasions she uses her sexuality to gain the upper hand.

This seems a common pattern in video games, possibly due to the fact that for a long time video games have been seen as a male-dominated medium. Therefore, the female characters who feature in the games tend to be attractive visually, and either strong or in need of rescue, depending on their role in the game. As video game technology has progressed, the audiences for them have widened to include a larger female demographic (audience group). You could explore whether this has led to a transformation in the representation of women in video games.

The Individual Media Studies Portfolio

Let's research

Research audience responses to the representations of women in video games.

■ Are strong women in video games empowering?

■ Does the image they are given work against this strength?

As well as Ada and Ashley, you may also wish to consider:

Lara Croft from *Tomb Raider*

▲ *Figure 1.61: Lara Croft*

Other texts to explore:

■ Games from the fighting genre: *Tekken*, *Soul Calibur*, *Street Fighter* or *Dead or Alive*.

■ Compare the representation of Yuna in *Final Fantasy X* for the PlayStation 2(R) and her representation in *Final Fantasy X-2*, also for the PlayStation 2(R).

■ Consider a historical approach, looking at characters such as Princess Daisy from the Mario Brothers franchise, and explore the progression in her image and role and ultimately her representation.

Case study 2 – The representation of video games in other media texts

Resources:

The Simpsons: Lisa Gets an A (1998)
South Park: Make Love not Warcraft (2006)
World of Warcraft

Exemplar task: Compare how video games are represented in different media texts, exploring how these may influence public reception to the medium.

VIDEO GAME CONTROVERSIES

Modern video games often feature scenes of violence and will often involve the player having to get the game character to commit acts of violence. There are two forms of censorship in place for these video games in the UK:

- The games industry itself, under the Pan European Game Information (PEGI) – this is not a legally enforceable rating system and participation is voluntary. It works, however, to inform the buyer about the recommended age rating for the game and informs them of the content of the game.
- The British Board of Film Classification (BBFC) – this is a legally enforceable form of censorship and works in the same way the certification for films works. However, it is only games with extreme adult content that receive these certificates.

In spite of these two forms of censorship, controversy constantly surrounds the violent content of certain video games. Some games have even been refused certification in the UK due to their extreme violent content.

Another aspect of video games that has often been criticised in the media is the addictiveness of playing the games. US television programme *The Simpsons* has included references to video games and their impact upon characters a number of times. One such episode is *Lisa Gets An A*. In this episode, eight-year-old Lisa falls ill and has to stay off school in order to recover. During this time she initially tries to keep up to date with her school work and watch educational programming. However, her mother, Marge, insists that Lisa takes a break and gives her brother Bart's games console to her to play with while she is ill. Lisa's initial reaction to the console and the game *Dash Dingo*, a parody of *Crash Bandicoot*, is not good and she seems uninterested. Yet, soon after, Lisa becomes addicted to the game. She is given a homework assignment but fails to complete it due to her addiction to the video game and drags out her illness in order to play more. Upon returning to school, Lisa cheats in a test to compensate for the uncompleted homework assignment.

The video game in this example is represented as being a very negative force in the Simpson family's life. Lisa, usually the most hard working and academically capable member of the family, becomes so easily and quickly addicted to the game, that it suggests that no one is safe from video game addiction. The consequences of this obsession are clearly negative and Lisa is put into a very difficult moral dilemma of whether to cheat or not and eventually whether to own up or not.

Another American animation, *South Park*, represents video games as being a very addictive and negative force on children. In the episode *Make Love Not Warcraft*, the four central characters go on a mission to level their characters up on the MMORPG (massively multiplayer online role playing game) *World of Warcraft*. To do this, they must dedicate a large amount of their time (two months) to killing boar in the forests in order to level up to a stage where they will be able to beat another player. There follows a montage of the characters playing the game at every available moment; they begin to put on weight, their hair becomes greasy and they develop acne. This implies that the addictiveness of video games can have a negative effect on the health and physical

appearance of the player, and once again the representation of the game itself is negative.

However, in both these examples there is something more complex than just a suggestion of video games being bad. Both Lisa Simpson and the characters in *South Park* become addicted to the games and it is this addiction that leads to the negative consequences. Therefore, we could make the suggestion that the games themselves are not negative at all, but when we become addicted to the games it can lead to negative consequences. So we could argue that in moderation there is no problem with video games, but when played in excess they may have negative effects.

▲ *Figure 1.62: South Park boys addicted to* Warcraft

Let's research

The two examples in the case study display the negative consequences of video games, and specifically of video game addiction. It is, however, clear that video games have many very positive qualities as well. In fact, a lot of research has been carried out on the positive effects of video games as well as the negative.

Professor James Paul Gee has written about the positive effects of video games. In his article 'Good Video Games and Good Learning', he describes the positive aspects of playing video games, including problem solving, sharpening players' reactions, the player becoming part of the production and interactivity.

- Explore other representations of video games in the media.
- See if you can identify media texts where video games are given a more positive representation.

Let's compare

- Pick a video game that has recently come out and been reviewed in the media. Compare how the different newspapers react to the video game and explore what messages the newspapers may be conveying to the audience.
- Look at a series of advertising campaigns for different video games. Explore how these advertisements represent the product and how they attempt to promote the product.
- Look at films such as *Tron* or *ExistenZ*, both of which feature futuristic video games, and explore how they are represented.

Let's produce

The production exercise has to show your teacher and moderator that you have a good knowledge and understanding of representations of or in video games. Remember that you need to cover at least two media in this unit as a whole. This means if you have chosen to study two video games for your comparative assignment you need to work in a different medium, such as print or television, for your production exercise.

Here are some suggestions for different exercises:
- Design a female video game character for a new platform game and provide a design for the first three screens.
- Put together an advertisement for a new video game featuring a male hero, aimed at a male audience.
- Storyboard a sequence for a new TV broadcast (for example, news, documentary or sitcom), where video games are featured and represented in a particular way.
- Put together a double-page spread for a video game magazine reviewing a new fighting game, exploring the representation of the violent content.

Let's evaluate

Your evaluation can be in the form of a written essay, a podcast, or a PowerPoint presentation. Remember to answer these questions in your evaluation:
- What area of representation (such as violence, war or gender) did you choose to focus on in your production exercise?
- What messages were you trying to convey?
- How did you plan and research for your exercise?
- How did you use media techniques, such as casting, framing, mise-en-scène and design to challenge or reinforce messages and values?
- What are the strengths and weaknesses of your finished exercise?

Key terms

Arcade game: a pay per play game played in a public locations as opposed to at home

Console: a system built almost entirely for game playing

Convergence: the merger of two or more media products or industries to create something new; for example, merging BluRay players with gaming to create the PlayStation 3[R]

Demographic: information on the characteristics of an audience, such as game playing habits, age, gender, etc.

FMV: full motion video – these are cut scenes in a video game. The player has no control during these moments and the graphics are usually at a higher resolution

Globalisation: the coming together of countries around the world. In this case the online communities help the process of globalisation by allowing increased communication

Graphics: the visual aspects of a computer system. The higher the computer graphic ability the more realistic the images will appear

MMORGP: massively multiplayer online role playing game – a fairly new genre of video game that emerged through the online gaming phenomenon

Multiplayer: a game that allows more than one player, often one player against another. However, online capabilities have now allowed more multiplayer functions

■ Useful websites

www.capcom.com: makers of the *Resident Evil*™ series among many others; their website features news and video clips from current and upcoming games

www.bbc.co.uk/news: a good source for news stories relating to video games

www.guardian.co.uk/media: a good archive source for news stories surrounding the release of certain games

www.gamespot.com: a gaming website providing reviews and news on video games, while also providing users with an opportunity to leave feedback and hold discussions on games

www.nintendo.co.uk: a great source of information, news and images from Nintendo, one of the longest-running games system manufacturers

www.youtube.co.uk: features a large array of FMV sequences from video games

Unit 2
Textual Analysis and the Media Studies Topic

Introduction to Unit 2

In this unit you will learn to:
- write a textual analysis of a film or magazine extract
- explain the scheduling of television or radio comedy programmes.

Writing a textual analysis means you will:
- accurately describe different aspects of a film or magazine extract
- explain why the people who made the extract chose each of those aspects
- explain what this extract says about the world.

Key concepts for textual analysis	genre
	media language
	representation

Explaining scheduling means you will:
- describe what day and time the comedies were transmitted
- explain why the channels chose those days and times
- explain why these comedies fitted the channels that showed them
- discuss why audiences enjoy these comedies.

Key concepts for explaining scheduling	audience
	institution

This unit is assessed through an exam with two sections:

■ Section A

Section A asks you to analyse either some pages from a lifestyle magazine or a short extract from an action/adventure film. The exam has either a magazine or a film extract, not both on the same paper, so you or your teacher will choose which exam you want to take beforehand. Both exams have three set questions on genre, media language and representation.

▲ *Figure 2.1:* Arthur *is an example of an action/adventure film*

▲ *Figure 2.2:* Elle *is an example of a lifestyle magazine*

■ Section B

Section B asks you to explain the scheduling of one or two comedies you have studied. These can be radio or television comedies, or both. The question covers two key concepts: audience and institution.

▲ *Figure 2.3:* Little Britain *is a BBC television comedy*

▲ *Figure 2.4:* South Park *is a comedy of a very different institution: MTV*

Key terms

Brand image: what we think and feel about a brand: if the brand is a television or radio channel, it's what we expect from that particular channel
Channel idents: the ways a television channel help us recognise what channel it is; these might be logos, short films or animations
Demographics: measuring audiences by gender, age, class, ethnicity, and region

Downmarket audiences: audiences with more lower-working-class and working-class people

Flagship programme: a programme that is used by a channel to promote itself, to lead the schedules, to add to its brand image

Institution: the organisation that makes programmes

Mainstream: appealing to a mass audience

Mass audience: an audience that includes most types of people; usually a large audience

Mixed schedule: when the programmes a channel shows cover a mix of different types of programmes (e.g. news, comedy, documentary, soap)

Multichannel television: where there are many television channels competing with each other

Niche audience: an audience that includes one group or a few different types of people; usually a small audience

Psychographics: measuring audiences by their tastes, attitudes, and lifestyles

Public Service Broadcasting (PSB): television and radio that has to follow regulations; it is meant to do more than just entertain audiences to make money

Specialist schedule: when the programmes a channel shows cover a few or only one type of programme

Stripped schedule: when a channel has the same programmes on at the same time every day

Upmarket audiences: audiences with more upper-middle- and middle-class people

Watershed: PSB rules about when programmes have to be suitable for children

▪ Useful websites

www.bbc.co.uk/info/channels/television/bbc_one: explains the remit for BBC1 – what the BBC wants it to do; see the navigation bar for the other BBC TV and radio channels

www.itv.com/aboutitv/: institutional information about ITV

www.channel4.com/about4/: institutional information about Channel 4

http://about.five.tv/corporate-information: institutional information about Five

http://corporate.sky.com/about_sky: institutional information about Sky

www.ofcom.org.uk/: Ofcom homepage

www.ofcom.org.uk/consumeradvice/guide/: a short summary of what Ofcom do

www.bbc.co.uk/comedy/archive/: the BBC's comedy archive

Section A: Textual Analysis – Introduction

■ What is textual analysis and how can you use it to impress your friends?

Textual analysis is writing about a media extract you are given. To do effective textual analysis you must do more than simply describing what is in the text.

Describing this image would be to say things like:
- This is a picture of Spider-Man.
- He is sitting high up on the ledge of a building.
- He is wearing a red suit.

All this is true, but it's never going to impress anyone.

▲ *Figure 2.5 Spider-Man*

Good analysis follows the **PEAT** model:

Point: you make a point about the text
Example: you give an example from the extract you are analysing
Analysis: you explain the example
Terminology: you use Media Studies technical terms if you can.

Those technical terms are how you impress your friends (and, more importantly, your examiners). To use PEAT analysis in an exam, you could explain how a sequence tries to look scary (*point*) by describing a shot of Spider-Man halfway up the outside of a tower block (*example*), and explaining how the wide angle lens (*terminology*) increases the sense of depth in the shot, making the drop below him look much scarier (*analysis*).

Obviously, to do this you need:
- to know terms such as 'wide angle' and 'telephoto' lens
- to be able to spot the difference between them.

This makes textual analysis *quite difficult* and *fun* at the same time.

Section A: Textual Analysis – Moving Image

■ What will you analyse?

AN EXTRACT FROM AN ACTION/ADVENTURE FILM

This will be between three to five minutes long and will be typical in some way of the action/adventure genre.

This means the extract will probably have a hero, a heroine, or a band of 'goodies'. This person or group will be in danger, often being attacked by a villain or some other dangerous force.

There will be some action, often with violence, or a sense of preparing for action, perhaps with a feeling of suspense. It may be set in a location that is exotic or unusual or spectacular in some way. If there is action, there may be fast-moving camerawork and fast-paced editing, along with a busy soundtrack, often dominated by exciting orchestral music.

The extract will be chosen because it not only fits the genre, but it clearly represents people in a certain way. It might, for example, have a male action hero protecting a vulnerable woman, or it might, by contrast, have a strong female character leading male characters.

▲ *Figure 2.6: Michelle Yeoh and Pierce Brosnan as male and female versions of the traditional action hero*

■ ## What aspects will you have to analyse?

You will be asked questions on:

- genre conventions
- media language
- representation.

■ ## Genre conventions

ACTION/ADVENTURE GENRE CONVENTIONS

These are the elements that we would expect to find in an action/adventure film. Conventions are what you find to be typical of the genre.

Now, you need to remember that there are lots of different kinds of films that fit into the action/adventure genre. They can be science fiction films, historical dramas, comic book superhero dramas, crime thrillers, spy thrillers, war films … the list goes on. This means that you don't want to get too specific about the conventions. You could watch two science fiction films and think that action/adventure films usually have aliens in them, or watch two spy thrillers and think they usually have spies in them, but you'd be wrong.

It is important to think about a wide range of action/adventure films and come to a very general list of what they have in common. There is no definite right and wrong answer to this; there is no list of conventions written down anywhere that the people who actually *make* films refer to. Moreover, there is nothing to stop a film breaking these conventions and heading out in a new direction. It is unlikely you would encounter this sort of film in the exam, however.

There are two main kinds of convention you might be asked to analyse:

- the characters and events in the extract (narrative)
- the media language conventions.

Let's go back to the description of what might be in the extract and break these down into these two sets of conventions:

1 Narrative conventions (characters and events):
   ' ... it will probably have a hero, a heroine, or a band of 'goodies'. This person or group will be in danger, often being attacked by a villain or some other dangerous force. There will be some action, often with violence, or a sense of preparing for action, perhaps with a feeling of suspense.'

2 Media language conventions

'It may be set in a location that is exotic or unusual or spectacular in some way. If there is action, there may be fast-moving camerawork and fast-paced editing along with a busy soundtrack, often dominated by exciting orchestral music.'

This film uses camerawork. Is that a convention?

No. You can say 'it uses camerawork' of any genre of film, so it is too vague.

The convention should be about what makes a film action/adventure. So you can say 'it uses spectacular camerawork' or 'it uses fast-moving camerawork to emphasise action', but avoid 'it uses medium shots so we can see people talking'.

How do you investigate what the conventions are?

This is the good bit. You need to watch action/adventure films, or at least key extracts from them, and see what they have in common. You can read lists of conventions in books like this one but this is only useful if you try to apply them to individual films and see how they work in practice.

How do you analyse the conventions?

Your job in a textual analysis is to spot any feature in the extract that fits the conventions you have discovered in your class (or in your own research). You can go into the exam with a memorised list in your head, but this isn't much use unless you've practised *applying* these conventions.

There are other genres in the extract too. Can you analyse them?

Yes. Most popular films mix genres. A film with more than one genre is called a hybrid (see Topic 2 on page 25). *Star Wars* is both science fiction and action/adventure. *The Mummy* is a hybrid of horror and action/adventure. As action/adventure is thought to appeal more to masculine audiences, it is often mixed (or 'hybridised') with romance to appeal to female audiences.

You could discuss how an extract might cover more than one genre if, for example, two attractive characters suggest a possible romance, but you must explain that this hybridity is typical of action/adventure films as a whole.

Do I have to name other films that share these action/adventure conventions?

You can do, but you should not spend a great deal of time writing about other films, as your job is to analyse the extract. You might name one or two other films, but only to show you know films with the same conventions as the extract.

So can I have a list of the generic conventions of action/adventure films?

Try this one:

1 There is a hero or band of heroes who may be on a quest or in some kind of danger.
2 The danger is due to a villain or band of villains or some dangerous force of nature.
3 This danger will lead to action, or preparing for action, such as violence, explosions, a chase or an escape.
4 The setting will often be exotic or threatening or trapping.
5 The film language will be fast moving, with active camerawork, fast-paced editing, and a dense and exciting soundtrack with sound effects and music adding to the action.

Are these conventions always present?

Maybe not. This is a large and varied genre.

Is there a problem if a film doesn't have all the conventions?

No. Remember two things:

1 That genre is a 'repertoire of elements'. This means that genre is like a repertoire of music that musicians know they can play. They do not have to play any one piece of music, but they can. A genre does not have to include all the elements, but it can.
2 It is reasonable to argue that there are no set rules with generic conventions. They can change at any time.

How do I decide what is an action/adventure film?

That is a very good question. One answer is to look at the list of conventions above and say: 'an action/adventure film is a film that has these elements'. This is what is called a 'circular argument' and philosophers won't like it, but it may be the way your examiners choose action/adventure films for the exam.

Another answer is to go into a DVD shop and look at the shelves that say 'action/adventure'.

Media language

What is media language?

- soundtrack
- camerawork
- editing
- mise-en-scène.

How do you analyse media language?

This unit tests your understanding of the media language of action/adventure films. So your PEAT analysis needs to be about the effects often found in these films – action, excitement, suspense, spectacle, and so on:

Point: what effect is being created

Example: examples of sounds, shots, edits and lighting/sets/locations/costumes/props

Analysis: how these examples create the effect or effects

Terminology: correct descriptions of, for example, shots, edits, styles of lighting, etc.

Camerawork

Camerawork examples	Useful terms for analysing action/adventure	Common relevant effects
00.04.52 in *The Matrix*	Tracking (camera moves fairly smoothly)	Creates a sense of movement within the scene, adds sense of action; emphasises spectacle. Very occasionally used for a point-of-view shot
01.18.10 in *Pirates of the Caribbean*	Hand-held camera (camera moves jerkily or wobbles)	May suggest urgency (as in a fight or flight scene) or realism (looks more like a documentary)
00.02.01 in *The Matrix* or 01.19.41 in *Pirates of the Caribbean*	Aerial shot: crane shot (camera swoops up or down) or helicopter shot	Expensive shot creating a sense of spectacle and perhaps making a character look small
00.02.50 in *The Matrix*	Close-up (head fills the frame) or extreme close-up (part of face fills the frame)	Emphasises emotion or action

Camerawork examples	Useful terms for analysing action/adventure	Common relevant effects
00.04.35 in *The Matrix*	Zoom in (magnifies)	Quick zoom in emphasises what is being zoomed in on, often used to focus on facial expression; may create sense of urgency or excitement
00.03.47 in *The Matrix*	High-angle shot (looking from above)	Can make subject look small and powerless; may emphasise spectacle (e.g. crane shot of a battlefield)
00.03.48 in *The Matrix*	Low-angle shot (looking from below)	Can make subject look larger and more powerful
00.01.18 in *Pirates of the Caribbean*	Whip pan (blurred extra-fast looking around from the same position, e.g. on a tripod)	Sense of action (especially with accompanying sound effect)
00.04.20 in *The Matrix*	Overhead shot (looking down on events)	May give a sense of power; may encourage the audience to survey the scene
00.05.29 in *The Matrix*	Dutch tilt (canted) (camera is tilted significantly off the horizontal)	May give a sense of unease or disorientation, or add to the action
00.05.04 in *The Matrix*	Focus pull (camera changes focus during a shot)	Creates a little more complexity, and so excitement, in a shot; can reveal things without cutting

Camerawork	Less useful terms for analysing action/adventure	Reason
	Medium shot (head to waist)	This is an everyday shot to show people talking to each other – it is used in action/adventure films, but in everything else as well
	Long shot (whole bodies)	This is an everyday shot to show where people are – it is used in action/adventure films, but in everything else as well

■ Practising camerawork

You may have used some of these shots in your practical production. If not, it is a good idea to try some out so you get first-hand experience of their effects.

TRACKING

Sit someone with a video camera in a chair with wheels or trolley and push them around until they arrive at the end of the shot (you need to plan this).
OR
Put a camera in a bag with a hole in the side and record the camera 'flying' over the ground and around objects until it arrives at the end of the shot.

HAND-HELD CAMERA

Shoot a dramatic 'event' with the camera on a tripod, then again holding it in your hand, but trying not to wobble or wave it around too much.

CRANE SHOT

If you cannot hire a crane, try shooting riding up an escalator or a lift with windows (assuming you can't get a helicopter!).

CLOSE-UP

Shoot someone acting scared in medium shot, then again in close-up and see the difference.

ZOOM IN

Students always use the zoom button too often, but try out one quick zoom in the middle of a shot when something important happens. See if you can keep it in focus (bright lights help).

HIGH- AND LOW-ANGLE SHOTS

Shoot someone from the top of the stairs looking down (high angle) and the bottom of the stairs looking up (low angle) – which would you use if the person was trying to get elected as Prime Minister?

WHIP PAN

Set up the shot so you suddenly whip from one part of a person (e.g. their face) to another (e.g. their mobile phone), and add a sound effect afterwards or get someone to make a whoosh noise.

OVERHEAD SHOT

You probably can't do these without breaking health and safety rules.

DUTCH TILT

Let your head flop down towards one shoulder until what were verticals are now diagonals.

OR

Shorten one leg of the tripod so the camera tilts more and more – notice that the Dutch tilt only looks good when it is tilted *a lot* (a small tilt looks like a mistake).

FOCUS PULL

You need a manual focus for this. Zoom in on someone in the distance so you have a telephoto lens, and the person in the foreground goes out of focus. Change focus from one person to the other (e.g. when the out of focus person pulls out a mobile).

■ Observing camerawork

Once you are familiar with different shots you should practise watching films with the sound turned off so you can concentrate on the camerawork, observing the range of shots being used in a sequence. Give yourself extra points for spotting unusual shots.

■ Editing

Editing examples	Useful terms for analysing action/adventure	Common relevant effects
00.03.05 in *The Matrix*	Fast-paced editing	Suggests excitement, action, confrontation, and so on
00.00.17 in *Pirates of the Caribbean*	Slow-paced editing	May be caused by complicated camerawork, such as long tracking shots, which follow the action without cutting – these long takes may add to the tension or give a sense of spectacle
00.02.54 in *The Matrix* – sudden increase in editing pace	Change of editing pace	Usually signals an important change, such as the start of an action sequence
00.02.00 in *The Matrix* – cross cuts from inside to outside the hotel then, at 00.02.47, back inside	Cross cutting (cutting from one action/ location to another, then back again)	Often adds to the excitement or suspense in a film

Editing examples	Useful terms for analysing action/adventure	Common relevant effects
There is currently a famous example on the jump cut page in Wikipedia.	Jump cuts	Rarely used cuts that cause the object to appear to jump within the frame – caused by cutting between two very similar shots of the same object or person. These were traditionally considered to be a mistake, but are very occasionally used on purpose to draw attention to an important moment in a scene or to suggest disorientation. A jump cut is NOT a cut from one object or person to a different object or person, not matter how surprising this cut may be.

Editing	Less useful terms for analysing action/adventure	Reason
	Cut	This is an everyday edit with no special meaning
	Shot-reverse-shot	Everyday editing, cutting from one speaker to the opposite shot of another speaker – will be used in action/adventure films but also in all other genres
	Continuity editing	Everyday editing that is designed so you don't notice it – will be used in action/ adventure films but also in all other genres
	Dissolve (last shot dissolves into the next shot)	May be used for smoothness, for peacefulness, for elegance – not normally for action/adventure effects
	Wipe (next shot moves across the screen wiping off the last shot)	Draws attention to the edit, but usually used in moments of quiet or ends of scenes

■ Practising editing

It is harder to practise editing if you don't have an editing program, but a very simple one will do. Otherwise, you could edit in camera.

FAST-PACED EDITING

Shoot a scene twice – once with three longer shots and once with ten shorter shots – and see the difference.

JUMP CUTS

Keep the camera on a tripod in one place, shoot three shots of the same person in different places within the frame doing different things, then play this back and watch the person jump about in the frame.

■ Observing editing

You can train yourself to watch out for editing by trying to spot every edit in a film (or television) sequence.

Another useful technique is to count in between edits to practise judging the speed of editing – if you can't get to 'two' then it is quite quick; if you get past '15' it is pretty slow.

■ Soundtrack

Soundtrack	Useful terms for analysing action/adventure	Common relevant effects
	Dialogue	Establishes character, relationships, conflict, action
	Music	Music may be used to emphasise suspense or reflect the excitement of the action; music may reach a climax (not a 'crescendo') to signal the climax of a scene
	Background sounds and sound effects	May be used to emphasise action or violence; may suggest events offscreen
	Diegetic and non-diegetic sounds	Diegetic sounds are those from within the fictional world (can be heard by the characters); non-diegetic sounds from outside the fictional world (e.g. stirring music) are common in action/adventure

■ Practising using soundtrack

It is easier to play around with sound if you have an editing program, but you can change sound by turning the sound down and playing something else over the top of a scene.

MUSIC

Take a scene from a film that has mostly music on the soundtrack and replace that music with something different – why was the original music right for that scene?

OR

Record different types of music or sound effects (e.g. babies crying, the sound of celebration, war noises) over a scene you have shot – show the different versions to audiences and see how they interpret the scene differently.

Listening to soundtrack

It is very easy to overlook the contribution of soundtrack when you are watching a film, so practise listening to films without looking at them. Remember that most of the sound – the footsteps, the people talking in the background, the traffic noises, the music and often the dialogue – will have been added after the film was shot.

Pay attention to how busy the soundtrack is: are there lots of sounds competing for attention? Which ones do you notice the first time round and which do you only hear on a second listening?

Mise-en-scène

Mise-en-scène examples	Useful terms for analysing action/adventure	Common relevant effects
Opening five minutes of *The Matrix*	Low key lighting (not very bright lighting so dark shadows are left)	Dark shadows and lots of contrast may suggest danger, suspense, horror
The flashing blue lights outside the hotel in the opening sequence of *The Matrix*	Unusual lighting effects, such as flashing lights, blue lights	Often used to suggest danger, especially in science fiction films
01.18.03 in *Pirates of the Caribbean*	Naturalistic lighting (lighting you don't notice) – might be high key lighting (more even, brighter lighting)	Less easy to spot, but naturalistic lighting may be used to make events look more 'real', which can add to a sense of suspense or sympathy. 'Natural' lighting, e.g. the use of sunshine in this extract from *Pirates of the Caribbean*, is usually naturalistic
The confining corridors in the opening sequence to *The Matrix*	Set or location	Sets and locations are important to the tone of action/adventure films – they may create spectacle, for example, or a sense of being trapped in a confined space, or freedom in an open space

Mise-en-scène examples	Useful terms for analysing action/adventure	Common relevant effects
The identical earpieces, suits and sunglasses that the agents wear in *The Matrix*	Costume and props	Often important in showing the hero's and villain's characters
	Casting (why particular actors have been cast in their roles)	Action/adventure films need to cast the right actors – those who can look and act the part, and those whose star image means that they fit the part – for heroes, villains, side-kicks and love interest
The three agents in *The Matrix* 00.06.04	Blocking (how actors – and objects – fit into the frame)	This might emphasise the togetherness of a team of heroes, or may show the conflict between opposing sides

■ Practising mise-en-scène

LOW KEY LIGHTING

Get a halogen torch (for a whiter light) and point it up under a subject's chin in a dark room – instant horror!

LOCATION

Find a location and shoot it to make your subject look trapped – strong vertical lines are good for this; get your subject into a small and fragile pose.
AND
Find a contrasting location that suggests freedom and openness and get your subject into a powerful or free pose.

CASTING

Play the casting game. Try to replace an actor in a film you know well with another actor (see page 133 on the commutation test). Try to work out why the other actor does not work as well (if he or she doesn't). Then decide what qualities the first actor had that made them fit.

For example: replace Elijah Wood, who played Frodo in *The Lord of the Rings*, with Orlando Bloom who played Legolas in the same film. Orlando does not work as well because his star image may be seen as too pretty. He appears to lack the sadness and depth that Elijah brought to the role. So Elijah Wood's star image includes the sad but edgy quality that he has brought to films like *The Lord of the Rings*.

BLOCKING

Get a group of people on camera and try to block them so they look like a team (close together in the frame, maybe forming a triangle); next try to block them so it looks as though one of them is an outsider.

■ Observing mise-en-scène

Pause the film. Start looking at the background then work towards the actors.

- ■ What kind of set or location has been used?
- ■ What sort of lighting?
- ■ What colours are the costumes and what do they tell us about the characters?
- ■ How are the actors blocked?
- ■ Why have those actors been cast?

Everything will have been designed or chosen for a purpose.

 Let's analyse

▲ *Figure 2.7:* I Am Legend

Look at the shot from *I Am Legend* (Lawrence, US, 2007) on page 129. What makes this fit the action/adventure genre?

This mise en scène is enigmatic – it is puzzling. There is a lot of meaning created by the combination of the empty, crumbling streets and the lone man and his dog. He looks vulnerable. The yellow sky and broken bridge suggest that some catastrophe has occurred. This fits the action/adventure genre as it looks like, instead of fighting a villain, the man is going to battle against a different kind of adversity: the disaster all around him.

The composition emphasises the empty sky and broken bridge and makes the building appear to tower over him. His is a small and lonely figure towards the bottom of the frame. His depressed pose and large gun suggest that he is battling on but he is not finding the struggle easy. We can guess he is the hero and likely to triumph against this adversity in the end because he is surrounded by a halo of white light and dressed in 'ready for action' clothes. Moreover, Will Smith, a big Hollywood star, has been cast in this role and such big stars seldom play 'losers'.

Now look at the still from *Romancing the Stone* (Zemeckis, 1984, US).

▲ *Figure 2.8:* Romancing the Stone

This shot gives an impression of peril. The two characters are in an exotic, possibly dangerous setting, suggested by the rain and vegetation. The quite loosely framed shot showing trees in the background and the out-of-focus greenery in the foreground suggest that they are surrounded by rainforest. The lighting is low key and the shadows in their hair and clothing emphasises how wet they are. They are dressed in unglamorous clothes and their make-up is very natural. However, they are both Hollywood stars so he is probably an action/adventure hero and she is possibly a 'damsel in distress'. His acting connotes confident action, while her acting connotes nervousness and vulnerability. Her hair is out of control (as her character is); his carefully packe backpack with a rifle butt sticking out of the top suggests that he is self-sufficient and ready for action. He might be rescuing her.

■ Representation

WHAT IS REPRESENTATION?

Representation, at its simplest, is about how people are depicted in the extract.

You can look at how other things are represented – places, events, aliens, monsters, ideas – but it is best to start with people.

You will have learnt that people are often stereotyped in the media (see the Introduction to the Individual Media Portfolio on page 12). Stereotyping is such a big issue in representation that it is often the best place to start.

What stereotypes of people do you often find in action/ adventure films?

Action/adventure films are usually based on heroes and villains, so this is a rich area to investigate.

Villains can often be foreign, whereas heroes stereotypically are not. This means that most American films will cast Americans as heroes (and quite often British actors as villains), and British films will cast British actors as heroes. If they do, this is stereotyping; if they don't, this might be an attempt to get away from the stereotype.

Heroes are stereotypically men. The hero is strong and resourceful and these are stereotypically masculine traits. There has been a long tradition of female action/adventure heroes, however, and you may find examples of anti-stereotyping where the female character is strong and resourceful.

Male action/adventure heroes often protect stereotypically weaker and vulnerable women. You may find examples of anti-stereotyping (especially in more recent films) where the woman is an equal team member to the man.

Older action/adventure films set in third world locations often reflected colonial attitudes. These usually represented the white man as civilised and the 'natives' as dangerous and uncivilised. This means that to have a white hero is stereotypical of the genre and that to have equal or superior characters played by ethnic minority actors is anti-stereotypical. This is becoming less true as African-American actors, such as Will Smith, routinely play action/adventure heroes, but is still worth commenting on.

Action/adventure heroes are strong and resourceful, so mature actors with no visible disabilities usually play the role. To cast older actors or ones with visible disabilities would be anti-stereotypical. Fatter people are not stereotypically heroic. People with obvious facial scars are stereotypically cast as villains, and given lank, unkempt hair. Heroes are clean cut and stereotypically attractive.

Heroes are stereotypically heterosexual. Traditionally, other sexualities have been cast as villains or were just absent altogether. There have not been any mainstream action/adventure films with clearly gay, lesbian or bisexual heroes.

WHAT ELSE COULD YOU ANALYSE?

Values

Representation also includes what the film is celebrating or valuing.

This means you could ask yourself: 'What does the film say is a good thing?' These 'good things' are called *values*. They are what the heroes act out.

Most action/adventure films celebrate values that most people can agree with so they can appeal to as many people as possible. This means they are mainstream values. Mainstream values include:

- the underdog defeating the powerful
- love
- teamwork
- fairness
- family
- self-sacrifice
- becoming a better person.

If you find any of these things being celebrated in an extract, then it is celebrating mainstream values.

Making sense

You could further ask: 'How does this representation make sense to the audience?' Many action/adventure films use very familiar plots and characters to make the film easy to understand. You might comment on how an extract does this.

For example, the still shot from *Romancing the Stone* on page 130 is a familiar situation in action/adventure films. A man is protecting a woman in a dangerous environment – the jungle. The jungle is often used in films to represent hostile surroundings and dirty clothes, and a sweaty appearance is often used to show people confronting new dangers. Audiences will be very familiar with this idea.

The *I Am Legend* shot on page 129, on the other hand, takes a familiar location and makes it seem strange. The audience may not immediately know what is happening as this is not so familiar, but will be confident that they will find out before long. The idea of a familiar world completely changed has been explored in many other films and television programmes, so audiences may have seen similar representations in other texts.

SO WHAT SHOULD YOU ANALYSE?

Analyse representation, not characterisation (describing the characters).

You should start with looking at stereotypes in an extract. You can get a top grade just by doing this.

You might comment on what the extract values – e.g. the qualities that the heroes have (that the villains don't) – and perhaps how the world it tries to create makes sense to its audience.

How do I learn how to analyse representation?
- By lots of practice.
- By learning to do what is sometimes called 'the commutation test'. This is easier than it sounds.

THE COMMUTATION TEST

Take the people in shots, for example, and mentally (or try this with real images) replace them with different sorts of people. It's a muscled man? Try replacing him with somebody very skinny. It's a young heroine? Replace with an older woman. It's a white action hero? Make him or her ethnically Chinese, or West Indian, or Pakistani and see if it makes a difference.

If the new image seems somehow wrong, then the factor you have changed is significant. If it doesn't, then it isn't. If replacing a white action hero with a black action hero doesn't look strange, then black people have not been excluded from this stereotype of heroism. If replacing an action hero with an actor with a missing limb does look strange, then people with disabilities are being excluded from this stereotype of what it is to be heroic.

The casting game is a particular variant on this (see page 128).

Textual Analysis Case Study 1
– *The Matrix*

Moving image textual analysis case studies

To get the full benefit from these case studies you will need to get the DVD of the following action/adventure films:

The Matrix

Pirates of the Caribbean

Let's analyse

■ Watch the opening six minutes and four seconds of *The Matrix* (Wachowski Bros, 1999, US). This is a 15 certificate film.

We will analyse the sequence from when we first see the Policeman's torch (00.01.24) to the line 'The informant is real'.

This makes the sequence four minutes 40 seconds long, which is within the usual three to five minute time scale for the exam.

▲ *Figure 2.9: Still from* The Matrix

■ Characters

Trinity   The woman in leather who fights and is chased
The Agents The three men in suits with earpieces
The Police In uniform

■ Genre

The first question on the exam is about genre conventions, so let's explore the action/adventure conventions in this extract. You should ignore what you know about the rest of the film, if you have seen it before, and only discuss the extract.

Let's start with characters and events – the narrative.

Trinity appears to be the *heroine* and the agents the *villains*. How do we know this?

■ Trinity is in danger.
■ She is an underdog – there are lots of people chasing her and only one of her, and she appears to be scared of the Agents.
■ This could make her a victim, but she is attractive and appears to be almost super-humanly competent, so she appears much more like a heroine.
■ We see her talking to herself trying to overcome her fear – we don't usually have these moments when we can identify with characters if they are villains or victims.
■ The Police Officers appear to be the victims in this scene – we know nothing, so care nothing for them and they have been cast to look less attractive.
■ The Agents lack personality, have very corporate-looking earpieces, are very confident, and are less attractive than Trinity – they seem like villains.

Fights and chases are common in action/adventure films; they are conventions of the genre. Chases and violence are very spectacular and exciting ways to suggest conflict. The film uses 'bullet-time' photography during the fight scene (we track around an apparently stationary Trinity) to create extra spectacle, and a daring roof-top chase with leaps over huge drops to create excitement and suspense.

The media language in the extract also fits the action/adventure genre:

■ There is a lot of complex moving camerawork, including crane shots (e.g. of the hotel sign) and an aerial shot of Trinity flying over the gap between two buildings.

- The editing in the fight scene is very fast paced.
- The soundtrack is dominated by exciting orchestral music which helps build up the action.
- The scene uses low key lighting, especially in the fight scene, which is lit by the Police Officers' torches, which helps build suspense.

Media language

The second question on the paper is about media language.

This is why the first question might restrict you to narrative conventions.

You will be asked to describe some elements of media language and explain how they create their desired effect. You may be told which effect to look for, or it might be your own choice.

Let's take the media language elements one at a time and explore what you might pick out from this extract. We will cover more than you would be expected to cover in the exam.

MISE-EN-SCÈNE

Element	Effect
The police walk down a very dirty, crumbling, cramped and dark corridor. The only lighting, apart from their torches, picks out some dangling wires. Much of the extract is set in confined spaces, such as corridors, windowless rooms and alleyways.	The confined mise-en-scène fits the fear that Trinity is trapped by the agents and adds to the sense of danger.
Trinity has been cast to look strong and attractive and is dressed in tight shiny clothing to emphasise this. The agents wear identical bland costumes and have very similar expressionless faces and voices. They are blocked in a triangular formation at the end of the sequence.	Trinity's character is an individual, which helps establish her as a heroine, while the Agents are portrayed as a group who simply carry out orders, which helps establish them as villains.
Low key side lighting is used throughout, casting dark shadows on the sides of people's faces and leaving large areas of the screen unlit.	The darkness helps add to the suspense as the audience cannot see clearly; it also adds to the portrayal of a crumbling, dangerous city, and suggests that Trinity has to work in the shadows.

CAMERAWORK

Element	Effect
Tracking shot as Trinity runs across the rooftop with bricks in the foreground. (00.04.52)	The tracking emphasises her movement and adds to the excitement of the chase.
'Point-of-view' shot from the door's perspective as the Police Officer kicks it down. (00.01.49)	Adds to the violence of the kicking down.
Focus pull from the ringing phone to Trinity in the background. (00.05.28)	Allows a close-up of the phone so the audience see it is crucial, then shows that Trinity is watching it – suggesting that she has to get there. This creates urgency.
Extreme close-up of Trinity's face as the police approach her with handcuffs. (00.02.50)	Shows that she is preparing for action.
High-angle shot of Agent looking down into the alleyway where another Agent awaits. (00.03.47)	Emphasises the spectacle of the Agent's long shadow filling the alleyway.
Crane shot of Agents arriving in their car. (00.02.08)	Makes them look more powerful and so more menacing.
'Bullet time' photography of Trinity's aerial kick. (00.02.58)	Creates greater spectacle and adds to the sense of her super-human powers.

EDITING

Element	Effect
Change of editing pace as the scene moves from the Agents outside to Trinity fighting inside. (00.02.54)	The slower pace in the Agents' conversation reflects their calm confidence; the faster pace in Trinity's fight reflects the action and danger.
The first part of the scene cross cuts from the police and Trinity inside the hotel to the Agents arriving outside.	The cross cutting helps build up suspense as the audience is given more information about what is going to happen from the events outside.

SOUNDTRACK

Element	Effect
Eerie music and sound of footsteps and guns being cocked as Police go to hotel room door. (00.01.34)	The audience has to listen carefully for the quiet sounds and this adds to the suspense.
Sound effects of police radios and car as camera tracks down hotel sign. (00.02.02)	Helps create a believable world, as we know already there are police cars outside the hotel.
'No Lieutenant, your men are already dead.' (00.02.44)	This line establishes that Trinity is a deadly opponent and that the Agents have experience of chasing her; it also sets up suspense as to what will happen next.
Loud sound effects on Trinity's kicks and punches in the fight, deep resonant gun shot sounds and ricochet noises. (00.03.01)	These add to the violence of the fight.
The music builds up during the chase sequence until it reaches a climax as Trinity leaps over the giant gap between buildings. (00.04.27)	The build-up adds to the suspense and excitement of the chase and the climax emphasises her incredible feat.
All we can hear, as Trinity lands on the foot of the stairs, is the sound effect of a creaking light. (00.05.09)	Trinity is scared and we, like her, are listening out for her chasers – the creaking symbolises this.

■ Representation

Does this extract use stereotyping, anti-stereotyping, or both?

GENDER

Trinity is a strong and resourceful action hero and a woman – this is anti-stereotyping. However, she is young, thin and attractive and her attractiveness is emphasised by her dress – this is a stereotypical representation of a woman.

GENDER AND 'RACE'

The police are represented in a slightly stereotypical way. They are all white and male. Is this a sexist and racist representation? The lieutenant is a typical no-nonsense hard-boiled cop – a character type familiar from many Hollywood films. There is an older cop and younger cop couple – again, this coupling is familiar from many films. There is a sense that these are deliberately stereotypical representations, as if they are 'comic book' cops, rather than it being a sexist and racist representation.

The Agents are also all white and male. Again, this appears to be deliberate stereotyping. The anonymous corporate security characters are recognisable types from the thriller genre.

You might note that there are no obvious ethnic minorities represented in the extract. You should ignore the fact that a major character later in the film is black because your job is to analyse the extract, not the whole film. One argument against the film being racist, however, is that the villains are both very white and middle class and some of the heroes are black.

AGE

There are some older characters represented in the extract (in the police) but they either make wrong decisions or are victims. The competent and powerful characters are all adults under 40. This is stereotypical.

DISABILITY

There are no characters with visible disabilities and, further, the extract celebrates extreme physical fitness (leaping across spaces) by comparing this unfavourably to the clumsier and less fit Police Officers. This is stereotypical.

SEXUALITY

There is no evidence of sexualities in the extract except that it does suggest a world that is not altogether straight.

THE CITY

The city in which the events occur is represented as a dangerous and depressing place. This is one stereotype of the city, seen in many other films.

So the answer to the stereotyping question seems to be: the extract uses both stereotyping (some of it deliberate) and anti-stereotyping.

THE WORLD OF THE FILM

The extract contains some quite shocking events, such as police officers being shot by a hero figure. This is part of the disturbing tone of the whole extract, during which the audience – like the

Police Officers in the extract – are shocked and don't quite understand what is going on. Though the extract contains very familiar situations – the police make an arrest, they are over-ruled by higher authorities, there is a chase – they are treated in an unusual way. This makes the world of the film both familiar and shocking. The audience will expect this world to be made clearer as the plot develops as this is the normal process in a Hollywood film.

VALUES

What is being valued in this extract? It is easier to analyse values by comparing the end of the film to the beginning of the film, but the extract still contains values that are common to many action films. It values resourcefulness, athleticism and the lone individual standing up to bureaucratic forces.

Textual Analysis Case Study 2 – *Pirates of the Caribbean*

 Let's analyse

■ Watch *Pirates of the Caribbean* (Verbinski, 2003, US) from 01.14.22 to about 01.18.42. This is a 12 certificate film.

We will analyse the sequence from the aerial shot of the ship to the line 'See that it's lost!'.

This makes the sequence about four minutes 20 seconds long, which is within the usual three to five minute timescale for the exam.

■ Main cast in order of appearance

Will Orlando Bloom
Elizabeth Keira Knightley
Barbossa Geoffrey Rush
Jack Johnny Depp

■ Genre

The first question on the exam is about genre conventions, so let's explore the action/adventure conventions in this extract. Ignore what you know about the rest of the film if you have seen it before.

Let's start with characters and events – the narrative.

Will and Elizabeth and the crew of the ship being chased appear to be the *heroes* and Barbossa and his pirate crew the *villains*. Jack, the cheeky pirate, appears to have a position in between the heroes and the villains. How do we know this?

■ Will and Elizabeth and the rest of their crew are in danger from a better-armed enemy.

■ They have been cast, dressed and made-up to be attractive in a conventional way – Will and Elizabeth are young and good-looking, the woman on the wheel looks 'plucky', and the man with the whiskers looks grandfatherly and 'reliable' – so we care for them.

■ They are being brave and resourceful in a tricky situation.

■ Barbossa has been made up to look unattractive – a pantomime villain – and his crew lack personality, so we care less for them.

■ Jack is a 'lovable rogue' – he is imprisoned by the villain and may cross over from a life of crime on the high seas to helping the heroes.

The 'magic object' that everyone seeks is a convention of the adventure film. In this case it is the gold medallion that Elizabeth gives back to Will, for which Barbossa is chasing them. The writer Propp suggests that the magic object, or agent (e.g. Aladdin's lamp), is a common feature of fairy stories, and this idea is often used in adventure films.

The chase is a common feature of action/adventure films; it is a convention of the genre. It is a spectacular and exciting way to suggest conflict. The film uses urgent music and fast-paced camerawork and editing during the chase to create extra spectacle.

The location – the high seas awash with pirates – again fits the adventure genre in that it is exotic and dangerous.

The hybrid nature of the extract – action/adventure hybridised with romance – fits the genre, as it is usually mixed with romance to extend its appeal to more 'feminine' audience tastes.

The media language in the extract also fits the action/adventure genre:

■ There is a lot of complex moving camerawork, including an aerial shot of the ship and some rapid panning on the *Interceptor*.

■ The editing in the flight scene is fast-paced.

- The soundtrack in the flight scene is dominated by urgent orchestral music, which helps build up the suspense.
- The scene uses spectacular location filming at sea.
- Barbossa has exaggerated make-up to emphasise his villainy.

■ Media language

The second question on the paper is about media language.

This is why the first question might restrict you to narrative conventions.

You will be asked to describe some elements of media language and explain how they create their desired effect. You may be told which effect to look for, or it might be your own choice.

Let's take the media language elements one at a time and explore what you might pick out from this extract. We will cover more than you would be expected to cover in the exam.

MISE-EN-SCÈNE

Element	Effect
Whereas the romantic scene is shot in a confined interior, the later scenes always show the sea in the background.	The confined mise-en-scène fits the closeness of the two lovers; the sea connotes open adventure.
The pirates have elaborate costumes (e.g. Barbossa's enormous hat), straggly, unkempt hair, and a ship with tattered black sails; our heroes have simpler, honest costumes, more restrained hair and a 'normal' looking ship.	The pirates' wild look connotes their wild and criminal life, but this is so exaggerated that it suggests they are like pantomime villains, and not to be taken seriously.
Golden low key side lighting is used in the Will and Elizabeth scene, casting shadows and suggesting candlelight.	The lighting adds to the romance of the scene which then emphasises Will's surprise when he finds that Elizabeth has his medallion.

CAMERAWORK

Element	Effect
Aerial shot of the *Interceptor*.	Creates sense of spectacle. Establishing shot to show us the exotic location of the interior scene that follows.
Series of close-ups of the lovers' faces after Elizabeth says, 'Don't stop'. (01.15.02)	Marks the emotional climax of the scene.

Element	Effect
Low-angle shot of Barbossa. (01.16.30)	Introduces him as a powerful man. Shows his monkey on its perch.
Tracking shot. (01.16.41)	Creates a sense of the two characters circling each other as they fail to make a deal.
Canted shots in the whole scene with Barbossa and Jack.	Gives the illusion that we are at sea.
Point-of-view shot down the telescope. (01.17.37)	Comic shot emphasises the comic moment.
Hand-held camera and a series of fast edits. (01.18.09)	Creates a sense of action and realism as they try to escape.
Whip tilt. (01.18.15)	Fast camerawork creates a sense of action; the tilt shows us the young woman at the wheel.
Close-up on dialogue: 'See that it's lost!'.	The close-up emphasises this dramatic dialogue at the climax of the scene.

EDITING

Element	Effect
Change of editing pace as the scene moves from Barbossa and Jack on *The Black Pearl* to our heroes trying to escape on the *Interceptor*. (01.18.03)	The slower pace in the conversation reflects their calm confidence; the faster pace on the *Interceptor* reflects the action and danger.

SOUNDTRACK

Element	Effect
Background sound effect of waves and the ships creaking throughout the scenes; this becomes louder and the sea sounds rougher once we see the *Interceptor*.	Emphasises the location and the crescendo in the wave sounds emphasises the *Interceptor*'s rush to escape.
Soft music starts when Elizabeth says 'Don't stop', but turns into more eerie music when she gives Will the medallion.	The music connotes romance at first, but the change emphasises the key role of the medallion in the plot (the magic agent).
Echo on Will banging his hand down on the table.	The echo stresses the violence of the action.
Hollow wind instrument sound as Will stares at the medallion at the end of the scene; this continues into the next scene.	This eerie noise again emphasises the key role of the medallion, almost giving it a character; then the sound acts as a sound bridge, linking this scene with the next.

Element	Effect
There is only the background ambient sound effect as Barbossa and Jack bargain, but as they step onto the deck the sound world changes to include wind, footsteps and sails flapping.	This gives a naturalistic effect but also stresses the movement from the private world of the captain's cabin to the public world of the deck.
Urgent music starts as we see the *Interceptor* trying to escape.	The music reflects their plight.
Accelerated sound effects of wood and rigging creaking and sails flapping during the *Interceptor* scene.	Adds to the action.

■ Representation

Does this extract use stereotyping, anti-stereotyping, or both?

GENDER

Elizabeth is a strong and resourceful woman; she suggests using the shoals to escape, for example – this is anti-stereotyping. However, she is young, thin and attractive – this is a stereotypical representation of a woman as defined by her beauty.

RACE

One black actor plays a stereotypical 'heavy' role – he is heavily built and wears fewer clothes than anyone else. On the other hand, the navigator on the *Interceptor* is played by a black actress – this is anti-stereotypical. Her character is strong and decisive and she appears to be a natural leader.

AGE

The characters we are supposed to find most attractive are the younger characters. Keira Knightley was 18 when the film was released and Orlando Bloom was 26. The oldest character appears to be the man with the grey whiskers, who gets a positive, rather fatherly role. So there is a stereotypical linking of attractiveness to youth, but at least the older people are not victims, as in *The Matrix*.

PHYSICAL APPEARANCE

The film strongly links physical appearance to morality. The villains are all cast and/or made up to look less attractive than the heroes. Geoffrey Rush is wearing a mask of make-up to make him look like he has a skin condition, for example. This is a stereotypical representation, but one that is done in such an exaggerated way as to suggest that it is a rather knowing, self-conscious representation – the film is deliberately stereotyping to fit in with pirate film tradition.

THE CARIBBEAN

The film uses the traditional stereotype of the Caribbean as a beautiful but dangerous place that was established in adventure literature and repeated in many films.

So the answer to the stereotyping question seems to be: the extract uses both stereotyping (some of it deliberate and conscious) and anti-stereotyping.

THE WORLD OF THE FILM

The film portrays a very familiar world. Not only is the representation of pirates very common and familiar to most audiences, but the film itself is also an easy-to-follow blockbuster rollercoaster ride in which a simple plot is used to set out a number of set pieces – this chase being one.

VALUES

What is being valued in this extract?

The qualities embodied in the heroes are: love, teamwork, resourcefulness under pressure, youth and physical attractiveness.

The villains are suspicious and unkempt but pleasingly exotic and naughty. The plot allows the audience to experience a very safe version of the outlaw life. Like many films, *Pirates of the Caribbean* gives the audience the thrill of escaping dull rules. Jack Sparrow is the bad man with a heart of gold who carries us across from the good but dull world into the bad but exciting one, then allows us to return.

Section A: Textual Analysis – Print

■ What will you analyse?

AN EXTRACT FROM A LIFESTYLE MAGAZINE

This extract will be between three and five pages long and will probably include the front cover, the contents page(s) and the editor's letter.

The extract will be typical in some way of the lifestyle magazine genre.

This means it will probably have a front cover with a photograph of a model or celebrity looking directly at the reader. There will be a strong sense of the magazine 'talking' to its readers. There will probably be a 'chatty' editor's letter. The contents of the magazine will be a mixture of items, but are likely to include topics such as fashion, shopping, celebrities and health. The tone will probably be aspirational – the magazine will be trying to help make the reader a better person.

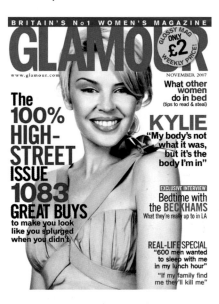

◀ *Figure 2.10:* Glamour *magazine has Kylie Minogue looking out at the reader; coverlines about shopping, sex, celebrities, and a sense that the magazine is trying to make its readers look attractive ('Great buys to make you look like you splurged')*

The magazine might be aimed at a range of different audiences, for example:
- women or men
- young adults, older adults, 'tweenagers' or older teenagers
- heterosexuals, gays or lesbians
- ethnic minorities or the ethnic majority.

The extract will be chosen because it not only fits the genre, but it clearly represents people in a certain way.

A women's magazine might feature a feminine role model on the front cover. *Glamour* magazine (see Figure 2.10) shows Kylie Minogue as a model of glamorous femininity that the readers might aspire to be like.

A men's magazine, on the other hand, might feature a model of masculinity (such as an actor), or a model of sexualised femininity (such as a woman showing her breasts).

◀ *Figure 2.11: Daniel Craig as a model of rugged masculinity*

■ What aspects will you have to analyse?

You will be asked questions on:
- genre conventions
- media language
- representation.

■ Genre conventions

What are lifestyle magazine genre conventions?

These are the elements that we would expect to find in a lifestyle magazine. Conventions are what you find to be typical of the genre.

This magazine has coverlines on the front page. Is that a convention?

No. You can say 'It has its coverlines on the front page' of any genre of magazine, so it is too vague.

The convention should be about what makes a magazine a *lifestyle* magazine. So you can say, 'It uses a mix of coverlines about a range of lifestyle topics', but avoid 'it uses coverlines to attract people to buy the magazine'.

How do you investigate what the conventions are?

You need to read a range of lifestyle magazines and see what they have in common. You can read lists of conventions in books like this one but this is only useful if you try to apply them to individual magazines and see how they work in practice.

How do you analyse the conventions?

Your job in a textual analysis is to spot any feature in the extract that fits the conventions that you have discovered in your class (or in your own research). You can go into the exam with a memorised list in your head, but this isn't much use unless you've practised *applying* these conventions.

There are other genres in the extract too. Can you analyse them?

Yes. A lifestyle magazine is really a hybrid of a range of genres: fashion, food, health, celebrity, and so on. It could easily stray over into music, film or hobbies too.

Do I have to name other magazines that share these lifestyle magazine conventions?

You can do, but you should not spend lots of time writing about other magazines, as your job is to analyse the extract. You might name one or two other magazines, but only to show you know lifestyle magazines with the same conventions as the extract.

■ How do you analyse media language?

This unit tests your understanding of the media language of lifestyle magazines.

So your PEAT analysis needs to be about the effects often found in these magazines – for example, warmth, friendliness and stylishness.

Point: what effect is being created

Example: quotes, examples of fonts, layout, photographs, use of colour

Analysis: how these examples create the effect or effects; you can use the word 'connote' as an all-purpose term for 'suggests', 'symbolises' or 'gives the effect of'

Terminology: correct descriptions of, for example, typography, layout, photography, language.

Here is a collection of terms you can use to describe print media language, with examples from the case study magazines you can see on pages 157–186.

Media language element	Key terms and concepts	Common effects
Typography *Good Housekeeping* uses a serif font for the 'Sarah Ferguson' coverline.	Serif fonts e.g. Times New Roman Note that there are little ornaments (serifs) hanging down from the horizontal line of the 'T'. **What is the difference between fonts and typefaces?** A typeface is a family of fonts. Times New Roman and Arial are both typefaces. A font is a typeface in, for example, a particular size. *Arial 12 point italic* is a font. Arial 10 point **regular** is another font.	Fonts with serifs (ornaments) may connote formality, tradition, seriousness or elegance.
Good Housekeeping uses a sans-serif font for the '10 years younger' coverline.	Sans-serif fonts e.g. **Arial** Note that there are no little ornaments (serifs) on these letters.	Fonts without serifs (ornaments) may connote informality, modernity, freshness or youthfulness.
Layout *Good Housekeeping* has a symmetrical layout on the front page.	Symmetrical layout.	A symmetrical layout may connote balance.
Good Housekeeping has an asymmetrical layout on the contents pages.	Asymmetrical layout.	An asymmetrical layout is usually more dynamic and interesting.

Media language element	Key terms and concepts	Common effects
Clint Eastwood in *Esquire* looks shot with a longish lens. Note how his arm looks foreshortened and out of focus.	Long lens. Shallow depth of field means that background or near objects are often out of focus; collapses depth within a shot.	More flattering for shooting people. Emphasises the subject of the shot over the environment.
The picture of George and Zoe under the *Bliss* editor's letter is slightly high angle; note how you can see the floor.	High-angle shot.	Can make subject look small and powerless, may emphasise spectacle.
Clint Eastwood in *Esquire* looks shot at a slightly low angle.	Low-angle shot.	Can make subject look larger and more powerful.
Mise-en-scène (for photos) The 'Perfect Taste' shot in *Esquire* is quite loosely framed; the cover shots are all tightly framed.	Framing. Tightly framed shots fill the photographic frame (the edge of the photo) with the subject; loosely framed shots give the subject lots of space within the frame.	Tightly framed shots emphasise the individual; looser framing emphasises the environment more.
The photo of the woman on a yacht in *Good Housekeeping* has been cropped to include the mast and lots of blue sky.	Cropping. Cropping is 'cutting' the photo to a certain shape or to create the desired framing.	Different shapes of photos may have different connotations.
The front covers of *Bliss* and *Good Housekeeping* have conventional, composed photographs; the photo on the front cover of *Esquire* has an unusual composition: Eastwood is pointing to the right but the photo has not left space for him to point into; he is central within the frame when his pose suggests he should be on the left of the frame.	Composition. Conventional composition means such elements as: ■ giving space in the frame in the same direction as the subject's gaze ■ placing main objects about one third of the way into a photo, not the middle ■ making the eyeline about one third from the top of the frame ■ triangular compositions.	Conventional composition is 'normal'. Unusual composition is designed to create a specific effect.

Media language element	Key terms and concepts	Common effects
Clint Eastwood in *Esquire* is shot with low key lighting; this emphasises his wrinkles.	Low key lighting. Dark shadows and contrast.	Low key lighting often connotes danger or artiness, so is not often used in lifestyle magazines.
Sarah Ferguson in *Good Housekeeping* is shot with high key lighting (but with a soft light) and lots of fill light to fill in any wrinkles.	High key lighting. More even, brighter lighting.	May connote realism or cheerful tones.
The photo of the woman on a yacht in *Good Housekeeping* is shot with 'natural' light (sunlight) that looks naturalistic; the shots in *Bliss* by the editor's letter also look naturalistic as they look like 'ordinary snaps', shot by artificial light.	Naturalistic lighting. Lighting you don't notice.	Not normally used to create an effect, except realism ('looking real').
It also deliberately uses location – on a yacht.	Set or location.	
The photo of the man in a towel in *Good Housekeeping* uses the towel costume, the gym props, and the rather open pose to suggest a man who is both powerful and vulnerable.	Costume, props and pose.	
Clint Eastwood in *Esquire* has been chosen for his looks and what he symbolises – a sort of no-nonsense success. The yacht woman in *Good Housekeeping* has been cast for her sophisticated good looks.	Choice of subject.	You might comment on how subjects have been cast for their looks or what they already symbolise.
House style *Esquire*'s house style is constructed through its red, black, white and yellow colour scheme, its consistently spacious layout, and its common use of serif fonts.	The different pages of a magazine look like they come from the same magazine. This effect may be created by a common layout format, a common colour scheme, a common use of fonts, and so on.	

■ How do I learn how to analyse media language?

You need to practise using lots of different magazines.

You should try creating your own pages:
- ■ trying different page layouts
- ■ using different fonts
- ■ putting in different photographs
- ■ cropping the photographs differently
- ■ using different styles of language
- ■ using different colour schemes.

■ Representation

WHAT IS REPRESENTATION?

Representation, at its simplest, is about how people are depicted in the extract.

You can look at how other things are represented – places, events, aliens, monsters, ideas – but it is best to start with people.

You will have learnt that people are often stereotyped within the media (see page 131). Stereotyping is such a big issue in representation that it is often the best place to start.

What stereotypes of people do you often find in lifestyle magazines?

Lifestyle magazines are usually aimed at supporting people in their masculinity or femininity, so this is a rich area to investigate.

Men's magazines commonly represent women as sex objects for the enjoyment of their male readers. They often use a 'laddish' stereotype of men as confident, jokey and only interested in sex, drinking, cars and football. However, not all men's magazines are the same, so you need to do a careful analysis of a range of magazines. Gay men's magazines, for example, tend to offer different representations of women and often represent men as sex objects.

Women's magazines commonly represent women as 'superwomen' who can hold down a job, be fashionable, look after a family, cook perfect meals, budget, look after their own and other people's emotional health and have exciting sex.

Lifestyle magazines tend to rely on stereotypical views of attractiveness. Women's magazines may represent older women as attractive, if they are aimed at that market, but only if they have 'kept themselves young'. Thus sexual attractiveness is still equated with youth, and women's magazines are full of advertisements offering ways of making you look younger. There are very few images of visibly disabled people or people with scars that are held to be models of attractiveness, and thin people dominate. So an extremely anti-stereotypical cover model for a women's magazine would be an older woman, showing her fat and a missing limb.

Lifestyle magazines traditionally used white models or celebrities on the front cover. This is less true today, especially of magazines aimed at ethnic minority audiences. However, you could still discuss whether it is anti-stereotypical to use an ethnic minority model on the front cover, especially if that model is not a celebrity.

In the same way, front cover images tend to be models of heterosexuality, except for magazines aimed at gay audiences.

Lifestyle magazines often use stereotypes of a rich lifestyle, so use stereotypes of middle-class or aristocratic ease. A model photographed on a yacht, for example, references traditional stereotypes of class. Notions of 'good taste' in Britain are closely associated with class.

WHAT ELSE COULD YOU ANALYSE?

Values

Representation also includes what the magazine is celebrating or valuing. This means you could ask yourself: 'What does the magazine say is a good thing?' These 'good things' are called *values*. They are what the people featured in the magazine act out (or deviate from).

Most lifestyle magazines celebrate values that most people can agree with so they can appeal to as many people as possible. This means their values are mainstream values.

Mainstream values include:
- good taste
- attractiveness
- becoming a better person and overcoming obstacles
- love and family
- buying things (materialism)
- defining yourself by your lifestyle (consumerism).

If you find any of these things being celebrated in an extract, then it is celebrating mainstream values.

Making sense

You could further ask: 'How does this representation make sense to the audience?' Many lifestyle magazines use very familiar representations to make the magazine easy to understand. You might comment on how an extract does this.

For example, take Kylie's statement on the front page of *Glamour* (Figure 2.10), that 'My body's not what it was but it's the body I'm in'. This is a familiar representation to the audience in a number of ways:

- They may remember Kylie's famous battle with cancer, which is itself one of a series of celebrity battles with illness.
- The experience of watching your body lose what it had is a common social stereotype (one based on real experience).
- The plucky 'but it's the body I'm in' reflects an age-old 'grin and bear it' attitude that is particularly associated with the acting profession (the show must go on).

SO WHAT SHOULD YOU ANALYSE?

Analyse representation, not characterisation (describing the characters).

You should start with looking at stereotypes in an extract. You can get a top grade just by doing this. You might comment on what the extract values – e.g. the qualities that the magazine celebrates – and perhaps how its world makes sense to its audience.

HOW DO I LEARN HOW TO ANALYSE REPRESENTATION?

You can learn to analyse representation by carrying out what is sometimes called 'the commutation test'. Take the people on the front covers, for example, and mentally (or you can try this with real images) replace them with different sorts of people. It's a Duchess? Try replacing her with somebody poor. It's a young model? Replace with an older man.

If the new image seems somehow wrong, then the factor you have changed is significant. If it doesn't, then it isn't. If replacing a beautiful white model with a beautiful black model doesn't look strange, then black people have not been excluded from this stereotype of beauty.

Print Textual Analysis Case Study

Case study – *Good Housekeeping*, *Bliss* and *Esquire*

Your textual analysis exam asks you three questions about a print extract:

1 how it fits the lifestyle magazine genre
2 how the media language creates the effects the editor was trying to achieve
3 how people are represented in the extract, plus an option to discuss the representation of something more abstract (such as 'femininity').

For our case studies we will compare three magazines to see what the lifestyle magazine genre has in common. Then we will analyse each in turn for both media language and representation.

1 Genre

THE FRONT COVERS

Look at the three front covers shown here and on the following pages. What do they all have in common?

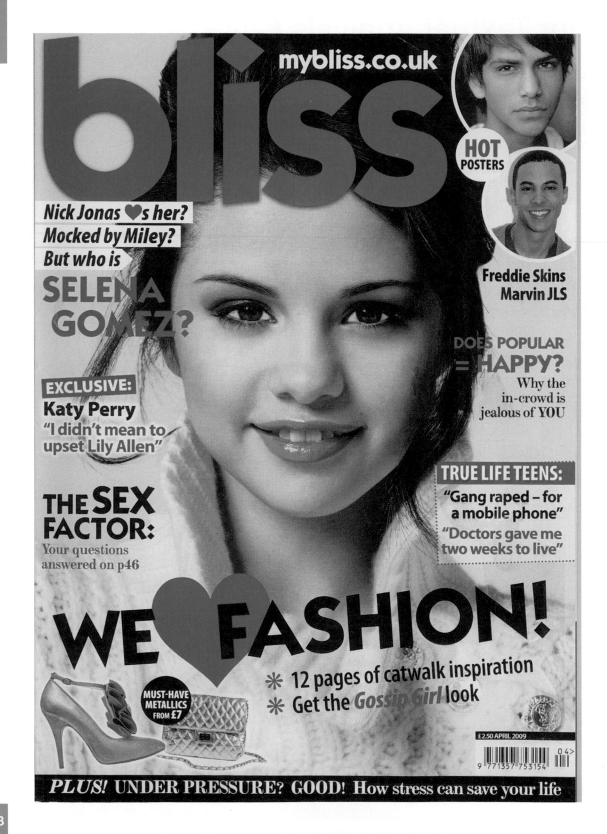

bliss

mybliss.co.uk

HOT POSTERS

Freddie Skins
Marvin JLS

Nick Jonas ♥s her?
Mocked by Miley?
But who is
SELENA GOMEZ?

EXCLUSIVE:
Katy Perry
"I didn't mean to
upset Lily Allen"

DOES POPULAR
= **HAPPY?**
Why the
in-crowd is
jealous of YOU

THE SEX FACTOR:
Your questions
answered on p46

TRUE LIFE TEENS:
"Gang raped – for
a mobile phone"

"Doctors gave me
two weeks to live"

WE ♥ FASHION!

* 12 pages of catwalk inspiration
* Get the *Gossip Girl* look

MUST-HAVE
METALLICS
FROM £7

£2.50 APRIL 2009

9 771357 753154

04>

PLUS! UNDER PRESSURE? GOOD! How stress can save your life

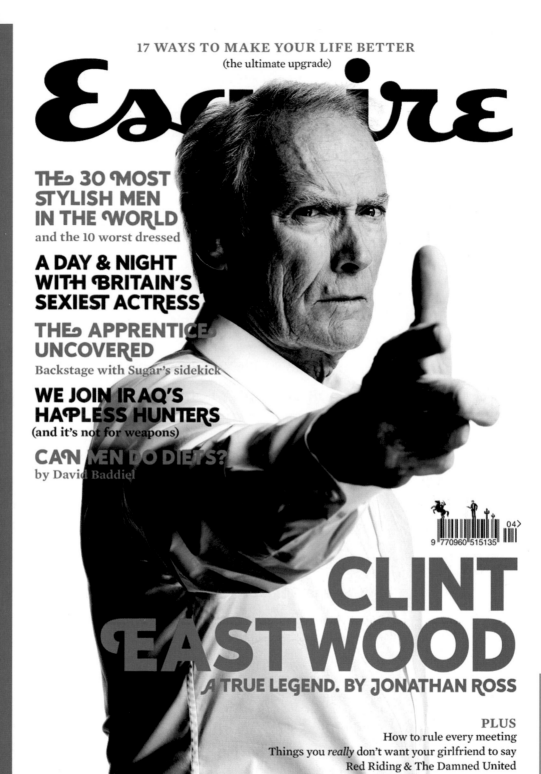

17 WAYS TO MAKE YOUR LIFE BETTER
(the ultimate upgrade)

Esquire

THE 30 MOST STYLISH MEN IN THE WORLD
and the 10 worst dressed

A DAY & NIGHT WITH BRITAIN'S SEXIEST ACTRESS

THE APPRENTICE UNCOVERED
Backstage with Sugar's sidekick

WE JOIN IRAQ'S HAPLESS HUNTERS
(and it's not for weapons)

CAN MEN DO DIETS?
by David Baddiel

9 770960 515135   04 >

CLINT EASTWOOD
A TRUE LEGEND. BY JONATHAN ROSS

PLUS
How to rule every meeting
Things you *really* don't want your girlfriend to say
Red Riding & The Damned United

ESQUIRE | APRIL 2009

THE MAGAZINE FOR MEN WHO MEAN BUSINESS

CLINT EASTWOOD | WOMAN WE LOVE | BEST-DRESSED LIST | HUNTING IN BAGHDAD

WWW.ESQUIRE.CO.UK

APRIL 2009 | £4.25

UNIT 2

159

WHAT THE FRONT COVERS HAVE IN COMMON

- The front cover is dominated by a photograph of a celebrity looking directly into the camera.
- The coverlines cover the mix of subjects expected under 'lifestyle'.
- There is a sense of direct address to the reader, both in the photograph and in the language of the coverlines.

Other common features include:
- the title at the top of the page
- the bar code at the bottom
- the shape of the page
- the one or two word title
- the mix of fonts.

This second set of features is so typical of magazines in general that it does not help define the conventions of the lifestyle magazine genre very well, so it is best not to use them in a genre answer.

So let's stick to the first three conventions.

MODEL OR CELEBRITY LOOKING DIRECTLY INTO THE CAMERA

Bliss and *Good Housekeeping* both have medium close-ups of celebrities – the actor Selena Gomez and the Duchess of York Sarah Ferguson; *Esquire* has a medium shot of the film actor and director Clint Eastwood.

These photographs are the 'face' of the magazine. They try to communicate the personality of the magazine and the aspirations of the reader.

Why Selena Gomez?

Selena Gomez is young and conventionally attractive. She appears confident. She is professionally made up. She would be considered successful by *Bliss* readers because she has a television show and is about to make a film and release an album. She is presented as a role model for the teenage *Bliss* reader, who can aspire to be like her.

Why Sarah Ferguson?

Sarah Ferguson is turning 50 but has an 'action plan'. She is a woman who is famous for having had difficulties in her life and dealing with them. She is conventionally attractive. She is easily recognisable as a 'personality'. She reflects the aspirations of the older, middle-class, rather conservative *Good Housekeeping* reader, which are to manage life effectively.

Why Clint Eastwood?

Clint Eastwood has a 'lived in' face. He has had a long and successful career as an actor and director, often playing roles of exaggerated masculinity. He can be shot in a serious, slightly aggressive pose and look like he means it. He is 'a true legend'. *Esquire* has a tagline: 'The magazine for men who mean business'. Clint Eastwood is presented as a model of 'meaning business'.

THE COVERLINES OFFER A MIX OF 'LIFESTYLE' SUBJECTS

Which subjects do **all three** magazines cover on the front page?

	Good Housekeeping	*Esquire*	*Bliss*
Celebrity interviews	Sarah Ferguson	Clint Eastwood, 'Britain's sexiest actress', and 'Sugar's sidekick'	Selena Gomez and Katy Perry
Sex/relationships	'Loving again after divorce'	'Things you really don't want your girlfriend to say'	'The sex factor'

Which subjects do **two** magazines cover on the front page?

	Good Housekeeping	*Esquire*	*Bliss*
Fashion		'The 30 most stylish men in the world'	'Get the Gossip Girl look'
Food	'25 recipes'	'Can men do diets?'	
Work	*Good Housekeeping* has 'Survive as a working mum'	*Esquire* has 'How to rule every meeting'	
Emotional health	'The value of true friendship'		'Why the in-crowd is jealous of you'

SENSE OF DIRECT ADDRESS TO THE READER

Lifestyle magazines like to present themselves as the readers' friend; someone who understands and can help.

This can show itself in a common use of the word 'you' – the magazine is talking directly to the reader:

- *Bliss* has 'Why the in-crowd is jealous of **you**' plus 'The sex factor: **your** questions answered'.
- *Esquire* has 'Things **you** *really* don't want your girlfriend to say'.
- *Good Housekeeping* has 'Time-crunched gardener? **Your** year starts here'.

It can show itself in the suggestion that the magazine is giving things to the reader:

- *Bliss* has '12 pages of catwalk inspiration'.
- *Esquire* has '17 ways to make your life better'.
- *Good Housekeeping* has '5 steps to tackle emotional eating'.

It can show itself in talking about the readers' assumed lifestyles:

- *Bliss* has 'Under pressure? Good!' – assumes teenagers feel stressed.
- *Esquire* has 'How to rule every meeting' – assumes reader is competitive and has a management job.
- *Good Housekeeping* has 'Survive as a working mum' – assumes reader is a working mum and finds that hard.

INSIDE THE MAGAZINES: THE CONTENTS PAGES

Look at the contents pages from the three magazines on the following pages.

CONTENTS
APRIL 2009

104 Plain sailing: bold, bright basics with a nautical flair

15 Treat yourself to the best

70 Hot topic: four real men discuss the real dangers of cancer

15 Fresh new ideas for your home

178 Unforgettable British holidays

173 Season-by-season gardening guide

128 Top marks: our 2009 Food Awards

Good Housekeeping Institute
TRIED ★ TESTED ★ TRUSTED

THE GOOD HOUSEKEEPING INSTITUTE is a leading research centre that has tested goods and stood up for consumers for more than 80 years. Our expert staff assess hundreds of products, triple-test thousands of recipes and respond to queries, feeding your concerns into the magazine. FOR ADVICE: go to www.allaboutyou.com/goodhousekeeping or email cookery.query@natmags.co.uk or consumer.query@natmags.co.uk.

COVER PHOTOGRAPH Colin Bell
STYLING Jane de Teliga STYLING ASSISTANT Lucy Goldring
Hair: Jonathan Malone. Make-up: Cheryl Phelps Gardiner at aart London. Sarah, Duchess of York wears: Dress, Boss by Hugo Boss at House of Fraser. Necklace, Erickson Beamon

▲ *Figure 2.12:* Good Housekeeping *contents pages*

Contents

I was bowled over by Jack and Luke from *Skins*

Enjoy this issue – write and tell me what us think at bliss@panini.co.uk

On the cover

bliss**Stalker**

bliss**You**

bliss**Style**

bliss**Boys**

bliss**Guide**

bliss**Regulars**

74 natural beauty

60 Red nose style

Letter from **bliss**…

Welcome to **bliss**! When I was younger, I had a really mixed view of celebrities. There were the ones I fancied, the ones I though were really arrogant, and the ones I aspired to be like because I thought they had perfect lives. But after having the opportunity to interview so many for the mag, it's clear that I had it all wrong. Really, they're just like us. They have the same hang-ups as we do, are into the same things that we are, and even though they might have fame and fortune, they're still just ordinary people.

I had a giggle with George Sampson during our dance lesson (p14) where he put me through my paces, and the *Skins* boys Jack (Cook) and Luke (Freddie) had me in stitches when I caught up with them at a bowling alley in London. I also interviewed r'n'b singer Akon in a posh London hotel, where we ended up munching on jam on toast and talking about hooking up Prince Harry. So, who said celebs weren't down to earth?

Zoe

Features writer

For talking boys over toast, Akon's your guy

Think George and I could win *Strictly Come Dancing*?

Panini UK Ltd., Brockbourne House, 77 Mount Ephraim, Tunbridge Wells, Kent TN4 8BS
Tel: 01892 500100 Fax: 01892 545666
Email: bliss@mybliss.co.uk
www.mybliss.co.uk
www.myspace.com/myblissworld
www.blissgirls.bebo.com

This month's question:
What's the best thing you've ever done for your mum?

Word girls
Assistant editor / features Angeli Milburn "Left home. Ha ha!"
Acting entertainment editor Louise Bennett "Cooked Christmas dinner when she was too ill"
Features writer Zoe Shenton "Took her on holiday"
Features intern Lucy Peden "Baked her a castle cake"

Production princesses
Assistant editor / production Jo Mellor "Made her proud"
Deputy chief sub editor Nic Hubbard "Baked her chocolate brownies as a special treat"

Team style:
Executive style ed Fatima Bholah "Graduated. All that money spent on uni wasn't a waste!"
Fashion & beauty assistant Lydia Thompson "Gave her a hug when she needed one"
Thanks to Lauren Grant

Arty farties
Senior designer Emily Hammond "Whisked her away to Paris for the weekend"
Designer Victoria Talbot "My mum said being born!"

Piccy queen
Picture ed Abby Wells "Took her to New York"

Web wonders
mybliss.co.uk **acting online editor** Frankie Mullin "Made her an 'egg tree' when I was eight"
Acting online assistant Nadine Brown "Learnt to wash my own clothes"

Other players
Managing director Mike Riddell
Marketing manager Jess Tadmor
Circulation manager Rebecca Smith
Managing editor Alan O'Keefe
Head of production Mark Irvine

FOR ADVERTISING SALES:
Contact: orange20 advertising sales
Email: paninidadsales@o20.co.uk
Tel: 020 7321 0701 or 01372 802800 **Fax:** 01372 723322

Account manager Michelle Fairlamb
Tel: 01372 802300 **Email:** michelle@o20.co.uk

Advertising sales manager Iona Spencer
Tel: 020 7389 0854 **Email:** iona@o20.co.uk

Marketforce (UK) Ltd
4th Floor, The Blue Fin Building, 110 Southwark Street, London SE1 0SU
Main Switchboard – 020 3148 3300 Trade enquiries – 020 3148 3333
marketforce.co.uk

If you had trouble finding **bliss** in the shops, email blisscirculation@panini.co.uk. **bliss** magazine is published monthly by Panini UK, part of the Panini group. **bliss** is a registered trademark. Nothing in this magazine may be reproduced in whole or in part without the written permission of the publishers. Any material submitted for publication is sent at the owner's risk and neither **bliss** nor its agents accept any liability for loss or damage. Subscriptions: call 0870 837 8504 or log on to subscription.co.uk/bliss.

bliss competitions are open to UK residents only, except employees of Panini, **bliss** printers and their families, and anyone connected to the competitions. No responsibility is taken for entries lost or delayed in the post. No correspondence will be entered into. Judge's decision is final. Send in an SAE to the usual **bliss** address for full competition terms and conditions.

All teen magazines in the UK must comply with the Teenage Magazine Arbitration Panel (TMAP) Guidelines designed to ensure sexual issues are addressed in an accurate, responsible and age appropriate way. If you have a specific complaint which cannot be resolved with the editor, contact TMAP. For more info and a copy of the guidelines, go to tmap.org.uk or call 020 7405 0819.

recycle

▲ *Figure 2.13: Bliss* (left) and *Esquire* (right) contents pages

CONTENTS

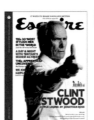

COVER

CREDITS
Photograph by Nigel Parry
White shirt by Prada (+44 20 7647 5000 www.prada.com)

SUBSCRIPTIONS
If you want a limited-edition, coverline-free version of Esquire delivered to your door, call +44 8448 481 601 and quote reference SB37

ORDER A LIMITED-EDITION COVER

DO CONVENTIONS CONTINUE INSIDE THE MAGAZINES?

The diverse mix of contents

This table shows how the different elements of the lifestyle magazine are covered on the contents pages of our magazines.

	Good Housekeeping	*Esquire*	*Bliss*
Celebrity interviews	'Good reading'	'Features'	'Bliss stalker'
Sex/relationships		'Inquire'	'Bliss boys'
Fashion	'Good Looks'	'Style and Grooming'	'Bliss style'
Food	'Good food'	'Critics'	
Work		'Business'	
Emotional health	'Good health'		'Bliss you'
Reviews		'Critics'	'Bliss guide'
Travel	'Good escapes'	'Design and travel'	
Homes and gardens	'Good homes'		
Shopping	'Good buys'	'Design and travel'	

Not all the elements of the lifestyle magazine are present in all magazines. This shows two important points:

1   That genre is a 'repertoire of elements'. This means that genre is like a repertoire of music that musicians know they can play. They do not have to play any one piece of music, but they can. A genre does not have to include all the elements, but it can.

2   That genres are 'inflected' differently when they target different audiences. You would not expect *Bliss* magazine to discuss homes and gardens when their target audience is teenagers.

DIRECT ADDRESS TO THE READER

We find this again in the contents pages.

	Good Housekeeping	*Esquire*	*Bliss*
Direct address in the language	'How to get the most of your budget'	'Everything you ever needed to know ...'	'Faultproof your future'
Giving things to the reader	'Six style rules that work'	'be the most stylish man about town'	'Get it or regret it'
Addressing the readers' assumed lifestyles	'Eating in is the new going out: plan the perfect Easter party'	'How to de-stress at home, at work, and abroad'	'The fashion guide to guys'

THE EDITOR'S LETTER

Another generic convention is a chatty editor's letter.

Esquire

EDITOR'S LETTER

THOUGH NOT AN AVID FOOTBALL FAN, I've seen my fair share of games over the years. My first match was Norwich v Arsenal at the former's home ground of Carrow Road. I was only six, and my form teacher, Mr Kennedy, took me as a special treat because my parents had just split up and he fancied my mum. Much to Mr Kennedy's discomfort, I decided that I would support the Gunners and insisted on wearing a red and white rosette.

A few years later, at boarding school in Ipswich, I got caught up in the game once more: Mick Mills, Ipswich's captain, had a son in my class, and manager Bobby Robson's kid was in the sixth form (he used to drive to school in a sports car). When they won the FA Cup in 1978 (beating Arsenal; I didn't mind) we all trooped excitedly down to the Town Hall to welcome the victors home. Despite being unable to recall any of the metaphysical poetry we were forced to learn back then, I can still remember what we all sang that day as we stood outside Grimwade's, the school outfitters, waiting for the open-top bus to arrive: "We're all part of Bobby's army / We've all been to Wembley / And we really shook 'em up when we won the FA Cup / 'Cos Ipswich are the greatest football team."

Attracted by Ipswich's success, I disloyally decided to switch teams and even bought tickets to watch the reserve team play one rainy Saturday afternoon. It was cold, and the match was boring, so I left at halftime to go and buy a packet of Minstrels; I found a misshapen one and sent it to Mars with a letter of complaint. They very kindly sent a replacement packet by way of apology.

That was it for football and me, until, 10 years ago, another men's magazine asked me to report on an Old Firm cup final at Hampden Park. I was astounded by the zeal of the Celtic fans I chatted to on the train up to Glasgow; impressed by how far the pieces of pie could fly from the mouths of the Rangers fans I was standing next to; and horrified when a young Catholic boy, Thomas McFadden, was stabbed to death that night for wearing the wrong colour scarf.

Disappointing England World Cup performances aside, I kept my distance from football until, a few weeks ago, while in Italy for business, I was taken by the designers Domenico Dolce and Stefano Gabbana to see AC Milan play Fiorentina at the impressive San Siro stadium. There were no pies flying in the designers' black velvet-clad box, just vintage Dom Perignon champagne corks, and there, only a few feet in front of us, were Beckham, Kaká and the rest of what must be one of the most stylish teams in the world. This was one occasion when the nickname "the beautiful game" didn't seem like an embarrassing misnomer.

Milan's residents are, naturally, a rather chic bunch and I'm not sure what Kaká would have made of the UK had he, as nearly happened, transferred to Manchester City. The place might have a swish restaurant scene and a plethora of well-stocked fashion emporiums, but Britain's footballers themselves tend to dress appallingly: they pile on the designer labels with gay abandon (Ronaldo), accessorise with far too many sparkly things (Ronaldo) and haven't yet discovered that logos a go-go have gone out of fashion (Ronaldo). So, while one footballer has made it on to our Best-Dressed Men list this year, it was a momentous task limiting ourselves to placing only two on the Worst-Dressed one. So it's a family-size packet of perfectly formed Minstrels for each of the winners, and a small piece of Hampden Park pie for the losers. Enjoy. ⓔ

Jeremy Langmead – Editor

ILLUSTRATION BY ANTONY HARE

030 | **ESQUIRE** | APRIL 2009

Textual Analysis and the Media Studies Topic

UNIT 2

▲ Figure 2.14: Esquire *editor's letter page*

Esquire magazine's editor's letter is **personal**:

> 'Though not an avid football fan, I've seen my fair share of games over the years.'

This gives us an insight into the **lifestyle** of the editor. This lifestyle is **aspirational**:

> 'a few weeks ago, while in Italy for business, I was taken by the designers Domenico Dolce and Stefano Gabbana to see AC Milan play Fiorentina at the impressive San Siro stadium. There were no pies flying in the designers' black velvet-clad box, just vintage Dom Perignon champagne corks, and there, only a few feet in front of us, were Beckham, Kaka and the rest of what must be one of the most stylish teams in the world.'

The letter suggests to us a lifestyle of sophistication, celebrity, foreign travel, highly expensive drinks, and 'class', plus the authentic manliness that football brings to the mix. This world of good taste and masculinity is designed to appeal to the *Esquire* reader, the man 'who means business'.

The letter **addresses** men who understand references to football, Italian designers and French upmarket champagne. It flatters its readers by assuming that they either live in this world, or could fit in if they did.

The letter further offers style advice in a way that avoids giving the impression it is doing so. Men, famously, hate to be told what to do. So the magazine instead has a feature on the most stylish and worst-dressed men in the world:

> 'Britain's footballers ... tend to dress appallingly: they pile on the designer labels with gay abandon (Ronaldo), accessorise with far too many sparkly things (Ronaldo) and haven't yet discovered that logos a go-go have gone out of fashion (Ronaldo).'

Readers are **flattered** by the letter, assuming that they know the latest fashion rules, and can share a joke with the editor about people who don't.

The letter ends with a personal touch, 'Enjoy', before, you sense, Jeremy is whisked off to his next party with the rich and stylish.

fromTHE EDITOR

WELCOME

If Christmas is all about family, then I always think the Easter Bank Holidays are for quality time with your friends. For the past few years we have spent the Easter holiday in a rented house in the Highlands of Scotland with two other families who have children of similar ages to my daughter. Plus assorted dogs. The idea behind choosing Scotland is that the brisk weather conditions will drive the kids indoors for at least an hour or two each day to study for their exams next term. And it gives the grown-ups (and dogs) the opportunity to go for long hearty walks down the glen and then recover by lounging in front of an open fire with a stack of novels to read (not the dogs, obviously). I can't think of anything nicer than when the 12 or so of us sit down to dinner around one huge table and the noise level reaches the rafters. Of course, the highlight is the Egg Hunt on Easter Sunday. Before the children are awake, the Dads get up early to assist the Easter Bunny in scattering dozens of chocolate eggs of all shapes and sizes around the gardens. Then, when the little darlings stir from their slumbers (not before 11am these days) they grab bags and containers of all descriptions and set off shrieking on their hunt. The youngest and fittest always get most of the eggs, which seems about right. The eldest 'child' in our party is now 22, but steadfastly refuses to be considered one of the adults. She says she's going to be part of the Easter Egg Hunt for ever. Good for her not to bow to the tyranny of worrying about calories or the pressure of wanting to be thought grown up. And good for the rest of us if we can take this one day a year to liberate our inner child – and feed her with chocolate! To get you in the mood, I'm delighted that we have partnered with Lindt, maker of wonderfully fine chocolate, to give you a bar of its new Dark Orange Intense. Your favourite magazine plus free chocolate – what could be better? Have a good Easter.

Here's photographer Juli Balla, hard at work shooting our fashion story with the temperature in the upper 20s (remember that?) on Sydney Harbour. Her gorgeous pictures of Riviera-style chic (page 104) promise a breath of spring.

Selecting (and tasting!) the array of delicious offerings that comprise this year's Food Awards (page 128) are (left to right) wine expert Richard Ehrlich, editor Lindsay, Prue Leith, associate editor Karen Barnes, chef Alan Murchison and Jane Asher

Our competition to find the best memoir about grandparents drew hundreds of entries. Here are the judges: books editor Kerry Fowler, Lindsay, Sarah Brown, Joanna Trollope, Gil McNeil of PiggyBankKids and Ebury's Fiona Macintyre

10   GH • April 2009

www.allaboutyou.com/goodhousekeeping

PHOTOGRAPHY BY TONY MCGEE, CHLOE CHLOE, PAUL, CHRISTIAN BARNETT, JANE DE TELIGA

▲ *Figure 2.15:* Good Housekeeping *editor's letter page*

The *Good Housekeeping* editor's letter is **personal**:

> 'If Christmas is all about family, then I always think that Easter Bank Holidays are for quality time with your friends. For the past two years we have spent the Easter holiday in a rented house in the Highlands of Scotland with two other families who have children of similar age to my daughter. Plus assorted dogs.'

This gives us an insight into the **lifestyle** of the editor. This lifestyle is **aspirational**:

'the brisk weather conditions will drive the kids indoors for at least an hour or two each day to study for their exams next term. And it gives the grown ups (and dogs) the opportunity to go for long hearty walks down the glen then recover by lounging in front of an open fire with a stack of novels to read.'

The letter suggests to us a lifestyle of family, close friends, achieving children (who revise for exams even when on holiday), healthy pastimes (walking), country leisure (lounging in front of an open fire), and the time and education to read 'a stack' of novels.

This world of happy families is designed to appeal to the *Good Housekeeping* reader, the woman who has to work hard to look after the family, look younger than her years, look after the house and garden, and take care of herself and her friends. It is a vision of community and happiness:

'I can't think of anything nicer than when the 12 or so of us sit down to dinner around one huge table and the noise level reaches the rafters.'

Even the Dads help out:

'the Dads get up early to assist the Easter bunny in scattering dozens of chocolate eggs of all shapes and sizes around the garden.'

The children are grateful, as they:

'set off shrieking on their hunt.'

The letter **addresses** women who understand references to comfortable middle class lifestyles. It offers an emotional ideal, an ideal of warmth and comfort, rather than the status ideal of *Esquire* magazine. Instead of flattering the reader, this editor's letter invites them in.

The relentlessly positive note that the letter strikes – no arguments or surly teenagers in this family – perhaps reflects the way the *Good Housekeeping* woman should always present her best face to the world. Lindsay has cleaned up her Easter holiday experience for the public, in the same way that the reader would clean and tidy the house before visitors arrived.

The letter ends with Lindsay's signature and a gift:

'To get you in the mood, I'm delighted that we have partnered with Lindt ... to give you a bar of its new Dark Orange Intense. Your favourite magazine plus free chocolate – what could be better? Have a good Easter.'

▲ *Figure 2.16: Bliss editor's letter page*

The *Bliss* editor's letter is **personal**:

'When I was younger, I had a really mixed view of celebrities.'

This gives us an insight into the **lifestyle** of the editor. This lifestyle is **aspirational**:

> 'I had a giggle with George Sampson during our dance lesson ... and the *Skins* boys Jack ... and Luke ... had me in stitches when I caught up with them ... I also interviewed r'n'b singer Akon in a posh London hotel.'

The letter suggests to us a lifestyle of fun, getting around and mixing with the stars. Compared to the *Esquire* and *Good Housekeeping* letters, however, this letter is much more down to earth. There is a sense that Zoe is just doing her job, rather than living in an ideal world.

Zoe's letter also stresses how 'normal' the stars really are:

> 'They have the same hang-ups as we do, are into the same things that we are, and even though they might have fame and fortune, they're still just ordinary people.'

Stressing how ordinary celebrities are assumes that the readers think of them as super-humans, so Zoe's sisterly insight into what it is like to hang out with important people **addresses** the reader as less knowing and needing helpful advice.

The editor's letter gets over this problem of appearing superior by adopting a very chatty tone, and by including photos that look like ordinary snapshots – Zoe really is just like the readers, only she has got a great job.

Zoe signs her letter not with Lindsay's sophisticated handwriting, but with a straightforward, felt pen signature, again stressing her ordinariness.

SO WHAT ARE THE GENERIC CONVENTIONS OF LIFESTYLE MAGAZINES?

- The front cover is dominated by a photograph of a model or celebrity looking directly into the camera.
- There is a diverse mix of contents expected under 'lifestyle'.
- There is direct address to the readers' lifestyles.
- There is a chatty editor's letter that gives personal information about the editors' aspirational lifestyles.

ARE THESE CONVENTIONS ALWAYS PRESENT?

Maybe not. We have established these conventions by looking at three magazines. You should look at other magazines and see if they fit these conventions too. It also does not matter if a magazine does not have all the conventions or if it contains other conventions.

HOW DO I DECIDE WHAT IS A LIFESTYLE MAGAZINE?

One answer is to look at the list of conventions on page 147 and say: 'A lifestyle magazine is a magazine that has these elements'. This is what is called a 'circular argument' and philosophers won't like it, but it may be the way your examiners choose lifestyle magazines for the exam.

Another answer is to go into a shop that sells lots of magazines and pick them off the shelves that say 'lifestyle'.

■ 2 Media language

The exam will ask you to comment on a set of media language elements. This will include some or all of the following:
- layout
- typography
- use of language
- use of colour
- use of images – photographs and graphics.

Let's take each magazine in turn and give examples of how you might analyse each element.

ESQUIRE

▲ *Figure 2.17: The* Esquire *magazine extracts*

ESQUIRE'S LAYOUT

Esquire has styled its layout to reflect how it wants its reader to think of the magazine. *Esquire* seems to be aiming to be an upmarket, stylish magazine for men, so the layout should reflect this.

All these pages featured have more white space than the pages of the other magazines. This spacious layout is a result of trying to look classy. Most downmarket magazines tend to cram their pages with content to look as though they are good value for money. *Esquire* is trying to look well-designed; so good that it doesn't need to sell itself to its readers.

Esquire's layout is very ordered. All the lines on these pages are horizontal or vertical and there is a strong use of columns to give a sense of order. However, *Esquire* doesn't want to look *too* ordered. It does not want to look too neat and tidy as that would not be very masculine.

Therefore, the reproduction of the pages in the first contents page does not form a complete column – the 'Biting the bullet' page is twice the width, which moves the 'Features' bar to the right and disrupts the next columns established above.

The text in the editor's letter is wrapped around the line drawings at the bottom of the first column.

ESQUIRE'S TYPOGRAPHY

▲ *Figure 2.18: Coverline from* Esquire *magazine*

Esquire's mixture of the formal and stylish, combined with slight informality, continues with its use of typography.

Esquire mixes serif and sans-serif fonts. It uses a sans-serif font for headings and a serif font for the copy. You can see this serif font in: 'and the 10 worst dressed'. It further mixes serif and sans-serif fonts in the coverlines.

Look at the first 'THE'. This font is a simple sans-serif font that would usually connote informality, freshness and youth, but *Esquire* has decorated the title font in an unusual way. Some letters join together , such as the 'H' and the 'E'.

Esquire is using a formal serif typeface as its house typeface. This gives it a sense of formality and seriousness. However, it doesn't want to look too serious and formal, so it uses a sans-serif typeface for titles and headings, and plays around with this typeface to give a 'designed' look to the magazine.

ESQUIRE'S USE OF LANGUAGE

Esquire uses many of the language conventions of the lifestyle magazine genre. Direct address to the audience gives the impression of communicating directly with the reader, as if a friend: 'Trading on your iPhone'. An advisory tone suggests that the magazine is in the know: 'Don't judge *The Damned United* by David Pearce's novel'. An informal register using colloquialisms creates a more friendly tone: 'Our new-look guide to looking buff'.

However, *Esquire* at times uses a slightly more formal register to suggest some seriousness and sophistication: 'The science of a slow-cooked winter stew'. This more formal language is always counterbalanced by a more jokey, masculine language, either in style or in content. The mention of metaphysical poetry in the editor's letter, for example, is in the context of the chants the editor sang when the victorious Ipswich Town football team came home.

ESQUIRE'S USE OF COLOUR

Esquire uses strong, masculine colours. Red, black and white predominate. Where the text uses yellow, it is not the bright yellow of *Bliss* magazine, but a sandy yellow with greater complexity. The red and yellow are used sparingly, giving the magazine a solemn but not grave look – this is a serious magazine for serious people, but one in which you can still find some laughs and interesting stories.

The pink pages used for business reflect the pink pages of the *Financial Times* – the main newspaper for business people.

ESQUIRE'S IMAGES

The photographs in the extract we have selected are either in black and white or have a very limited colour palette. Black and white photography is often used for documentary photography as it suggests more realism than colour photography. This is a convention that has probably evolved as colour photography replaced black and white photography, so we notice the black and white of old photographs and come to see them as having more authenticity. Much art photography still uses black and white, so it is often seen as more artistic.

The black and white photograph of Clint Eastwood, for example, not only has a connotation of authenticity, but the high contrast film and the low key lighting that have been used emphasise his wrinkles and the strong eye light. This makes him look both grizzled and full of life, an appropriate look for 'a true legend'.

The use of line drawings for the editor's letter page instead of a photograph of the editor is worth commenting on. This unconventionality fits the 'designed' look of *Esquire*. It restricts the colours on the page to black, white and yellow. It adds an air of irony to the page. Someone has made this drawing to illustrate the somewhat self-congratulatory tone of the letter and, in doing so, parodies it.

GOOD HOUSEKEEPING

▲ *Figure 2.19: The* Good Housekeeping *magazine extracts*

GOOD HOUSEKEEPING'S LAYOUT

Good Housekeeping has styled its layout to reflect how it wants its readers to think of it. *Good Housekeeping* seems to be aiming to be an upmarket but practical magazine for women, so the layout should reflect this.

These pages have less white space than *Esquire*, but more than *Bliss*. This layout is trying to look full but still classy. *Good Housekeeping* fills its pages in a no-nonsense way that reflects its more practical approach.

The layout is very ordered. Nearly all the lines on these pages are horizontal or vertical and there is a strong use of columns to give a sense of order. There is a clear header on the contents page and editor's letter page – both have the same design, which runs throughout the magazine and gives a strong sense of house style. However, *Good Housekeeping* doesn't want to look too ordered. It wants to look neat and tidy but to suggest that it has a sense of fun as well.

To achieve this look, the photographs on the editor's letter page are at slight angles to the page, as if to suggest a photo album, and they also break out of the text box of the accompanying copy. Plus, the text at the bottom of the editor's letter wraps around the photo of the chocolate bar, which is also at an angle.

The front cover has a fairly symmetrical layout, which works with the cover image to present a solid and reliable look – this is an established magazine that knows itself and its readers and is not going to undergo radical change.

GOOD HOUSEKEEPING'S TYPOGRAPHY

▲ *Figure 2.20: Coverline from* Good Housekeeping *magazine*

Good Housekeeping's mixture of formality mixed with informality continues with its typography in the way it consistently mixes serif and sans-serif fonts.

Good Housekeeping mixes serif and sans-serif fonts for the coverlines. '25 recipes' is in a serif upper-case font. 'World's easiest chocolate cake' is in a sans-serif lower-case font. The mix of fonts in upper and lower case on the front cover gives it a more busy look, which is restrained by restricting the coverlines to white. *Good Housekeeping* is sensible but fun.

Good Housekeeping uses sans-serif fonts for the contents page, apart from the heading and subheadings. Sans-serif fonts are often considered easier to read where the blocks of text are not very long. So the editor's letter page uses a serif font for the letter, but sans-serif for the shorter column on the right.

GOOD HOUSEKEEPING'S USE OF LANGUAGE

Good Housekeeping uses many of the language conventions of the lifestyle magazine genre. Direct address to the audience gives the impression of communicating directly with the reader, as if a friend: 'Our five-step plan to help put your relationship with food in perspective'. An advisory tone suggests that the magazine is in the know: 'Expert advice for using bright colours with confidence to give your home a new look'. There is, however, less use of the informal register or colloquialisms, apart from: 'Four men get their kit off', which, in referring to men, seems to adopt a more masculine style.

Good Housekeeping's language is clear, direct and to the point. It is woman to woman, friend to friend. When it does start getting jokey – the references to dogs not reading in the editor's letter, for example – this is short and understated: 'lounging in front of an open fire with a stack of novels to read (not the dogs obviously)'. The language seems to suggest that one can never let up in the constant battle to maintain modern femininity, that this is a serious business to be taken seriously.

GOOD HOUSEKEEPING'S USE OF COLOUR

Good Housekeeping uses similar colours to *Esquire*. Red, black and white predominate. However, compared to *Esquire,* the photographs in *Good Housekeeping* are a riot of colour. The photographs of food, flowers and landscape on the second contents page introduce blues, greens, and oranges into the mix. *Good Housekeeping* has chosen a strong set of colours for the house style colour scheme (though these change slightly throughout the magazine) but here they do not connote masculinity. Rather, they suggest a clean, fresh, well-ordered magazine – one that is working hard to make everything clear for the readers.

This is a good example of how you should not assume that colours have one set meaning. The same reds in *Esquire* and *Good Housekeeping* have different meanings because of their different contexts.

The front cover for *Good Housekeeping* is dominated by skin tones, giving the magazine a very human look. Nothing in the writing or background overshadows the colours of the face, which thus becomes the face of the magazine.

GOOD HOUSEKEEPING'S IMAGES

The photographs in the extract we have selected vary in size, style and content, giving a sense of variety to the magazine.

There are formal portraits using the conventions of glamour photography for the front cover and the image of the editor. Both use soft lighting (to minimise wrinkles) with lots of fill light (to avoid shadows) and light in the eyes, though the cover photo has been lit with more care to avoid shine, apart from that reflecting off the eyes and the gloss on the lower lip. The Duchess has been made up to minimise flaws in the skin, and she is smiling.

There are very naturalistic looking 'snapshots' on the right of the editor's letter page. These are quite poorly lit and look more 'amateur', giving them, perhaps, a sense of realism.

The photographs on the contents pages have all been cropped to give of different shapes, creating variety on the page. The 'woman on a yacht' photograph has been cropped to leave a lot of sky at the top of the shot, which matches the white space around the 'Contents' heading. There is a mix of model, man, mug and makeup on the first contents page, landscape, food and flowers on the second, suggesting the cornucopia of delights within the magazine.

BLISS

▲ *Figure 2.21: Front cover and contents of* Bliss *magazine*

BLISS'S LAYOUT

Bliss has styled its layout to reflect how it wants its reader to think of it. *Bliss* seems to be aiming to be a fun magazine for teenage girls, so the layout should reflect this.

These two pages are more ordered and less cluttered than the rest of the magazine, but they are still, as we would expect, more cluttered and less ordered than *Esquire* and *Good Housekeeping*.

The *Bliss* front cover has a number of elements that break out of the horizontal and vertical: the 'Exclusive' on the left, the fashion item towards the bottom of the page, the textbox for 'True Life Teens', and the circular borders for the photographs in the top right-hand corner.

The *Bliss* contents page photographs are mostly on an angle and the top one breaks out of the top of the page. The contents and editor's letter are organised into columns, but the rigid organisation of the contents columns is broken up by the large *Bliss* logo in the background.

This visual clutter is to try to give the impression of a magazine overflowing with content, to reflect the busy lifestyle of the *Bliss* reader, and to look more energetic and fun.

BLISS'S TYPOGRAPHY

▲ *Figure 2.22: Coverline from* Bliss *magazine*

Bliss uses overwhelmingly sans-serif fonts, as we would expect of a magazine aimed at a young reader. These look more chatty and informal.

The heart symbol is used twice on the front cover instead of 'love'. This symbol is an icon of young teenage communication about emotional matters (e.g. on social networking sites), so its use is designed to suggest direct teenage to teenage communication.

BLISS'S USE OF LANGUAGE

Bliss uses many of the language conventions of the lifestyle magazine genre. Direct address to the audience gives the impression of communicating directly with the reader, as if a friend: 'Why the in-crowd is jealous of you'. An advisory tone suggests that the magazine is in the know: 'Your questions answered on p46'. An informal register using colloquialisms creates a more friendly tone: 'Who said celebs weren't down to earth?'.

The language register is more informal than in the other two magazines. The sentences are short, the vocabulary is simple and there are a lot of colloquialisms. For example: 'Brit's Booky Wooky'. This language register is for creating a sense of community between the writer and the reader, and a warm and inclusive mode of address. 'Warm' means that the magazine is trying to make the reader feel good about themselves and the magazine. 'Inclusive' means that the magazine is trying to make the reader feel included, as part of the '*Bliss* community'. The magazine is prioritising this over giving information.

BLISS'S USE OF COLOUR

Bliss uses a saturated pink throughout the extract and this becomes a neon pink on the front cover. This neon pink is an icon of the magazine's femininity; it seems to suggest the fun-loving, party animal that is the ideal *Bliss* reader (that is, they hope, what the actual reader would like to be). It's bright, it's bold and it's not ashamed of itself.

Bliss uses yellow like *Esquire* does, though a brighter, younger yellow that contrasts with the pink, as if they are partying.

There are more colours used to establish the difference between the different sections on the contents page. These colours are more muted so they do not disturb the overall pink of the page.

BLISS'S IMAGES

The photographs in the extract we have selected vary in size, style and content, giving a sense of variety to the magazine. However, *Bliss* relies more on blocks of colour and typography on these pages to create a busy look, compared to *Good Housekeeping's* reliance on photographs.

There is a formal portrait using the conventions of glamour photography for the front cover. This uses soft lighting but with less fill light than the *Good Housekeeping* front cover photo (thus creating the shadow on her face). There is also less light in the eyes but the same shine on the gloss on the lower lip. Again, the actress has been made up to appear to have flawless skin, and is smiling.

There are very naturalistic looking 'snapshots' on the right of the editor's letter page. These are quite poorly lit and look more 'amateur', giving them, perhaps, a sense of realism. The shot of Freddie on the front page uses black and white. The shot of Marvin even includes the shadow cast by the flashlight on the wall behind. These more 'amateur' shots give the impression of being snatched in the middle of a busy social occasion – snaps of a celebrity lifestyle.

SO WHAT DO I NEED TO DO WITH MEDIA LANGUAGE?

You need to be able to:
- spot an interesting *example* of how it has been used
- describe this using *terminology* if possible
- *analyse* what effect the producers of the magazine were trying to create.

3 Representation

WHAT IS REPRESENTATION?

Representation, at its simplest, is about how people are depicted in the extract.

You may be asked to look at how other things are represented, especially masculinity or femininity.

You will have learnt that people are often stereotyped within the media (see page 131). Stereotyping is such a big issue in representation that it is often the best place to start.

LET'S COMPARE OUR THREE MAGAZINES

  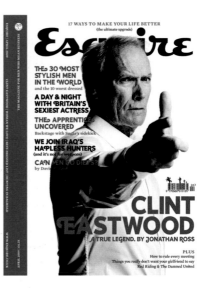

▲ Figure 2.23: The magazine covers

GENDER, RACE AND AGE

Gender, race and age are always present in any photograph of a person.

Gender stereotypes are strongly present in the three front pages. One of the most common gender stereotypes is that women are passive – to be looked at – and men are active – doing things or doing the looking.

Sarah Ferguson and Selena Gomez are represented as two different kinds of feminine beauty. They are lit in a flattering way in order to emphasise this. Their static poses place all the emphasis on their looks.

Clint Eastwood is represented as the embodiment of masculine power. His pose is active and aggressive and he looks like he is giving an order. There is no need to disguise his age as there is with most female subjects; his wrinkles testify to his long experience and serious lifestyle. He is a patriarch – a father figure with power.

The women are passive while the man is active. This is stereotypical.

Racial stereotypes are also present, but more subtly. Sarah Ferguson and Clint Eastwood are clearly white, where Selena Gomez could be mixed race. Replace Clint Eastwood with a black film director with a long reputation and the meaning would hardly change. Similarly, you could replace Selena Gomez with a young star of any ethnicity. But Sarah Ferguson was part of a very white institution – the British royal family. She is the embodiment of traditional British culture trying to adjust to the modern age, so her whiteness is a part of this meaning. This is because traditional Britishness is stereotypically thought of as white, despite the fact that there have been ethnic minority populations in Britain for centuries.

The model on the yacht in the contents page is also white. Yachting is another symbol of class and tradition in Britain, so that might explain why the model chosen for the yachting photoshoot is white. The stereotype of rich country pursuits is a very white one.

Age is clearly present, and its meaning changes with gender. Clint's age, as we have seen, is linked to his authenticity and fame and part of what makes him 'a true legend'. It connotes his experience and know-how. These are the qualities that make him the right man for *Esquire* magazine. Clint Eastwood is a 'real man', so he doesn't have an action plan for his undefined age. Sarah Ferguson is 'turning 50' and does have a plan. She is a woman who is known to have struggled in life and her age is an important part of this; this makes her the right woman for *Good Housekeeping* magazine. But both magazines could have a younger person, such as Selena Gomez, on the front cover. This is because older audiences are thought to relate to both older and younger people.

Younger audiences are thought to relate more to younger people, so *Bliss* magazine does need a young person on the front cover. Replacing Selena Gomez with Sarah Ferguson, for example, would be a shock to the *Bliss* reader, though not so much of a shock as replacing her with Clint Eastwood.

VALUES

What do these magazines value?

Good Housekeeping spells this out on the front cover: 'What really matters'. But the other contents also carry messages about 'what matters':

- Good Reading – finding out about celebrities
- Good Health – fighting disease, keeping the family healthy
- Good Choices – shopping
- Good Looks – thinness and fashion
- Good Food – eating well and impressing guests
- Good Homes – improving your home
- Good Escapes – holidaying
- Just for you – being looked after.

All these are consumerist values. Consumerism is about buying things to display who you are. It is about looking and being 'your best'. It is about having a 'lifestyle'.

Haven't people always bought things? Yes, but before the consumer society many people lived like their parents. They inherited attitudes along with their parents' furniture. With the consumer society it became 'normal' to rebel, to find out 'who you really are', and to define yourself by the way you look, where you live, the car you drive, where you holiday, and so on. Celebrities are the stormtroopers of a consumer society as they publicly experiment with lifestyles and fashions.

Are *Esquire's* values different? There is less emphasis on home, health and looking after others. There is more stress on celebrities that achieve, like 'the genius behind Borat', and much more emphasis on work. Consumerist values again, but the *Esquire* reader's lifestyle is defined by work as well as leisure.

The world of *Bliss* is simpler again. Celebrity, friendship, boys, fashion and beauty rule the life of the *Bliss* reader. Disappointingly, there is nothing about how to do well at school.

MAKING SENSE

The representation of the world in *Good Housekeeping* makes sense because it fits with the stereotype of the middle-class housewife. The very way that *Good Housekeeping* represents the role as applying to women and not men fits the traditional gender stereotype of women looking after the home. (The fact this stereotype is grounded in reality might explain why there aren't lots of *Good Housekeeping* magazines aimed at men.)

This world is familiar. We see representations of this world in other media texts, such as lifestyle television and some drama. We see it in a range of lifestyle magazines. We also see it in the advertising that largely pays for this genre of magazines (cosmetics, home furnishings and equipment, clothes, travel, food, medicines and detergents).

The representation of the world in *Esquire* makes sense because it mixes the more niche world of men's style and fashion (which provides most of its advertising) with some of the laddishness that will be familiar from other men's magazines, TV (such as *Dave*), popular newspapers, and so on.

The representation of the world in *Bliss* makes sense because it fits with the stereotypical world of teen drama in film and television, of young teenage ('tweenage') magazines and of popular music.

■ What you do in the exam

You will be given an extract from a lifestyle magazine. This extract will normally be the front cover, the contents page or pages, the editor's letter page and perhaps one other page.

You will need to answer three questions on:
■ generic conventions
■ media language
■ representation.

You should practise this using a wide range of lifestyle magazines. This is especially true of the generic conventions – you can only be sure of these if you look at lots of different magazines. If you only looked at women's lifestyle magazines you might decide that articles about recipes, for example, are one convention, but we found little about recipes in *Esquire* and *Bliss*.

It doesn't matter if you have studied the magazine used in the exam or not – you do not need to know anything about the particular magazine that you analyse. You just need to be able to analyse the extract. Good luck!

Section B: Television and/or Radio Comedy – Introduction

What do you study in Section B?

- You study how television (or radio) comedies are scheduled – what time and what channels they are on.
- You study the audience pleasures of those comedies.
- You study at least two programmes.

Investigating audiences and institutions

'Audience' can be a tricky subject in Media Studies because everyone thinks they know what it means. This can lead students into making common sense judgements about audience tastes that are based on their own stereotypes. Teenagers, for example, will write in exam essays about 'old people in their 30s' not enjoying TV programmes unless they are 'really boring'. This is just repeating a stereotype, not analysing audience. It is important, therefore, to use evidence to back up what you say about audience.

Where can you get evidence for audiences?

It is difficult to discover hard facts about audience figures and those that are easily available do not usually break down audiences into different groups, such as age and gender. So the evidence you are most likely to be able to use is 'textual'. You could investigate the **schedules**, **the programmes** and how channels **promote** themselves (trailers, their channel idents, and so on).

▲ *Figure 2.24: MTV and ITV logos*

Channel idents, like these two logos for MTV and ITV1, can tell us a lot about what kind of audience the channel is aimed at. They also give us clues about what kind of channel they are – this is what we mean by 'institution' – and how they want to communicate this to their audiences.

One of the above channels is aimed at a mass audience – that is, a wide range of people who may be young and old, men and women, rich and poor, and interested in mainstream entertainment.

The other channel is aimed at a niche audience – that is, a narrower range of people who share similar interests and attitudes.

How do these idents reflect the different institutions? The MTV logo style is more edgy – using a graffiti-style 'TV' and a three dimensional 'M', with the 'TV' breaking out from the confines of the 'M'. MTV describe themselves on their website as 'fresh, honest and groundbreaking' and the ident reflects this ambition.

The ITV logo, by contrast, is more ordered and so more sober in style. The ITV websites frequently use the words 'quality' and 'popular' to describe their programmes and this logo reflects the channel's desire to be accessible and friendly while still showing quality.

The ITV logo reflects ITV's mass audience, and the MTV logo reflects their niche audience. We might also guess that the MTV audience, as it was originally music television, is likely to be younger and less socially conservative ('wilder') than the ITV audience. To investigate this further we need to look at the schedules.

The schedules

A typical ITV schedule for February 2009 includes a wide range of programmes:

- *Emmerdale*, a soap opera
- *The Jeremy Kyle Show*, a talk show
- *Midsomer Murders*, a detective drama
- *News at Ten*
- *Golden Balls*, a game show
- *In the Line of Fire*, documentary on police firearms officers
- *Doctors and Nurses at War*, a documentary.

This mixed schedule is typical of a **mass audience** TV channel in Britain between the 1950s and the 2000s.

A typical MTV1 schedule for February 2009 includes a far narrower range of programmes:

- 10 showings of the reality television show *The Ashlee Simpson Show*, running from 6 am until 11 am
- 10 episodes of the reality television show *The Hills*, running from 11 am till 4 pm
- Five episodes of the reality television transformation show *MTV Digs*, running from 4 pm till 7 pm
- Two episodes of the reality television show *The City*, running from 7 pm till 8 pm

This specialist schedule is typical of **niche audience** television channels in Britain between the 1980s and the 2000s. This schedule is **stripped**: the same shows are shown at the same times every day, often several episodes back to back. This is another feature of niche audience television. The main characters in these shows are all young, addressing a young audience. The main characters in the ITV1 programmes, on the other hand, are from a wide variety of age groups.

We have found evidence for the different audiences for MTV and ITV from analysing their schedules, and from comparing their channel idents. We could look as well at their websites, how they advertise themselves, even their reports and policies. But it is time to mention the audience pleasures offered by the **programmes**, the last part of the jigsaw.

■ The programmes

You have to study two television (or radio) comedies. Let's pick a comedy from each of the two channels we have looked at.

Let's compare

MTV1 shows *Nick Cannon's Short Circuitz* in the 11 pm till midnight slot. This offers comedy players, sketches, impersonations and 'laugh-out-loud hi-jinx as only Nick and MTV can bring it' (www.mtv.co.uk/channel/mtvuk/schedule).

ITV1 shows *Harry Hill's TV Burp* at the same time, from 11.05 pm to 11.35 pm. This show, 'takes a surreal look at the week's small-screen highlights, subjecting the latest soap sagas, reality shows, documentaries and other assorted oddities to (Harry Hill's) unique brand of scrutiny through his collection of TV clips' (www.itv.com/TVGuide/TextOnly/default.html).

The next move is to watch both these programmes and analyse the audience pleasures they offer, picking examples from the programmes to illustrate these pleasures. We shall do this later on in the case studies. For now, the important point is to see that the differences in audience pleasures should reflect the differences between the two channels that show the programmes.

Therefore, *Harry Hill's TV Burp* should be accessible and popular with a wide-ranging audience, whereas *Nick Cannon's Short Circuitz* should address a younger audience.

This difference can be seen in the choice of presenters. Nick Cannon is a 28-year-old African-American rapper, record producer, songwriter and comedian with his own clothing line. Harry Hill is a 44-year-old white British comedian who offers family-friendly humour (catchphrases and clean language) with a surreal twist – hence the title 'TV burp', a title that is slightly naughty but not rude, and strange yet comforting.

Short Circuitz offers sketches like 'Working with White People' whereas *TV Burp* offers 'TV Highlight of the Week', which will show some very ordinary event from a programme, such as a character pouring tea.

These two pieces of evidence suggest that *TV Burp* addresses its audience as British people who watch mainstream television, and that *Short Circuitz* addresses its audience as African Americans or people who are willing to explore the experience of African Americans. MTV1 is offering more edgy pleasures than ITV1, as we would expect.

▲ *Figure 2.25:* Harry Hill *and* Short Circuitz's Nick Cannon

■ Studying audience and institutions

You need to study two comedy programmes that offer different audience pleasures, such as *TV Burp* and *Short Circuitz*.

These different pleasures should reflect the differences between the television (or radio) channels that show these programmes, such as ITV1 and MTV1.

One important difference between television channels is that some are aimed at mass audiences and others are aimed at a niche audience. ITV1 is an example of a channel for mass audiences, whereas MTV1 is for a niche audience.

The evidence for differences can come from studying:
■ the programme
■ the channels' schedules
■ how the channels market themselves (websites, idents, trailers, advertisements)
■ the institutions' policies.

ITV1	MTV1
Family-friendly comedy	More edgy comedy
Mixed schedule	Specialist, stripped schedule
Friendly yet serious channel ident	More youthful looking channel ident
Claims to offer quality, popular programmes	Claims to offer 'fresh, honest and groundbreaking' programmes

■ And finally …

ITV might appear to be one of the 'big boys' from this analysis, but MTV is part of Viacom, one of the largest media companies in the world, who own the Paramount Hollywood studio.

See http://www.viacom.com/ourbrands/globalreach/Pages/default.aspx for a map of their global reach.

ITV is tiny in comparison.

Section B: Television and/or Radio Comedy – Institutions

■ Institution

'Institution' means the organisation(s) that transmit the television or radio programmes that you study. There are several key elements to look at when you are investigating a television or radio channel.

■ Target audience

MASS AUDIENCES AND NICHE AUDIENCES

We have already come across the distinction between mass audience and niche audience channels with our comparison of ITV1 and MTV1. A quick look at the schedules for a channel should be enough evidence to tell whether the channel is mass or niche.

A mass audience channel needs a mix of programmes that appeals to all different sorts of viewers or listeners. They need to be mainstream enough to be popular. Niche audience channels will schedule very similar programmes, either in terms of their genre or their audience appeal.

 Let's research

Investigate the BBC channels and decide whether their audiences are mass or niche.

TV channels	Audience	What the BBC says they are for
BBC1	Mass	Popular programmes
BBC2	Niche – upmarket audiences	Knowledge-building programmes (plus comedy, drama and arts)
CBeebies	Niche – young children	Learning through play for children under six
CBBC	Niche – older children	Safe and trusted informal learning for six–12-year-old children
BBC3	Niche – teenagers	Innovation for younger audiences
BBC4	Niche – upmarket audiences	Culturally and intellectually enriching programmes (arts and factual)
BBC News	Niche – news audience	Reporting the news
BBC Scotland	Niche – Scots	Reflecting Scottish culture and heritage
BBC Wales	Niche – Welsh	Reflecting Welsh culture and heritage
BBC Northern Ireland	Niche – Northern Irish	Reflecting Northern Irish culture and heritage

DEMOGRAPHICS AND PSYCHOGRAPHICS

These might be two rather frightening words, but don't worry. All this section is trying to do is to tell you that there is more than one way of describing audiences, and that you can make up your own way of doing this, so long as it communicates something important about the audience.

Demographics sort audiences into groups by such factors as their **age**, **gender**, **region** or **nation**, **class** and **ethnicity**. These are known as demographic categories.

Many BBC channels are aimed at a demographic category:
- the 'upmarket' audiences listed above – for BBC4 and BBC2 – are defined by class (middle-class audiences)
- the audiences for BBC Scotland, Wales and Northern Ireland are defined by nation
- audiences for BBC3, CBBC and CBeebies are defined by age.

The main difference between Radio 1 and Radio 2 is that Radio 1 targets a niche audience of 15–29-year-old popular music listeners, whereas Radio 2 is a mass audience channel aimed primarily at 25–44-year-olds.

Psychographics sorts audiences into groups on the basis of shared **tastes**, **attitudes** and **personality types**. Science fiction enthusiasts, for example, are a psychographic group as they are defined by their shared enthusiasm for science fiction. The SciFi Channel is aimed at this psychographic category. Radio 3 targets another psychographic group – classical music fans (plus jazz and world music fans).

There are lots of different versions of psychographics, so no one version can claim to be correct. One famous American system analysed what people bought. They found that people who bought 'in-bowl toilet fresheners' were very unlikely to buy 'snow blowers'. In the same way, you could investigate what other programmes the fans of a particular show all like and what programmes they dislike. That would help build up a picture of the show's audience.

Let's discuss

Daytime MTV1 programmes, as we have seen, tend to be reality television shows about young girls trying to make their way in the celebrity world. This probably makes young girls their core demographic. Look at this list of personality types and discuss which ones fit MTV1 viewers:

- the virtuous
- admiration seekers
- pleasure seekers
- security and stability seekers
- anti-authority rebels
- joiners
- those who don't want responsibility or commitment
- those who don't know or care what they want
- materialists
- complainers

- do-gooders
- survivors
- achievers
- belongers
- experimentalists
- succeeders
- working-class puritans
- struggling poor
- resigned poor
- innovators
- followers

Let's research – Investigating target audience

- Examine the schedules to see if you are dealing with a mass audience or niche audience channel.
- See how the channel defines its audience on its website.
- Investigate what other programmes (or films, music, magazines, newspapers, websites, etc.) fans of the programme like and dislike to build up a psychographic profile.
- Try applying personality types.

■ Brand image

Back in the 1980s, my father-in-law used to go through the *Radio Times*, read the descriptions, and circle which television programmes in the coming week he wanted to watch. If he had a cable or satellite subscription today he would be spending more time going through the schedules than he would spend watching the programmes.

Once upon a time, if you wanted to change channel you had to get up, go to the television, turn the knob until you reached the right channel, hit the television a few times to get it working properly again, then sit down again. Unsurprisingly, once audiences had tuned in to a channel they would often stick with it.

We are now in the age of **multichannel television**. Audiences flit from channel to channel, checking what's on. So how does a channel try to persuade us to try them?

They need a strong brand image.

A brand image is the identity or 'personality' of a brand that has been constructed by a particular institution. It is what we all think about a brand once we know its name, see its design, see its advertisements, know what it costs and, possibly, use it.

BBC

The BBC has a strong brand image. People will recognise the name, and most will recognise the logo. Many will have positive feelings about the BBC. This is because it is a very well-established brand with a long tradition that links in some way to the very idea of 'Britishness'. When the BBC set up new channels, they kept the same brand name and extended it to BBC2, BBC3, and so on.

UKTV – WHAT'S IN A NAME?

UKTV is not such a strong brand. This is despite the fact it is partly owned by the BBC and uses lots of BBC programming. So when UKTV rebranded the rather forgettably-named UKTV G2 they chose a name – Dave – that is very recognisable and appropriate for a channel aimed at men. They came up with a tagline – 'The Home of Witty Banter' – that again made the channel sound masculine and ironic. The relaunched channel was given a slot on Freeview. Dave quickly developed a strong brand image and attracted a larger audience than UKTV G2. Men looking for something to watch would stop and check out Dave.

UKTV took one look at how successful Dave had been and then decided to rebrand their other channels:
- UKTV Gold became G.O.L.D. – 'Go On Laugh Daily'
- UKTV Drama became Alibi – 'The Deadliest Place on TV'
  UKTV People became Blighty – 'One Nation Under a Channel'
- UKTV Documentary became Eden – 'One Amazing Channel, One Amazing World'
- UKTV History became Yesterday

FLAGSHIP PROGRAMMES

An interesting or very familiar name is not enough in itself. A television or radio channel that is trying to attract audiences in a busy market place needs a flagship programme to attract audiences and build up its brand image.

Sky1, for example, used the series *Lost* to promote the channel. Sky used the fact audiences could only watch *Lost* on Sky in an extensive advertising campaign in 2007.

You can investigate what programmes are being used by a channel to build up their brand image by looking at their advertising and websites. Flagship programmes will feature prominently in both of these.

Flagship programmes need to be high quality, popular and long-running. *Fawlty Towers*, a sitcom from the 1970s, was high quality and popular, but famously only ran for two series. It would be hard to build a schedule around that show. American sitcoms usually run for much longer. *Will & Grace* ran for eight seasons of 22–27 episodes each. *Friends* ran for 10 seasons, at an average of 22 episodes per season. *The Simpsons* is now into its 20th season, with around 20 shows per season. These are all highly recognisable, popular shows that can draw audiences to a channel.

ADDING VALUE

A flagship programme, if it works, brings more than audiences. It will transfer value from the programme as a brand to the channel as a brand. What does this mean? The channel is hoping that by showing *The Simpsons*, a witty, sophisticated and successful programme, the audience will think of the channel as witty, sophisticated and successful.

What if it doesn't work? FIVE bought *Joey*, the spin-off from *Friends*, for a lot of money and gave it a primetime slot on Saturday nights. The show was dropped by NBC in America during its second series and received a lukewarm reception in Britain. Thus the so-called flagship was neither long-running, nor successful. The wrong values were transferred to FIVE – a good try, but a failure. FIVE quietly moved the programme to a less important slot.

For a programme to add to the channel's brand image it must fit that image. Living has a very feminine brand image, so it made sense for it to buy *Will & Grace* (a sitcom about a gay man and his straight female fashion designer friend) and to schedule it alongside shows like *Queer Eye for the Straight Guy*. Neither show would fit the 'lads down the pub' brand image of Dave. Dave does represent gay men (e.g. Stephen Fry in *QI*), but is the wrong channel for the glossy, 'fashionista' world of these programmes.

Let's research – Investigating brand image

You need to investigate how the programme you are studying reflects the brand image of its channel.

- Look at the channel's name, its channel ident, advertising, website and, most importantly, its schedule, and find some key words that you think describe that channel and how it presents itself to the world.
- You can find out what the channel wants to put forward as their brand image by looking at the corporate sections of their website.
- Then think about how that programme fits into that channel's brand image. Imagine swapping it with a programme from another channel and see if it fits. If it doesn't, why not? What does that tell you about the channel?

Public Service Broadcasting (PSB)

Why don't we just watch American television? American programmes can be imported for a fraction of what it costs to make programmes. Sky1, for example, has always been dominated by American imports. Look at the evening schedules in 2009 for the BBC, ITV, Channel 4 and FIVE – they are full of British programmes. Why?

The answer is: Public Service Broadcasting.

Once upon a time all television and radio in Britain was Public Service Broadcasting, operated by one public organisation – the BBC. This meant that television and radio were not about making money, but rather they were about informing and educating the public, making us all into better people.

Why didn't this disappear with commercial television? Surely that is about making money?

Television was a rare thing, to start with. When ITV was given the right to run a commercial television channel in 1955, it made a lot of money. There was little competition for advertisers – it was either ITV or the cinema if you wanted moving image advertisements – so ITV could charge a lot of money. Slowly, more channels were set up

(BBC2, Channel 4, FIVE, etc.), but the number was restricted by the available bandwidth.

There was therefore very little television, but it made a lot of money. This meant the regulators could tell TV companies what they could or couldn't do in exchange for giving them the right to transmit. This is why the commercial channels – ITV, Channel 4 and FIVE – all fitted into Public Service Broadcasting. They were controlled by regulators – called Ofcom in 2009 – who laid down the rules.

Examples of PSB rules:

- You must make quality programmes.
- You must have a proportion of British-made programmes.
- You must reflect the diversity of Britain, e.g. represent the different regions and nations.
- A proportion of your programmes must be made outside the M25.
- You must have certain genres of programme, e.g. news.
- You must show a balanced mix of genres (so no stripped schedules with repeated showings of the same programme).

The contract behind PSB – that channels could spend more money to make quality, home-grown programmes in exchange for valuable analogue transmission rights – will not survive the digital switchover. Ofcom, the regulator, is worried about this. They suggest that the BBC and Channel 4, who are both publicly owned and therefore don't have to make a profit, will have to keep to PSB rules. All the other channels may be allowed to compete without any special rules. This means they can buy in cheap American imports, if they want, and drop unpopular genres that cost them money in lost advertising.

While PSB still exists, however, any comedy that is made in Britain and that reflects the diversity of British culture (e.g. regional or ethnic differences), or says something about Britain today, is fitting in with Public Service Broadcasting.

Two Pints of Lager and a Packet of Crisps, for example, is set in Runcorn, a town not often represented on television, and thus fits the BBC's PSB obligations. *The Kumars at Number 42* reflects the experience of British Indians, again not often represented in British television, so again fit the BBC's obligations. *Friends* is neither British nor about Britishness, so it can be repeated in blocks in a stripped schedule on E4, a non-PSB channel, but not on Channel 4.

Let's research – PSB

- Is the programme you are studying shown on a PSB channel?
- If so, is it a British programme?
- Does it reflect the diversity of Britain in some way?

The watershed

The watershed is a term that applies to programmes on television. Ofcom has stated that programmes unsuitable for children (defined as 14 or younger) should not be shown before 9 pm or after 5.30 am. The watershed is 8 pm for a subscription channel that is not protected by a PIN.

This means there are certain rules about drugs, violence, swearing and the paranormal:

- Illegal drug-use, smoking and alcohol misuse should only be represented with strong justification, and not glamorised.
- Any violence must be limited and clearly justified.
- Violence or dangerous behaviour that can be easily imitated by children must not be shown unless there is strong justification.
- Frequent use of offensive language (mostly swearing) must be avoided and the most offensive words must not be used.
- Representation of sexual intercourse must not occur unless 'there is a serious educational purpose', and nudity should be avoided.
- Documentary representations (which are supposed to be real) of exorcisms, occult practices or the paranormal must not be shown. They are allowed in comedies.

These restrictions also apply to radio at times 'when children are particularly likely to be listening' (e.g. during the school run).

The transition to adult material after 9 pm must not be abrupt. This means a programme cannot feature a foul-mouthed, drunken exorcist having sex at two minutes past 9, but would have to wait until much later in the schedule. Even then, it would not be allowed on a very mainstream channel like ITV, which 'someone's grandmother could have fallen asleep watching', as a regulator once put it in a television programme on the subject.

- Is the programme you are studying scheduled before or after the watershed? If after, is it only just after it?
- Check how the programme meets the Ofcom rules.

■ History and ethos

Some channels have a history that gives them a particular atmosphere (or 'ethos').

CHANNEL 4

Channel 4 was originally set up to be the new force for creativity in British television, to go where no mainstream channel had ever gone before. It retains a flavour of this still, and it is still required by Ofcom to have 'a distinctive character'. This means a programme that appears on Channel 4 should have something about it that makes it distinctively 'Channel 4'. Let's take *Shameless* as an example.

What makes *Shameless* distinctively 'Channel 4'?
- It is a quality programme, winning Best Drama Series at the 2005 BAFTAs.
- Its affectionate and realistic portrayal of the British council estate underclass is unusual in British comedy.
- It has an unusual visual style for a comedy, with agitated camerawork.
- It is edgy comedy that does not patronise its audience.

THE BBC

The BBC was the original guardian of Public Service Broadcasting (see Topic 1 on Documentaries, page 13). It prided itself on its high standards and its role in 'educating the nation'. It has loosened up a great deal with changes in radio and television, but the BBC still has a special role in broadcasting. Its mission is: 'To enrich people's lives with programmes and services that inform, educate and entertain.'

The BBC does not usually aim to educate and inform through comedy, but it prides itself on quality in all it does. Hence the public outcry and denunciations in Parliament over the crude language and rude behaviour of Jonathan Ross and Russell Brand in a Radio 2 programme in 2008.

What makes *QI* distinctively 'BBC'?

- It is a quality programme, nominated for four BATFA awards.
- It combines entertainment with education as it is a comedy programme about general knowledge.
- It stars a 'national treasure', Stephen Fry, making it both clever and accessible.
- It has followed the route of many other BBC comedies in starting on niche channels (BBC4 and BBC2) and working its way up to the mass audience channel (BBC1).

Let's investigate

- Choose two very different comedy programmes from two distinct channels.
- Using the examples of *Shameless* and *QI* above, write down four ways in which your two programmes fit their channels.

Let's remember

You don't need to know a lot about the institutions that show the programmes you are studying. You *do* need to be able to argue why that channel has bought, or made, the particular programme you are studying.

You don't have to use all of the factors we have looked at, such as brand image, channel ethos, target audience, PSB rules, the watershed, etc. Use only what helps you to explain the institution's choice of programme.

Section B: Television and/or Radio Comedy – Audiences

■ Scheduling and audience pleasures

You need to study two radio or television comedies in two different ways, so that you can explain:

■ *how* and *why* they were *scheduled* on British television or radio
■ the audience pleasures of the two programmes.

The exam questions will ask you:

■ *either* to compare the **two** comedies
■ *or* to examine **one** comedy in detail.

This means you need to study the comedies in enough depth so that you can write about one programme in detail, and you will need to know the similarities and differences between them.

It is probably a good idea to pick two programmes that are:

■ of a different type
■ aimed at different audiences
■ on two different sorts of channels
■ offering different audience pleasures.

The case study below is based on shows that are scheduled at the time of writing. You will be expected to select your own case studies using comedies that are shown at the time you are studying.

Case study – Picking two different comedies

Resources: *Have I Got News For You* and *Scrubs.*

Have I Got News For You is shown on BBC1 at 9 pm on a Friday night.

Scrubs is shown on E4. It shows four episodes a day at 12.15 pm, 12.45 pm, 6 pm and 6.30 pm every day during the week but not at weekends.

Have I Got News For You is a game show where two regular panellists and two guests compete to answer questions about events in the news. Their aim is to be as funny as

possible while doing so, so the two regular panellists are the comedian Paul Merton and the satirical journalist Ian Hislop.

▲ *Figure 2.26:* Have I Got News For You?

Scrubs is an American sitcom set in a hospital that follows the lives and loves of the staff. It is unusual for a sitcom in that there is a voice-over letting us hear the thoughts of the main character JD, who is a doctor at the hospital. The comedy comes mostly from rapid-fire dialogue and JD's comments on what is going on, but also from strange 'daydream' sequences.

▲ *Figure 2.27:* Scrubs

■ How are *Have I Got News For You* and *Scrubs* two different sorts of comedy?

Scrubs is a situation comedy. *Have I Got News For You* is a comedy panel game.

Scrubs is a drama. The actors play characters delivering a script. *Have I Got News For You* is a performance. The panellists play themselves and it is supposed to be unscripted. *Scrubs* has a narrative that is resolved in some way at the end of the episode. *Have I Got News For You* has a loose narrative in which players compete for points and the teams win or lose at the end, but this is far less important than the laughs generated along the way.

The humour in *Scrubs* comes from everyday situations, whereas the humour in *Have I Got News For You* comes, for example, from attacking the stupidity of people and events in the news.

How are *Have I Got News For You* and *Scrubs* aimed at different audiences?

The audiences for the two programmes would overlap considerably, but the average *Have I Got News For You* audience member is older than the average *Scrubs* audience member.

Have I Got News For You is aimed at an audience with an interest in the news – it often asks questions about political events, for example, so it addresses an audience that would be more likely to read newspapers.

Scrubs is aimed at a younger adult audience, probably younger than the *Have I Got News For You* audience. It has a fast pace, young adult main characters, often incorporates rock, pop and indie music and has a similar visual style to other sitcoms aimed at young audiences, such as *Everybody Hates Chris*.

How are *Have I Got News For You* and *Scrubs* on two different sorts of channels?

Have I Got News For You is on BBC1. This is a mass audience channel that aims to attract the full range of the British audience.

Scrubs is on E4. This is a niche audience channel that aims to appeal to the young audience that is very attractive to advertisers (as they are hard to reach).

The BBC is not funded by advertising but by the licence fee. This means it has a special public service broadcasting (PSB) duty to educate, inform and entertain the whole British public. This means BBC1 programmes have to be popular, but have to have an extra quality – being very well made, having educational value or representing all the different parts of Britain, for example.

How does *Have I Got News For You* fit this bill? It proved itself popular when it was shown on BBC2, so this justified moving it to BBC1. It is an entertaining programme for a fairly wide target audience. It was set up to be more than funny, however. Ian Hislop was chosen as he is a moralistic journalist who has serious opinions about news. It was originally expected that Paul Merton would provide the jokes and Ian Hislop would provide the opinion. This gives the programme the opportunity to inform, as well as entertain.

E4 is part of a public institution – Channel 4 is owned by the British public (but may not be by the time you read this) and is not designed to make a profit. However, E4 is a commercial channel and a non-PSB digital channel. This means that E4 can show any programmes that it thinks will attract an audience, in any order. PSB channels have to show a lot of original material; non-PSB channels like E4 can import lots of cheap American programmes like *Scrubs*. PSB channels have to have a mixed schedule with different genres of programmes; E4 can show the same programme twice in a stripped schedule (e.g. at 12.15 pm and 12.45 pm every day). E4 are competing with lots of different digital channels, so it needs to have a schedule that is easy for the casual viewer to understand – so it strips programmes across the week.

How does *Scrubs* fit the bill for E4? E4 is a young channel that, like Channel 4, aims to be more daring and exciting than its competitors. It needs a programme that is popular, entertaining, but not too mainstream to fit this brand image. *Scrubs* attracts the right target audience and is fresh and different enough to fit E4's brand image.

■ How do *Have I Got News For You* and *Scrubs* offer different audience pleasures?

This follows from them being two different types of comedy.

The situation comedy offers narrative pleasures – we can follow a story as it unfolds throughout an episode and, in the case of *Scrubs*, from one episode to the next. JD, for example, can have a relationship in one episode (buying a porch with his girlfriend), then ruin it in the next episode and end up curled up in a ball while his friends Turk and Elliott try to console him.

Following a story means:
- We identify with one or more of the characters – we feel for them and want the best for them, though in JD's case this can be spoiled by his obvious weaknesses and stupidity.
- We are rewarded as loyal viewers by understanding events that are only explained by what happened in previous episodes. For example, only viewers of the pilot episode know why the Janitor is constantly playing practical jokes on JD.

- We get the pleasure of narrative resolution. A sitcom will have one or a few storylines that come to some conclusion at the end of the episode. For example, in the episode 'My Lips Are Sealed', Turk and Carla are struggling with their marriage, so JD takes Carla to a bar to talk. They get drunk and kiss. They decide that they should not tell Turk. Carla tells Turk she will move back in with him. The episode concludes with Carla being honest to Turk about her kiss. This resolves the disruption caused by the kiss.

- *Scrubs* offers a mix of serious and comic storylines. We might sympathise with characters as well as laugh at them. For example, in the episode 'My Boss's Free Haircut', Carla is staying with Elliot when she realises it is nearly the two-year anniversary of her mother's death. Elliot tries to cheer her up but Carla is upset when she hears her mother's voice on an answering machine complaining that Carla doesn't call her enough. Elliot tries to rescue the situation by taking Carla to the graveyard to talk to her mother. Elliot falls into an empty grave, and the episode ends with her stuck there.

Have I Got News For You also has a narrative, but who wins the game is much less important to the audience than the laughs they get along the way.

One pleasure that *Have I Got News For You* offers that *Scrubs* doesn't is that it gives a viewpoint on events in the news. This can add to the audience's sense of security brought about by the feeling that you know what is going on in the world and listening to other people's opinions about these events (see the uses and gratifications theory in Topic 4 on Celebrity on page 45).

Have I Got News For You also has a track record in attacking the rich and powerful, such as top politicians and business people. This satire, apart from being entertaining, may also help the poor and less powerful feel better about themselves.

■ How do *Have I Got News For You* and *Scrubs* offer similar audience pleasures?

- Both programmes use verbal comedy.
- Both programmes have regular characters that become familiar to regular viewers.
- Both programmes deal with real-life issues.

Why are *Have I Got News For You* and *Scrubs* scheduled on those days and times?

Have I Got News For You is scheduled at 9 pm on Fridays. It is repeated the next day.

9 pm is when BBC1 schedules its showcase dramas and documentaries. For example, this week it is showing the family history documentary *Who Do You Think You Are?*, the nature documentary *Nature's Great Events* and the drama series *Mistresses* and *New Tricks*. This suggests that 9 pm is the premier slot on weekdays on BBC1.

The slots before *Have I Got News For You* from 8 pm to 9 pm on BBC1 are filled with very mainstream programmes, such as *Eastenders* at 8 pm, and the slot after *Have I Got News For You* is filled with a comedy – making the 9 till 10 slot on Friday nights a regular comedy slot. This suggests that *Have I Got News For You* is being aimed at a large, mainstream audience that likes to wind down to comedy at the end of the week.

Have I Got News For You is scheduled just after the watershed. This means it is allowed to feature adult content, which is important for a topical news show.

Scrubs is scheduled at 12.15 pm and 12.45 pm, and 6 pm and 6.30 pm every day on weekdays.

The midday slot is part of the rolling programme of repeats with which E4 fills its daytime schedules.

The double showing of *Scrubs* at 6 pm kicks off the evening schedule. It is followed by the first showing of *Hollyoaks* (repeated the next day on Channel 4), which is the channel's biggest show in terms of ratings. This slot is in competition with Channel 4's early evening teenage slot, with *The Simpsons* followed by *Hollyoaks*, and Five's showing of *Home and Away* at 6 pm. This suggests that the early evening slot is hotly contested for teenage viewers.

Scrubs is scheduled before the watershed, so has to be a programme that is suitable for children. It fits this requirement because, though it does contain some sexual content, it is not sexually explicit, or violent, and it does not contain excessive bad language. It is, however, a slick and reasonably adult comedy that would appeal to a teenage audience.

■ Tim's exam answer

Here is an answer to a specimen exam question on the Media Topic using these two comedies. Let's see how well Tim does.

4(a) Pick two TV or radio comedies you have studied. Discuss why they were scheduled: ■ **on the channels that chose them** ■ **on the days and times they were transmitted.** [15]	**Examiner's comments**
My two comedies are *Have I Got News For You* (*HIGNFY*) and *Scrubs*.	
HIGNFY is scheduled on BBC1 at 9 pm on Friday nights and is repeated the next day. It fits BBC1 as it is a mainstream programme that will appeal to a wide audience because it is funny. It is also educational as it covers serious subjects like politics, so this makes it fit public service broadcasting. It is essential the BBC fits public service broadcasting because it is funded by the licence fee and so has to have some reason for charging everyone to watch it.	Covers the BBC1 audience Covers BBC as an institution
Friday night is good for comedy as it is a wind-down time of the week, so BBC1 always shows comedy at this time. After 9 pm is good as it is after the watershed and therefore the programme can contain swearing and rude subjects. The programme that follows is usually a comedy as well, because it can inherit *HIGNFY*'s audience. The programme can also be downloaded on BBCi.	Explains why Friday night and explains why after 9 pm, but not in much detail
Scrubs is shown on E4. It shows four episodes a day at 12.15 pm, 12.45 pm, 6 pm and 6.30 pm on every weekday, but not at weekends. *Scrubs* fits E4 because it is a channel aimed at young people – the same target audience as the programme. It also fits because E4 shows a lot of comedy shows, especially 'cool' shows from America. E4 can do this as it is a niche audience channel that is not covered by PSB regulations as it is not a terrestrial channel. This means it can have stripped schedules and repeat programmes over and over again that are aimed at young people. This makes it easier for young people to know what is going to be on E4.	Covers E4 as an institution and how it targets its audience Explains times, but not in much detail
Scrubs is shown at the moment at lunchtimes and early evenings because these are repeated episodes and not considered important enough for prime time. It can also be downloaded on 4oD.	Explains how programmes fit their channels
The BBC does not show lots of imported programmes such as *Scrubs* because it is supposed to make its own programmes. E4 would not show *HIGNFY* because most of its audience will be older than the E4 audience.	This answer does what the mark scheme asks for, so it just needs more detail for a higher mark

4(b) Show how these two programmes offer their audiences different pleasures. [15]

HIGNFY is very different to *Scrubs* as it is almost live comedy about recent events in the world, whereas *Scrubs* is a sitcom where the is comedy based on characters and everyday situations.	Understands the differences between the programmes
HIGNFY is 'infotainment' as it offers some education on the events of that week, whereas *Scrubs* episodes are simply for entertainment.	
HIGNFY has regular stars – Paul Merton and Ian Hislop – that the audience can tune in to see sparring with each other every week. This is similar to the regular characters in *Scrubs*, such as JD and Turk, who are in some ways like a family that the audience can drop in on regularly. One big difference is that *HIGNFY* is presented by different people every week and has different guests, and the audiences can tune in to see who is presenting this week and how well they will do. *Scrubs*, on the other hand, usually has more or less the same cast in every episode, but different storylines for the audience to follow.	Shows understanding of how the programmes offer different pleasures, but where are the examples?
Scrubs is a drama, so it has episodes with narratives that are resolved at the end of the episode. This gives the audience the pleasure of a story being told. *HIGNFY* follows a similar pattern every week, but there is little sense of narrative resolution – one team will win the competition, but this is really a throwaway ending. The quiz is an excuse for people to be funny.	Develops this understanding further, but still no detailed examples from the programmes
Scrubs will have situations where we can sympathise with characters as well as laugh at them or with them. For example, when JD is unlucky in love. *HIGNFY* is more about people performing for TV as themselves, so we tend to judge them on how well they have performed instead of feeling for them.	This answer does what the top level mark band asks for, except for 'detailed and appropriate exemplification'. Tim needs to study some episodes in detail

Tim has done pretty well. He only had just under half an hour to write these answers, so we can't expect lots of writing. He must learn to give more examples from the text, though. For this answer, he could have used an example of the panellists in *HIGNFY* being funny, an example of a storyline in *Scrubs* that is resolved, and perhaps an example of an everyday situation that is explored in one episode of *Scrubs*.

■ What other comedies could I study?

How about comparing children's and adults' comedies, such as *Spongebob Squarepants* and *QI*? Let's look at these programmes to see if they fit the bill.

■ They are two different sorts of programmes – animated comedy and comedy quiz.

■ They are aimed at different audiences – children and adults.

■ They are on two different sorts of channels – Nickelodeon (niche, non-PSB channel) and BBC1 (mainstream, PSB channel).

■ They offer different audience pleasures – comedy drama pleasures and 'infotainment' pleasures.

 Let's research

■ Take a look at the television schedules and pick out two contrasting comedies.

Here's a list of television comedies for two days in 2009. This should show you how much choice there is. Remember that ITV might not still be a PSB broadcaster by the time you read this, so you need to check.

Saturday PSB	Saturday non-PSB
BBC1 9.20 pm *Outnumbered*	Sky1 8 am *Malcolm in the Middle*
BBC2 6.35 pm *Porridge*	Sky1 5 pm *The Simpsons*
BBC2 9.05 pm *Have I Got a Bit More News For You*	Living 6–7 pm *Will & Grace*
BBC2 9.45 pm *Never Mind the Buzzcocks*	Virgin1 5 pm *The Fresh Prince of Bel Air*
ITV 6.35 pm *New You've Been Framed*	Paramount1 9 am–9 pm *The King of Queens/Everyone Loves Raymond*
ITV 7.05 pm *Harry Hill's TV Burp*	Paramount1 9–10 pm *South Park*
	Paramount1 10 pm–2.40 am *Sex and the City*
	FX 8–9 pm *King of the Hill*
	FX 9 pm–12 am *Family Guy*
	Nickelodeon 6.30 am, 9.30 am, 1 pm, 1.30 pm, 5 pm, 8.30 pm *Spongebob Squarepants*

Friday PSB	Friday Non-PSB
BBC1 3.40 pm *Watch My Chops*	Sky1 5.30 and 6 pm *Malcolm in the Middle*
BBC1 3.50 pm *The Secret Show (crime comedy)*	Sky1 6.30 pm *Futurama*
BBC1 9 pm *Have I Got News For You*	Sky1 7, 7.30, 10 and 10.30 pm *The Simpsons*
BBC1 9.30 pm *Gavin & Stacey*	Dave 7 pm *Who's Line Is It Anyway?*
BBC2 10 pm *QI*	Dave 9 pm *Never Mind the Buzzcocks*
ITV1 10.30 pm *TV's Naughtiest Blunders*	Dave 9.40 pm and 12.40 am *Live at the Apollo*
Channel 4 7.25 am *Everybody Loves Raymond*	Dave 10.40 pm and 12.40 am *Argumental*
Channel 4 7.55 am *Just Shoot Me*	Dave 11.20 pm *I'm Alan Partridge*
Channel 4 8.25 am *The Class*	Living 7pm, 7.30 pm and 1 am *Will & Grace*
Channel 4 8.55 am *Frasier*	Living 8 and 8.30 pm *Nothing to Declare*
Channel 4 6 pm *The Simpsons*	Virgin1 12 pm *My Wife and Kids*
Channel 4 10 pm *The IT Crowd*	Virgin1 12.30 pm *Home Improvement*
Channel 4 10.35 pm *Jimmy Carr Live: Comedian*	Virgin1 1 pm *The Fresh Prince of Bel Air*
Channel 4 12.15 am *Star Stories*	Nickelodeon 8 am, 8.30 am, 1 pm, 1.30 pm, 3 pm, 6.30 pm and 8.30 pm *SpongeBob Squarepants*
	Nickelodeon 5.30, 10 and 10.30 am *King Arthur's Disasters*
	Nickelodeon 7.30 am and 5.30 pm *iCarly*
	Nickelodeon 6.30 am, 3.30 pm and 5 pm *Drake & Josh*

■ What about radio?

The same principles apply if you want to study radio comedies instead of television comedies, or one of each. The only difference is that there is a narrower range of stations that play comedy – most is found on BBC stations – so it is harder to find very different institutions.

One possibility is to compare BBC Radio 7, a dedicated comedy channel, with BBC Radio 4, a mixed talk channel, or Radio 2, a music channel that occasionally plays comedy.

Radio 7 is currently playing an American import – *A Prairie Home Companion* – which they have rebranded *Garrison Keillor's Radio Show* and have scheduled at 5 pm on a Saturday. This use of an import reflects Radio 7's comedy specialism and its lower status as a station that is only available on digital radio.

Radio 4 has two regular comedy slots – 6.30 pm and 11 pm – and these are always filled with original programming. For example, the long-running comedy game show *Just a Minute* plays regularly in the prestigious Monday 6.30 pm slot on Radio 4. This slot is usually reserved for new versions of old favourites.

Radio 2 has a dedicated 'Comedy Hour' at lunchtimes on Saturday. This again demonstrates original programming, such as the topical satire show *Clive Anderson's Chat Room*.

Because most radio comedy is transmitted by the same institution, the main object of study becomes the different brand identities and target audiences of these stations. Luckily, the different BBC radio stations have very distinct identities. This is because BBC radio gave up always trying to target a mass audience back in the 1960s and the different stations have moved in different directions ever since. It is easy to imagine someone watching both ITV and BBC4 television in the same night. It is harder to imagine a Radio 3 listener tuning in to Radio 1.

You will find Topic 5 on Talk Radio (page 54) useful if you are studying radio comedy.

 Let's remember

You must choose programmes that are:
- two different sorts of programmes
- aimed at different audiences
- on two different sorts of channels
- offering different audience pleasures.

Let's investigate

Choose programmes you know and enjoy.

Here is a 10-point plan for each programme:

1 Watch several episodes of these programmes so you get a feel for what is repeated and what changes.

2 Find out what you can about the two channels by looking at their schedules, their channel idents (if television), how they promote themselves, their websites, and any audience figures you can get for the channel.

3 Decide what you think the target audience is for that channel.

4 Look at the slot the programmes have been scheduled in, and see:
  ■ what else is scheduled in that slot on different nights
  ■ what is scheduled before and after the programme
  ■ what is scheduled on competing channels at the same time.

5 Discuss why you think the programme has been scheduled in that slot.

6 Look at the narrative pleasures of the programme – does it offer narrative resolution (stories that end), identification with characters, rewards for the loyal viewer, etc.?

7 Look at the media language pleasures of the programme – does it offer fast pace, attractive actors, glossy style, appealing mise-en-scène, etc.?

8 Look at the form of comedy it offers – is it slapstick, character comedy, black comedy, satire, verbal comedy, punch lines, flights of fancy, etc.?

9 Watch some more episodes of the comedy; this is a good idea in itself, but it also provides a number 9, which leads on to ...

10 ... Number 10! Practise writing essays comparing two comedies and also writing about one comedy in detail.

Unit 3
Production Portfolio in Media Studies

Introduction to Unit 3

The Production Portfolio in Media Studies is likely to be the final unit in your GCSE course. You will have the opportunity to apply everything that you have learnt about theory to the production of a practical piece. It may well be the unit that you look forward to the most, as you will get the chance to be really creative and to use new media technology in the construction of your work. This unit will allow you to become a media producer, or author, of a media production. Once you have completed your piece make sure you get it out to its intended audience and get some real audience feedback.

The purpose of this unit is to give an overview of the briefs on offer, with some guidance on researching, planning and constructing the productions. The unit will not teach you how to use computer software packages or teach technical skills, as this is best learnt in the classroom.

What is the Production Portfolio?

Reading and writing about the media is a very important part of Media Studies, and practical work is about putting that knowledge and understanding into context. It can be argued that students' knowledge of the media can only really be cemented after they have had the opportunity to see how the process of production works. The Production Portfolio gives you this opportunity. It is a controlled assessment unit that will help you to develop practical production skills, and will then ask you to reflect on your finished piece in the form of an evaluation.

In this unit you will:

- plan, research and create a major practical production, chosen from a list of briefs that are set by OCR
- work either individually or in a small group
- collect evidence of your own contribution to the research and planning process, whether you are working alone or as part of a group
- complete an evaluation of your finished piece of work.

The briefs

The briefs come under five different areas:

- print
- video
- audio
- website
- cross-media.

The print options are:

- the front page and one inside page for a local newspaper
- an extract from a new magazine
- an advertising campaign for a new product
- the cover and two magazine advertisements for a new video or computer game.

The video options are:

- a music promo video
- an extract from a new television programme
- the opening sequence for a new film, with titles.

The audio options are:

- an extract from a magazine-style programme
- an extract from a scripted radio drama.

The website options are:

- four linked pages for a new TV channel
- four linked pages for a new entertainment website.

The cross-media options are:

- a promotional package for the release of a new album, which must include material from more than one medium.

Whichever option you choose, you will need to complete appropriate research and planning before you put together your production.

■ Group or individual?

If you were employed in a media industry then it is likely that the projects you worked on would be collaborative, working closely with other people to produce work to tight deadlines. For that reason working in a group for GCSE Media Studies is desirable as it most closely replicates the real-life practice. However, there are some obvious advantages to working on your own, as you can be your own boss and be confident that you will meet your own deadlines!

GROUP PROJECTS

Some of the production briefs lend themselves best to group working and would be difficult to complete on your own. The video and audio briefs are best completed in a small group, because of the variety of tasks involved. Small groups can be made up of up to five people and work best if individual group members are assigned particular roles. In this way, each person can take on responsibility for their own input and this should help keep the group focused and balanced. For example, if you have chosen Video Brief 6, then because of the variety of different elements involved, group members could take a lead in storyboard production, sound, lighting, camerawork or editing. It is good to try to play to each other's strengths wherever possible.

▲ Figure 3.1: Group planning a production

▲ *Figure 3.2: Group planning a moving image sequence*

The nature of working in a group will mean that you will need to rely on each other to be organised, and listen to everyone's input. This can sometimes be difficult, particularly if one person dominates discussions and the decision-making process. Remember to treat working in a group as if you are a real media production team – all the processes that you will go through will mirror what really happens in real production teams. The skills that you will develop through working in a small group are invaluable and can then be adapted to many other areas of your study. Learning to negotiate, getting your ideas heard and listening to others are valuable skills that you will develop during the course of this production.

■ Problems and suggested solutions

Before you embark on a group project, you may find it helpful to draw up some guidelines with the rest of your group about what to do if a problem arises.

Very quiet group members who don't say much

- Make sure that everyone in the group has a very clear role.
- Assign these roles based on individual strengths.
- Encourage the quieter members of the group to get on with jobs that they feel comfortable with, such as storyboarding or editing.
- Make sure all members feel comfortable about getting on with their assigned role or task.
- Make sure all members feel included and that they are contributing to the overall production.

Very bossy group members who take over

- Again, make sure that everyone has a clear role.
- Try not to let these roles overlap with each other too much.
- Try to use the confidence of louder members to lead your pitch and negotiate your idea with your teacher.
- Try to use louder, bossier members for asking for permission for location shooting or for other similar jobs that require the ability to speak out.

Someone in the group repeatedly fails to show up for filming/ production sessions outside lesson time

- Someone in the group should speak to them on a one-to-one basis to find out if there is a specific reason for their absence.
- They may feel their views are not being heard – if this is the reason it can be easily resolved.
- It could be something as simple as them having difficulty in getting to the location chosen.
- If all else fails, let your teacher know about the problem.

■ Access to resources

When deciding which brief to choose, you will need to start by thinking about the resources that are available to you. As this is a controlled assessment unit, you will need to produce your practical piece during the school day, where practicable, and possibly under the direct supervision of your teacher. If you have access to InDesign or QuarkXPress at home but not in school then you may find that you cannot use this programme to construct your magazine layout. Each section of this unit will look at specific resources in more detail.

■ What are you good at?

If you have the opportunity to choose the brief yourself, start off by thinking about what you are good at or enjoy doing before deciding on a brief.

- If you have no experience of using web design software but have made a short film before, then you may well enjoy one of the video options.
- If you are studying for an art-based GCSE, such as photography or design, then choosing one of the print options could play to your strengths.
- If you enjoy writing, then Print Brief 1 or 2 or either of the audio briefs, could give you the opportunity to combine your creative skills with your writing skills.

- If you are not able to choose your own brief then you can still play to your strengths. Working in a group to produce a video or television sequence will still give you the opportunity to take on a designated role and this is where you can do something that you are good at or enjoy. You could draw the storyboard if you enjoy drawing, or if you enjoy or are good at photography, then you could produce a digital storyboard and you might also enjoy the magazine or newspaper briefs, as both have requirements for original photography and writing.

■ Research and planning

Research and planning is a very important part of this unit, and you will find more specific guidance on researching and planning individual briefs later on in this unit.

Vital parts of the planning process include:
- conducting research into similar products
- identifying your target audience
- producing draft storyboards or mock-ups of front covers
- taking test shots for original images.

With any media production, whether it is a new BBC TV drama or an edition of a new celebrity magazine, careful planning and research must be completed so that the production is successful in meeting the needs of the target audience. If you are choosing a video brief you will need to select actors carefully, hunt for appropriate locations and source costumes and props. Planning for a print brief will involve drafting and redrafting articles, and taking test shots in preparation for your image selection.

WHY IS PLANNING SO IMPORTANT?

A well-planned production goes a long way to ensuring that the end product is successful in meeting the objectives in the original brief. Being organised and managing your time effectively is vital; allow time to think through your initial ideas and make sure that you have a fallback plan should you encounter technical difficulties during the construction process. Set yourself a clear deadline and work to it. Set yourself interim deadlines too – points by which parts of your production should be completed in draft.

Before you can get your hands on the equipment, this planning process should be well under way, if not finished.

Pitching

If you were working in a real media industry and had an idea for a new production, you would be required to pitch your idea to potential producers. The producers would then decide whether your idea was worth investing in. The pitch is therefore a very important part of the production process.

Task: In your group, prepare a five-minute pitch of your initial ideas and present this pitch to your class and teacher. Make sure you include:

- your idea, condensed into two short sentences
- a clearly identified target audience
- an explanation of how your idea would directly appeal to your target audience
- a statement outlining when and where your production would be positioned in the marketplace
- a schedule stating how long it would take you to plan and construct your production.

It is quite possible that you will have to formally pitch your idea towards the end of the planning process, so this 'mini-pitch' is useful for getting your ideas ready.

Production log

Evidence of the research and planning that you've completed will need to be put together in the form of a Production log. You will need to think about how you would like to collect and present this information. This is a crucial part of the Production Portfolio and carries 30 marks (25% of the overall marks for the unit). It will provide evidence for your teacher of your work and any contribution that you made to a group product, be it camera work, layout design, photography or audience research. Within it you will collect together materials that are specific to your brief. You can find out more about what is needed later in this unit.

Keeping a diary

Keeping a diary is a useful way of remembering what you did in each lesson when you come to look back on the construction process at the end. It can also form part of the evidence for your Production log. Give yourself 5–10 minutes at the end of each practical session to write a few notes on what went well and what could be improved. You can then amend your production schedule accordingly.

Production schedule

Week 1		Week 2		Week 3		Week 4		Week 5		Week 6	
Lesson 1	Lesson 2	Lesson 1	Lesson 2	Lesson 1	Lesson 2	Lesson 1	Lesson 2	Lesson 1	Lesson 2	Lesson 1	Lesson 2

▲ Figure 3.3: Production schedule diagram

After the research, planning and pitch are completed you will need to finalise your production schedule. A production schedule is a plan to help you organise your time effectively, so that you make the most of the time that is available to you. It should contain the key dates and deadlines for your production.

Draw up the grid with the dates of the lessons that you have available to you for completing the project (see Figure 3.3). Then work backwards from your final deadline and write down exactly how much time you have available for the construction process. At the end of each lesson, reflect on what went well and make any necessary amendments to your production schedule in light of this. Remember that part of your evaluation will require you to consider any revisions you had to make during the project.

Key media concepts

Throughout the course of your GCSE in Media Studies you will have been developing your knowledge and understanding of the key media concepts, which are:

- audience
- institution
- genre
- media language.

You will have learnt to write about these concepts for the Textual Analysis and Media Studies Topic Paper, and now you will have the opportunity to demonstrate your understanding of these concepts through the creative process.

■ Audience

Be clear about who your audience is and what will appeal to them, as a product without a clear target audience could have a very confused reception. It is important to define your audience as clearly as possible because you want them to be attracted to your end product – in a real media industry this would equate to sales and profit. Part of the mark allocation will come from how successfully your product meets the needs of your target audience. You need to consider the following:

- Is your production aimed at a mass audience, such as the potential audience for a new BBC primetime situation comedy?
- Is your production aimed at a niche audience, such as those readers targeted by a local newspaper?
- How do the overall tone, language and style of your production aim to attract your target audience?
- What is the age, gender and background of your target audience?
- What are the likes, dislikes and aspirations of your target audience?
- How and why will your audience engage with your production?
- What pleasure will your production bring your audience?

Let's research

▲ *Figure 3.4: The 'audience bag' test*

Building up a profile of your audience can really help you to understand what will appeal to them, and this in turn should make it easier for you to target your product successfully.

- Look at the audience profile for *Grazia* magazine (www.bauer.co.uk):

  '*Grazia* readers are upmarket women in their 30s. They are affluent, high spenders on fashion and beauty. The majority are married or living with a partner and working full-time. They read *Grazia* avidly and cite its fashion content as their main reason to buy the magazine.'

- Think about what kinds of products the average *Grazia* reader would carry around in her bag.
- Remember she is working full-time and does not usually have children, so would have disposable income to spend on products such as perfume, make-up, clothes, etc.
- It is likely she will have a hectic social life, so will have the latest mobile phone to keep in touch with her friends.
- Think about specific brands of products too.

Can you see how you can begin to build up a profile of the audience from this activity?

What sorts of things would your target audience carry around with them in their rucksack or bag?

▇ Institutions

- Who would be responsible for getting your product into the market place?
- Where and when would your product be 'consumed' by its target audience?

These factors should be considered during your research and planning stage. As you begin your research you will examine real media output from your chosen genre. As part of your research you should look at where the product is placed, and who was responsible for producing it. If you are making a promotional music video for either Video Brief 5 or Cross-Media Brief 12, you should look at how the internet has become part of the distribution process. Many artists, such as Lily Allen, will use social networking sites, such as MySpace, as a way of getting their latest musical offering to their fans by placing their videos online.

Media language

Your understanding of media language will be demonstrated partly through the technical construction of your finished product. For example, if you have chosen a video brief, then your understanding of how the camerawork and editing communicate with the audience will be evident. You will also have the opportunity to demonstrate your understanding of media language in your evaluation, where you will be asked to reflect on how well your production uses the codes and conventions of the genre in which you are working.

Genre

Genre is essential to media producers and audiences alike. (See Topic 2 on Film Genres on page 23). Audiences will have particular expectations of media products, based on their understanding and recognition of genre, and institutions use genre as a way of ensuring that they will get the right audience and therefore make money. Think about how important film genres are to both the audience and the institution. The horror genre, which is one of the most popular genres with young audiences, is constantly repeated and reworked. It continually draws in large cinema audiences because it is popular. Audiences recognise the genre, enjoy being frightened by gory images, and so will pay their money over and over again to see horror films. Through your thorough research you will demonstrate that you understand how your chosen genre uses media language to communicate with the audience, and how institutions use genre to attract audiences. Can you see how the key concepts are all interconnected?

Topic 1: Print Briefs

■ Print

The print brief is often a popular choice for GCSE students. It is a very manageable production to undertake, particularly if you are not working in a group, as the briefs can easily be attempted on your own.

Things to consider

Choosing Brief 1 or Brief 2? These two briefs will require some original writing, so you will need to plan your articles carefully and ensure that you are using the correct style and tone in your writing.

■ Overview

There are four print briefs to choose from:
- the front page and one inside page from a local newspaper
- an extract from a new magazine aimed at a specific audience
- a print-based advertising campaign for a new product
- a new computer/video game cover in an appropriate format and two magazine advertisements for the release of the new game.

■ Original photography

Each of the print briefs has a requirement for original photography. Original photography means photographs that you have taken yourself. All print briefs apart from the advertising brief ask for 'some' original photography, which means you can also include some images from other sources that you have not taken yourself. For part of your video game cover, for example, you may want the image of a volcano, which would be very difficult to photograph yourself. Whichever brief you choose, you will have to plan your original photography carefully, taking plenty of test shots and paying attention to lighting and framing.

Framing and lighting your photographs

Framing and lighting your photographs correctly is crucial, as is the choice of shot.

- Think carefully about the placing of your subject(s) within the frame – where do you want your audience's attention to be drawn?
- Consider carefully the shot type that will work best – remember that using a close-up can lead to a very different interpretation of an image compared with using a long shot.
- Would it be appropriate for your subject to look directly into the camera? This will be a definite requirement for some photographs.
- How will you light the shot? The lighting used in an advertising campaign for a women's fragrance is likely to be markedly different to the lighting used in a photograph to accompany a story in a local newspaper, as both images will convey different messages and moods.

Above all, don't leave lighting and framing to chance. Make sure you consider both aspects as your original photography will form an important component of your planning for a print brief.

▲ *Figure 3.5: Student taking an original photograph*

■ Equipment checklist

A digital camera will be fairly essential to any of these briefs, although many mobile phones now have the facility to take reasonably good quality digital photos, so you may not need to invest in or borrow a camera. You will need the ability to upload your photos and to edit them if necessary, so it is worth checking first if your school computers will support the uploading of photographs from your make and model of mobile phone or camera. If your school or college is lucky enough to have the latest iMacs it may be possible to bluetooth your photos, which will save the need for attaching cables.

Each of the print briefs has slightly different technical requirements, and for that reason you should think carefully before you make your final decision. As this is a controlled assessment unit you will be unable to create your print production at home, and so your final decision is likely to be governed by the packages there are on the computers in your school or college.

QuarkXPress, Adobe InDesign and Microsoft Publisher are appropriate packages for the production of newspaper layouts as they all let you insert text and image boxes and give you the ability to move them around the page easily. You can create columns and a masthead and can quickly produce an effective front cover. They are not, however, very useful for the manipulation or editing of images. For this you would need to use a package similar to Adobe Photoshop, which will allow you to create excellent print advertisements. Check out what software is available to you in school before you make your final choice.

You will be assessed on:
- your understanding of the codes and conventions of your chosen genre, through the selection and integration of appropriate illustrations and text
- accurate use of language
- effective construction and manipulation of images.

The following should go in the Production log:
- plans and mock-ups of your final product, including any test shots for your photos
- your production schedule, which should include key dates, decisions and deadlines
- a record of your contribution to the production if you have worked in a group.

If you have additional materials, such as rejected photos or very early layout designs or mock-ups, these can be included in an appendix.

■ Production processes

Once you have completed your print mock-up, and have finalised your deadlines in your production schedule, you can get started. If you are working on an individual print product you will need to be quite organised and self motivated. The technical construction of a print project, be it an advertisement, newspaper or magazine can take longer than you may imagine, because of the level of editing and fine detail required. If you are producing Brief 3, then you will be manipulating and editing images, while Briefs 1 and 2 have more of a focus on layout and manipulation of text with images. More detail on the specific production processes for each brief can be found on the pages that follow.

■ Brief 1

▲ *Figure 3.6: Example of a front cover of a local newspaper*

The front page and one inside page from a local newspaper, including some original photography.

Remember, if you are producing this in a group, then you must produce *at least* one inside page.

This brief will test your skills in layout and design, as well as writing for a purpose. If you choose this brief you should start by researching local newspapers to get a feel for the contents – what makes 'local' news as opposed to 'national' news? Although circulation figures for many local newspapers are in decline, due partly to the internet providing a source of local news, many people still rely on a local newspaper to find out what is going on in their area. Most British towns and cities will have their own local newspapers, and if you live in a large city like London then most boroughs have their own local newspapers, catering specifically to the needs of people in that area.

The Audit Bureau of Circulations, or ABC as it is known, is a non-profit organisation that is funded by the industry. It is responsible for monitoring circulation figures for newspapers and magazines. It will be a very useful research resource for you.

Researching your local newspaper

Carry out some initial research into the local newspaper in your area. It may be posted free through your front door every week or you may have to pay a visit to your nearest newsagent and scour the shelves. It is likely that this newspaper will have its own website too, which could prove to be a good source of additional information. Visit www.abc.org.uk and find out the circulation figures for the newspaper (how many copies were sold/distributed) in the last quarter of the year. Find out who owns your local newspaper – you may find out that it belongs to a company that owns several local newspapers in other areas, and may even own national newspapers or other media products. Think about how this may affect the content or tone of the newspaper.

Next, carry out a content analysis of the newspaper. Based on your content analysis and initial research you should now be able to identify broadly who the target audience is for your local newspaper. Once you have completed this you will begin to get a feel for the service that local newspapers provide for their readers.

 Let's research

A content analysis is a good way to get to grips with the variety of different components of a newspaper or magazine.
- Count the number of pages.
- Count the number of articles and the topics that the articles cover.
- Make a tally of the number of advertisements and where they mainly feature in the newspaper.
- Make a list of the other features in the newspaper, such as: letters pages, jobs section, property section, forthcoming events, classified section, editor's letter, etc.

Establishing who reads local newspapers will form an important part of your research, because it is a crucial aid in helping you to pitch your articles at the right level. You will be able to find out some of this information from www.abc.org.uk or from the website for the paper itself. Your content analysis should also help you to establish who the newspaper is pitched at.

▲ *Figure 3.7: Two students researching local newspapers*

■ Planning your own local newspaper

When you begin planning your newspaper production you will need to consider:

- house style
- layout
- content
- pitching your articles at the right level for the intended audience
- how accompanying images support the mood and tone of your writing
- the 'audience bag' activity (see page 222), as you will be required to reflect on this in your evaluation.

■ Images

Images can capture the mood of an article in a newspaper and are therefore as important as the words that you write. The choice of shot that you use is also very important. If you are writing an article about a personal experience of someone local then you could use a medium close-up so that your reader can clearly see who the article is about. If you are writing an article about the proposed development of a new shopping centre in your local area, then a long shot of the location would be needed to show clearly the area referred to.

Articles

When planning your articles try to find some real local stories. It may be possible to photograph and interview someone local for your newspaper article. Carefully plan the tone of your articles and make sure that you spend time drafting your words. Study the tone and style of articles from your local newspaper and see how journalists use persuasive language in order to engage the reader. Journalistic writing is very different in style, sentence structure and length to other forms of writing. Very long and complicated sentences tend to be avoided and the style is clear and direct, as newspapers want to engage their audiences and not make them switch off with overly long articles.

Layout and design

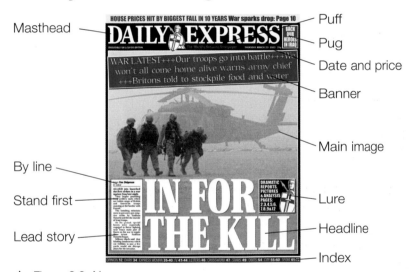

Masthead — Puff — Pug — Date and price — Banner — Main image — By line — Stand first — Lead story — Lure — Headline — Index

▲ Figure 3.8: Newspaper cover

Newspapers have a very distinctive style. A masthead of the newspaper title is always found at the top and the copy is written in columns. Images with appropriate captions that anchor (pin down the meaning of) the story and headlines are used to grab the attention of the reader. You will need to make sure that your newspaper front cover is following these codes and conventions of the genre.

Let's research

Visit http://www.fodey.com/generators/newspaper/snippet.asp and see what your articles might look like in print before you create your front cover (see Figure 3.8).

Key terms

Anchor: written text that fixes the meaning of an image
Banner: a strip of text that stretches the width of a newspaper or magazine front cover, often advertising the contents
Byline: details of the author of the associated article
Caption: written text that anchors the meaning of an image
Column: narrow strips reading down the page
Graphics: aspects of design, such as symbols, borders or stylised images
Headline: title of main article on newspaper or magazine front cover
Layout: term used to describe the positioning of the components of a magazine or newspaper front cover and inside pages
Masthead: large title at top of front cover of magazine or newspaper

■ Brief 2

An extract from a new magazine aimed at a specific audience, to include the front cover, contents page and a double-page spread article using some original photography.

The magazine industry is vast, and although circulation figures are decreasing, as they are for local newspapers, there is still a relatively buoyant market for magazines, as you will see when you complete your research activities. The brief is broad, allowing you to choose any genre, so one of the hardest parts of this brief could be deciding what sort of magazine to construct. It will test your skills of design and layout, as well as writing for a purpose. You will need to demonstrate that you understand how the codes and conventions of the genre work to attract an audience, so the placing of the model or cover image, coverlines, the masthead and banner, choice of font and colour will all need to be carefully planned in advance.

Things to consider

You could produce a specialist magazine aimed at a niche audience, or you could decide to produce a magazine with a mass appeal.

Case study – Bauer

Bauer is the largest privately owned publisher in Europe and publishes many of the titles that you see on the shelves in British newsagents.

- Visit the Bauer website www.bauer.co.uk.
- Select 'key facts and rate cards' from the top menu.
- Compare the circulation figures, target markets and average age of the readers for each magazine.
- Build up a profile of the audience for each magazine.

▲ Figure 3.9: A Bauer magazine – Take a Break

Let's compare – Genres

Before you can begin to sketch out ideas for your front cover layout you must investigate the magazine industry and magazine genres.

- Carry out a comparative textual analysis of the front cover of a range of different magazines: a young women's weekly, a home-interest magazine, a leisure magazine such as a walking or cycling magazine, and a men's monthly. Explore:
  - Colour – How many different colours are used? What mood and tone do the colours convey to you?
  - Font – Is the font serif or sans-serif? How many different types of font are used? How does the font support the overall tone of the magazine cover?

  > sans-serif
  > serif

  - Coverlines (sometimes referred to as sell lines) – How do the coverlines link with the genre of the magazine?
  - Language – Do the magazine title and the coverlines use formal or informal language? Do they speak to the reader on a personal level?

The magazine front cover is made up of several other elements, but from looking at these four alone you should be able to detect a difference in tone and mode of address, and the mode of address should also give big clues as to the target audience for the magazines.

Masthead

Puff

Date and cover price

Model

Main coverline

Tagline

Coverlines

Barcode

▲ Figure 3.10: Magazine cover features

Let's research – Magazine audiences

Who reads magazines? Before you decide on the sort of new magazine that you want to produce you should start by finding out who reads magazines. You wouldn't want to produce a magazine aimed at a niche audience of people who would rather use the internet than read a magazine.

- Ask your friends and family the questions below. Try to ask as wide a variety of people as you can, so that you can begin to get a broad picture of people's consumption of magazines. Ask:
  - How often do you read magazines?
  - How often do you buy magazines? (This might seem like the same question but some people will read magazines that other people have bought or may only read the sorts of magazines that come as free supplements in newspapers.)
  - Why do you read magazines?
  - Do you 'read' the magazine or concentrate on the photos and other content? (You may be surprised by some people's answers to this question.)
  - Which section do you turn to first?

It is important to record basic information about gender and age when collecting this information. Reflect on the information you have collected. Can you see any trends or patterns in magazine consumption emerging?

Audience categories based on income and occupation

You may have noticed from your research that reference is often made to ABC1, or C2DE. Referred to as demographics, these groupings of letters and numbers are used to refer to the income and background of the audience. The table below aims to illustrate this but is by no means exhaustive in terms of jobs within the categories. You must conduct your own research into income background and audiences in order to supplement this information.

A	Doctor, accountant, dentist
B	Teacher, police inspector, librarian
C1	Receptionist, salesperson, call-centre agent
C2	Electrician, plumber, heating engineer
D	Waiter, farm worker
E	Road sweeper, window cleaner, pensioner (without any other income)

(Key Note Ltd, 2000 – internet publication)

Media companies will use this information in order to pitch their product at the right level for the income and background of their audience.

 Case study – The *Take a Break* audience (January 2009)

Demographic: C1C2 background
Age: median of 45
Price: 78 p
Relationships: most have children

It is unlikely that *Take a Break* would carry advertisements for very expensive high-end cosmetics and perfume as this group is unlikely to spend their money on these products and would not aspire to do so. The content of this sort of magazine must appeal to the likes and dislikes, lifestyle and background of its readers to ensure that it sells copies, and ultimately makes a profit.

Visit www.abc.org.uk to check out the circulation figures for *Take a Break* magazine.

Let's analyse

As with any media product, it is important to ensure that your magazine will appeal directly to its target audience. The content must interest them, the house style (font and colour) must appeal to them and above all the magazine must talk to them on a personal level.

Once you have decided what sort of magazine you are going to produce you should look closely at other real magazines from the same genre. This will give you a guide to the tone to aim for in your production.

- Count the number of pages.
- Count the number of articles and the topics they cover.
- Make a tally of the number of advertisements and where they mainly feature in the magazine.
- Make a list of the other features in the magazine, such as letters pages, horoscopes, real-life stories, fashion or beauty, editor's letter, etc.

 Case study – *Eye Candi* magazine

▲ *Figure 3.11:* Eye Candi

Does your school or college have a student magazine? If it does, you could decide to produce a rival magazine. If it doesn't, then you can become a real media producer and create one! You are the target audience for a school or college magazine, and you should have a good idea about what appeals to this market. Conducting preliminary research should be easy as you can ask your classmates.

Eye Candi is the student magazine for City and Islington College in London, and is entirely produced by students of the college. It is available free online via the college's website and editions are produced and distributed throughout the college every quarter. Examine the front cover and see how it is constructed to appeal to its target audience of students.

Planning – the mock-up

Although you will use a computer software package to produce your magazine extract, you will have to produce a paper mock-up first, so that you can get a real sense of what the finished piece will look like. This can then be used as excellent evidence of research and planning in your Production log. It will give you the opportunity to try out different fonts, colours and layouts to see which works best for your target audience.

- Decide on your house style:
  - How many colours will you choose? Most magazines use a limited palette of, on average, four colours that directly appeal to their audience. For example, bright vibrant colours such as yellow and pink would be used for a magazine aimed at young teens, such as *Sugar*, and darker, bolder colours like red, black and grey would be used on a men's magazine, such as *Men's Health*.
  - What fonts or combination of fonts will you choose? There are marks specifically allocated to showing an awareness of the need for variety in fonts and text size, so you must bear this in mind when planning and constructing your front cover. Ensure you carry your house style through into the contents page and double-page spread.
- Practise writing your coverlines. Study the language used in the coverlines on the magazines you have analysed. You will see that they do not contain full sentences, but are constructed to lure you into the magazine without giving too much away on the cover.
- What will your double-page spread focus on? Remember that the tone of the writing and overall layout design must appeal to your target market.
- Show your mock-up to its intended audience and get some real feedback.
- Remember to use original photography and plan your photos. (See the specific guidance on page 226 on framing and lighting your photos.)
- Plan the layout and style of the contents page.
- Pitch your ideas to your teacher. You will need to identify:
  - who would publish your magazine
  - its cover price
  - how often it would be published
  - where it would be sold.

■ Brief 3

A print-based advertising campaign for a new product, such as a new clothing range, to include a brand name design, two full-page advertisements and a billboard poster, using original photography.

Understanding how the conventions of advertising work in print adverts is crucial, as you will need to demonstrate this knowledge and understanding through the production of your own advertising campaign. Traditionally, print advertisements would:

- contain a slogan
- show the product (image)
- name the product
- provide some product information
- contain a logo.

▲ *Figure 3.12: Two students researching advertisements in magazines*

Let's analyse

Choose a contemporary print advertisement for a cleaning product, some cosmetics or a car. Describe what you see (denotation):

- Describe the product being advertised.
- Can we see the entire product?
- Where is the product placed in the advertisement?
- What sorts of colours are used in the picture?
- What objects or people can be seen in the advertisement? Describe what you see.
- Have any special effects been used, such as CGI?
- What shot distance has been chosen to show the product?
- Is the shot at an angle?

- Can you see evidence of any lighting effects? How would you describe the lighting?
- What is the central focus of the advertisement?
- Can you identify the main conventions of print advertising?

After you have finished this part of the analysis you should move on to thinking about possible meanings or interpretations of the advertisement (also called connotations):
- What parts of the product do you think the advertisement is emphasising to the audience, and why?
- How is the advertisement encouraging you to 'buy into' a lifestyle or way of living?

Audiences for advertisements

Audience research is absolutely crucial to the success of a finished media product. Advertisers will spend a lot of time collecting profile information on their potential audiences, such as:
- education
- voting habits
- leisure time
- patterns of spending
- where they buy their groceries
- what brands they buy
- what make and model of car they buy
- where they go on holiday.

This helps advertisers tailor their advertisements accordingly. It will help ensure the product is reaching the right audience, and that this audience will buy the product.

The choice of colour, positioning of the product, lighting and text will all be very carefully planned in order to reach the audience. Ultimately, the advertiser wants to encourage us to buy into the lifestyle that the advertisement is offering us, and so will attempt to appeal to our aspirations.

Persuasive techniques

The advertisers will try to persuade us that we need the product on offer because it could enhance our lives in some way. They will do this by using persuasive techniques, or ways of appealing to us, such as:
- making the advertisement humorous
- providing us with 'expert' evidence for the success of the product
- using a famous person to endorse the product (we can be like them too!)

- emphasising the parts of the product that will make us successful or part of a special group of people
- making us feel insecure if we don't buy the product (because we will feel more secure and happy if we do!).

There are many more techniques of persuasion that advertisers use and, the more advertisements you analyse, the more familiar you will become with them.

Case study – Ford car advertisement

▲ Figure 3.13: Ford car – advertisement

An interesting way of identifying the unique selling points (USPs) of a product is to analyse an advertisement for a product from the past (see also Topic 9 on page 95).

The Ford advertisement in Figure 3.13 emphasises the 'newness' of this particular Ford model by inserting 'new' in the slogan: Take the wheel…try the new Ford 'Feel'. A woman is seen standing next to the driver's door and two women are seen sitting on one of the car's 'sofa-wide' seats. There is also a woman's foot applying the brakes, being in control of the car. Women are being targeted and the tactile 'feel' and comfort of driving a Ford is being emphasised.

The product information contains technical details on the performance of the car, but still with an emphasis on the word 'feel'. This technical information is clearly targeting men, as it discusses the specification for the steering and the engine's capacity, but the inclusion of the word 'feel' is to appeal to the audience of women, even though the advert is really only focusing on the way the car handles or drives. The word 'feel', more than the way a car 'drives', is thought likely to appeal to women, as they were (and still are) considered to be the softer sex, concerned with the look and comfort of a product over the function.

The colours used in the advertisement give a suggestion of the stars and stripes of the American flag, with the red of the car, white background and blue of the flag. It could be interesting to take this analysis further by thinking about when the advertisement was made and what this tells us about America at the time. The unique selling point, or the focus of the product that sets it apart from similar products, would be the way the car handles, or specifically the 'feel' of the car.

- Look at an early print advertisement. You can find old print advertisements for almost any product by looking on Google images or www.oaa.org.uk.
- Try to work out what the unique selling points (USPs) of the product are.
- Choose a recent advertisement for a similar product and compare the two.
- Analyse a range of advertisements for similar products, using a similar approach to the Ford analysis opposite.

■ Planning your advertising campaign

Once you have decided what your product is and have conducted your own research into your specific target audience, you can begin to plan the look and style of your advertising campaign. Use the following questions to help:

- How will your advertisements link together?
  - Some advertisers will place more than one advertisement in the same magazine or newspaper, on subsequent pages. The first advertisement may pose a question, to get the audience's interest, and the second advertisement on the following page may answer the question.
  - Your advertisements could contain a short narrative, with each advertisement becoming part of the 'serialisation' of this narrative. This could be an interesting way to encourage your target audience to 'look' for the product, as they may want to find out 'what happens next'.
- Where will your advertisements be placed?
  - Ensure that the target audience for your product is also the target audience for the medium in which the advertisement is placed. This may sound like a very obvious statement, but it is particularly important when considering the placement of advertisements in magazines and on billboards. Placing a billboard advertising the USPs of a new car at the side of one of Britain's busiest motorways would work well, but placing a billboard in the same place for a product aimed at young children would not work so well.
- Will you go for a hard sell (clearly identifying what the product is all about) or a soft sell (a more vague suggestion of the product without specifying many facts or details)? The latter sort of advertising is more concerned with creating an atmosphere around the product.

Production Portfolio in Media Studies

UNIT 3

- What aspect of your product will your advertisements focus on (your USPs)?
  - What are your product's USPs?
  - How will you draw attention to these USPs in your advertising campaign?
  - Will you draw attention through careful placing and lighting of the product (soft sell)?
  - Will you draw overt attention to your product by providing specific technical detail (hard sell)?

Brief 4

A new computer/video game cover in a appropriate format (PC, PlayStation, Nintendo, etc) and two magazine advertisements for the release of the new game, with some original photography.

Many of the skills that you will need to tackle this brief have already been covered in this chapter, along with some ideas for initial planning and research.

You should start by researching similar products. Take a selection of games covers, trying to choose games that are aimed at as wide an audience as possible, such as education games, Nintendo DS Lite games, Nintendo Wii sports games and 'action' games for the PlayStation. Next conduct a close image analysis, as described in Brief 3, of each of the covers. From this you should be able to see similarities and differences in the technical construction, such as shot-type and mise-en-scène. This will help you to understand how the construction of the game cover is an integral part of the marketing of a new game. It must stand out on the shelves of the shop and attract the right target audience.

Next think about surveying your target audience, finding out what attracts them to particular games. Do they buy games because they have seen them advertised? Do they buy games in a series if they have played the first instalment? Do they buy games that are recommended by friends? You could conduct a survey of your classmates or friends, as teenagers are the target market for many computer games.

When you construct your brief you will need to ensure that there is a clear visual link between the game cover and the advertisements, as the target audience will need to be able to identify the game on the shop shelf/online shop from the advertisement in the magazine.

Topic 2: Video Briefs

◼ Overview

Video work is a very popular choice for many students, and all of the briefs offer great creative opportunities. You will get the chance to work on a collaborative project and learn about how to work effectively in a group. Before you embark on any of these briefs you will need to ensure that you have access to the right equipment in your school or college (see the equipment checklist on the next page for guidance).

▲ *Figure 3.14: Filming a production*

◼ Things to think about

The video briefs all require 'acting' in some form. Perhaps you are you able to enlist the acting skills of drama students in your school or college, or you have confident friends who are happy to help out. You could even hold auditions as part of your planning process. Although Oscar-worthy performances are not a requirement of this unit, it is fairly important that your actors feel comfortable in front of the camera, particularly if you are choosing Brief 5.

The video option has a choice of three briefs:
- Brief 5 – a music promo video (maximum three minutes)
- Brief 6 – an extract from a new television programme (maximum three minutes)
- Brief 7 – the opening sequence from a new film, including titles (maximum three minutes).

■ What is being assessed?

The video briefs will test your technical skills in:

■ using the camera to shoot appropriate material
■ using shot types, angles and camera movement effectively
■ using sound with images
■ editing so that the audience can understand what is being shown to them.

■ Equipment checklist

If you have chosen this brief then you should have access to a Mini DV, SD or DVD camera and suitable editing software. If you are using an Apple Mac you could use iMovie or Final Cut Express software and if you are using a PC you could use Adobe Premier or even Moviemaker.

It is possible to produce relatively good quality moving image work using something like a Flip Mino mini-cam, although adding multiple soundtracks is not possible. This unit will not teach you how to edit, as packages are updated regularly. However, digital editing is pretty straightforward and packages such as Moviemaker and iMovie work in a drag-and-drop way, with large icons showing your clips. You can add several different soundtracks and titles to your video and you may be lucky enough to have the opportunity to make your own music using GarageBand or Soundtrack Pro.

Remember that this unit is a controlled assessment unit, and your production will therefore need to be completed under teacher supervision. For that reason it will not be possible for you to use your own editing software on your home computer.

■ Planning for a video brief

LOCATIONS

Decide which locations you are going to film in and when. Plan this part carefully – there is no point in trying to film in two locations that are quite far apart during the same lesson as you could waste valuable filming time travelling between the places. Also remember that it is essential that you get permission to film in the locations before you show up with your kit, or again, you could waste valuable filming time.

PRODUCTION SCHEDULE

Once you have decided which locations you are going to shoot in on which days you can put this in your production schedule. Then you can make a list of the props and costumes that you will need for these locations – write this on the schedule too. If you need to take lighting equipment with you for one location then make sure you remember to put that down as well.

DEADLINE SETTING

After you've completed the schedule for the filming sessions you should then be able to see clearly how many sessions you have for editing. Planning ahead should ensure that you don't run out of time! It is quite a useful idea to start by planning your actual production time allocation from the final deadline backwards, which might sound like an odd idea, but it works. Start by putting your edit deadline on your production schedule, and then add in sufficient time to edit. You may want to add in a rough cut deadline, which is a deadline for a preliminary assembly of your footage on the timeline. Doing this will should give you a clear idea of how long you have to film and plan, and that way you should meet your deadlines without any problems.

▲ *Figure 3.15: Boys editing their film*

RISK ASSESSMENTS

If you worked for a real media film or video production company you would have to conduct a risk assessment before you began filming. This would assess the level of risk involved at any of the chosen locations, or through the act of filming itself, and would hope to minimise any potential risk by drawing up a plan. Once you have decided where and when you are going to film you should aim to draw up your own risk assessment plan. Take each location in turn and list the possible risks involved, such as busy traffic, and then think of ways of minimising the risk, such as keeping to the pavement.

THE PRODUCTION LOG

Items to include:
- storyboards
- shot lists
- test shots from location hunt
- production schedule outlining rough cut, final deadlines and other key dates
- a record of your own contribution to the project.

Very early discarded storyboards, shot lists and other material not used towards the final production can be put into an appendix.

Whichever brief you choose from the video selection, you will have to produce a storyboard and you must organise a production schedule.

STORYBOARDING

Elements of a storyboard frame

Every cell should contain certain elements...

▶ Figure 3.16: Example storyboard

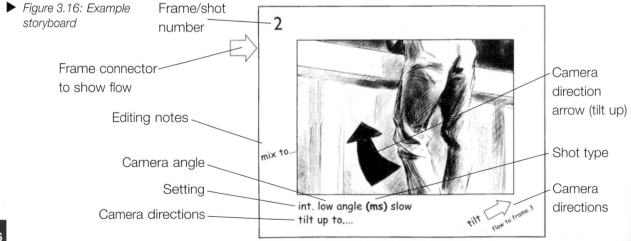

Frame/shot number

Frame connector to show flow

Editing notes

Camera angle

Setting

Camera directions

Camera direction arrow (tilt up)

Shot type

Camera directions

mix to...

int. low angle (ms) slow tilt up to....

tilt   flow to frame 3

Storyboarding is an essential part of the planning of any piece of moving image production work and as a result is a requirement of all three video briefs. It is a visual plan for each of the shots that you will record, with detail on camera movement, shot type and any sound direction. It should help you to see how your shots will go together when edited and how the flow of the narrative will work (see Figure 3.17).

▲ Figure 3.17: Digital storyboard

You don't need to be good at drawing to storyboard as you can produce a very effective storyboard with stick-men. Alternatively, you may want to produce a digital storyboard, which will involve you taking pictures of the exact shots you will record and downloading them into a timeline. With a digital storyboard you will need to sketch camera movement and direction, so that it is clear what is happening in the shot. The storyboard will then become a visual cue for the camera operator when you are out filming your production.

The kind of storyboard that is suitable for your production work can vary. Figure 3.17 shows a digital storyboard for the production of Brief 6 (genre: soap). The students have used a digital camera to record their shots and have added a written abbreviation of the shot type in the box below. You will see how this has been turned into a video later on in the unit.

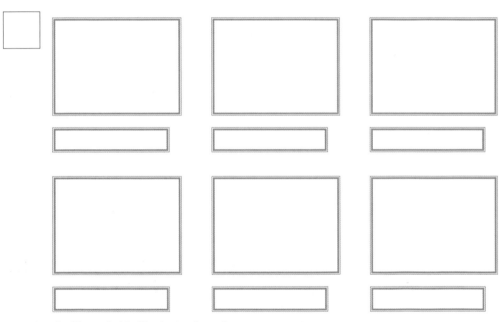

▲ *Figure 3.18: Blank storyboard*

You can design your own storyboard, similar to Figure 3.18, or there are many templates that are available to download from the internet.

■ What is mise-en-scène?

Mise-en-scène is everything that you see on screen, or within the frame. This includes:

- lighting
- props
- make-up and hair
- location
- costume
- shot composition
- set
- gesture or movement.

Shot types

Every shot in a music video or film is very carefully planned out beforehand. The shot type is not down to pot luck, but thought through in terms of what needs to be shown or conveyed to the audience at that time. You need to select each shot type for your production carefully.

Close-up shots

Extreme close-up (ECU)

Big close-up (BCU)

Close-up (CU)

Medium close-up (MCU)

Medium and long shots

Medium shot (MS)

Medium long shot (MLS)

Long shot (LS)

Very long shot (VLS)

Special shots

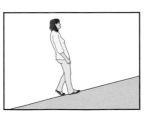

Tilted frame

Low angle shot (looking up)

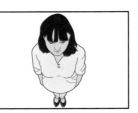

High angle shot (looking down)

Special types of shots

Two shot (CU/MCU/MS)

Over the shoulder shot

Interviewee looks/talks into space in the frame (and towards the interviewer)

Moving subject walks into space

▲ *Figure 3.19: Shot types diagram*

■ Framing

There are marks dedicated in the mark scheme to effective and appropriate framing, so it is worth spending some time learning about framing. Find out about the 'rule of thirds' and how it is applied to the composition or make-up of a frame. There is often a temptation, when you take a photo or record some footage, to place the head of the subject in the centre of the frame. What this does, however, is provide 'dead space' in the top of the shot (see Figure 3.20) which can draw the eye of the audience away from the subject. Unless there is a reason for the audience's attention to be drawn to the space above the subject's head, such as a bird or plane in the sky, then you should avoid drawing attention to it.

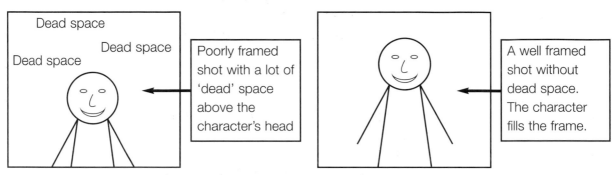

▲ Figure 3.20: Dead space diagram

Key terms

Dissolve: a cross-fade between two shots, often used to show change in location

Dolly: frame with wheels that tripod sits on – used for tracking shots

Fade in/out: transition used in editing, usually to black, often used to show passing of time

High angle: camera shoots from high up, looking down

Low angle: camera shoots from low down, looking up

Pan: movement of camera – pivoting from left to right or right to left while in a fixed position

Tilt: movement of camera up or down while in a fixed position

Track: movement of camera – camera placed on dolly or track and moves along with the action

Zoom: camera appears to move closer or further away from subject without physically moving – achieved through zoom lens

Video production process

Once you have drawn up your production schedule, prepared your props and completed your risk assessment, you are ready to roll! As soon as you collect your equipment from school or college you should shoot some test footage to check that everything is working properly. Record 30 seconds or so of the classroom, checking the zoom, and that the camera can pan on the tripod. Travelling to a location only to find that the battery is dead, or the tripod leg is wonky can waste valuable filming time.

A rule with producing video work is that you will never record enough footage on your first day of filming. Bear this in mind and make sure you get several takes of each shot, being careful to watch footage back after each take to check framing and lighting (and remembering to fast forward your tape back to the right place to avoid recording over something important!).

The five-second rule

Anticipate edits during the filming process by using the five-second rule: set up your shot, press record, count down 5-4-3-2-1 and shout 'Action!'. At the end of the action, shout 'Cut!', but keep recording for an additional five seconds. These five seconds of 'dead' time at the start and finish of your shot will help when you come to add dissolves or fades during the editing process, as without them you may find adding transitions is impossible. You must remember to log this 'dead' time when you come to copy your clips from your tape to the computer.

The zoom

To zoom or not to zoom – that is the question. Some teachers ban the use of zoom in student productions, as sudden and jerky zooming can give your project the feel of a badly-made wedding video, and can make cutting shots together very difficult indeed! However, some teachers will allow careful and controlled use of the zoom (in one direction only during any one shot) as a way of conveying a message to the audience. The secret to effective zooming is practice. Learning how much pressure should be applied to the zoom button and for how long, in order to achieve a desired effect, will greatly improve the quality of filming.

■ Continuity

Are you filming in sequence or out of sequence? Remember the rules of continuity if you are filming out of sequence (see page 257 on continuity in video work).

■ Base-tracks

If you have chosen Brief 5 then you may want to think about recording several 'base-tracks'. A base-track is a recording of the entire song from start to finish without pausing the camera. Producing base-tracks can make the editing process of a music video more straightforward as you can synch them one by one and lay them one on top of another. You can then cut between the tracks to create your video. It is useful if you are following a verse/chorus/verse structure.

If possible, download your footage at the end of every filming session, even if you've not finished the filming process. Taking time to watch and evaluate your footage is an important part of the construction process. You may have to make adjustments to future filming plans or re-shoot short sections to perfect them. These kinds of mid-project adjustments can feed into your Production log.

■ Brief 5

A music promo video, with storyboard. The length of the promo will reflect the length of the music track, but it is expected to be no longer than three minutes.

All material must be original, produced by the candidate(s), with the exception of the music or audio effects.

If candidates are working as a group, each group member is expected to take on a specific role, such as director, camera operator or editor.

■ The purpose

Music videos regularly cost tens of thousands of pounds to produce but do not, on their own, bring money back into the pockets of the music producers. You cannot really 'buy' a music video, although some bands do release DVDs of collections of their videos. Essentially, music producers will use the music video as a promotional tool to generate interest in the artist's new single or album, or to raise the profile of a new artist or band.

The concept

Music videos are based around a concept or clear idea, and this is something that you will need to have established before you pitch your idea to your teacher and class. For example: 'A group of rebellious teenage girls taking over the gym at high school' is the overall concept for Britney Spears' *Hit Me Baby One More Time*. This concept is clear and to the point, and most importantly, clearly identifiable as the concept for the well-known video.

Genre of music

If you were working for a real production company it is unlikely you would have any choice over the artist or genre of music you would work with. Bear this in mind when you come to select your track – do not simply pick your favourite song or artist unless you have a very clear concept for the video. Some music genres, for example r'n'b, demand high concept videos in order to closely follow the genre. It is important to consider what you have at your disposal in terms of setting and props before you make your final decision; be realistic about what you can do.

Making a music video will most definitely test your skills of editing; one of the conventions is for videos to cut to the beat, so if you choose an upbeat track this could mean that you will have a lot of logged clips in your bin! The Ting Tings' video for *That's Not My Name* has 29 different shots in the first 33 seconds of the video alone, while Beyoncé's video for *If I Were A Boy*, a much slower track, has only nine edits in the first 33 seconds. Music videos also tend to have a large number and great range of different shots, and most will utilise lip-synching, which is where the mouth and singing match. This is another technical skill that you will need to master, possibly by using 'markers' on your timeline.

Do you need to be able to sing to make a music video? No – it is useful for your 'artist' to sing while you record as it makes the job of matching the movement of the mouth with the words easier (and miming can make you look a bit like a goldfish!), but you will lay down the original music track to edit to, so that is what the audience will hear in the end.

Let's research

- Look at a variety of different genres of music video on the internet or by scanning the available music channels on your television.
- Compare hip-hop, heavy metal, r'n'b, indie guitar band, bubblegum pop and a typical boy band video.
- Develop an understanding of the typical conventions of music videos by comparing:
  - the range of shots
  - the structure (verse/chorus)
  - the speed of the editing
  - the mise-en-scène.

You can see that all videos have similarities but also that different genres follow their own codes and conventions.

Let's analyse

Carry out detailed textual analysis of a couple of videos from your chosen genre. Ask yourself the following questions:
- Is there a clear structure of a verse and chorus? What happens in each part?
- What sorts of camera angles and distances of shot are evident in the video?
- What locations are used?
- Is the video edited to the beat effectively?
- If the video uses lip-synching, when and where is it used?
- Does the artist wear different outfits during the video?
- What camera movement can you see and when is it used?
- Is the artist performing the song, taking part in a narrative or dancing?

Let's research

- Look at http://www.bemuso.com/musicbiz/labelsandpublishers.html. This website outlines the main record companies and how the money is distributed between the companies and the artists.
- Look at record labels as part of your research, so that you can understand how the recording industry works.
- Once you've decided on your track and have created an image for your artist(s), identify which record company is likely to sign you.
- Examine the website for Lily Allen (http://www.lilyallenmusic.com/lily/) or The Ting Tings (http://www.thetingtings.com/), as both of these artists premier their new videos on their sites for the benefit of loyal fans. Would you plan to develop a webpage for your artist and screen the video there?

■ Planning
BAND IDENTITY

Begin by creating your band image or identity. You won't be making a music video for the original artist, unless you are lucky enough to know someone who has recorded his or her own music track, or manage to track down an unsigned band from MySpace or YouTube (which has been done!), so it is likely you will be creating a brand new artist or group. Remember that the music video itself is simply a vehicle for promoting the image of your artist to their audience.

Let's create

Creating a mood board (see Figure 3.21) is a good way of drawing together an array of influences and ideas for your artist/band's image. Collect ideas and photos on:

- ■ fashion
- ■ colours
- ■ hairstyles
- ■ make-up styles
- ■ music influences.

Paste them on a large piece of cardboard. This mood board can then help you to choose a costume and style for your artist and can form part of your pitch.

▲ *Figure 3.21: Student mood board*

■ The next steps

Now you need to:

- ■ develop the concept for your video
- ■ plan particular shots or sequences
- ■ think about appropriate locations
- ■ decide whether you want a strict verse/chorus structure, if it is appropriate to the genre you have chosen
- ■ do the 'audience bag' activity (see page 222), as you will be required to reflect on this in your evaluation.

Production Portfolio in Media Studies

UNIT 3

■ Storyboarding for a music video

SHOT LIST

If you are having difficulty in starting your storyboard you might find it useful to begin by creating a shot list. This can be a list of individual shots or short sequences, with a description of the shot type, any camera movement, and detail of the location. The good thing about starting with a shot list is that you don't have to write it in the order that it will appear in the finished video – you can simply use it as a place to record your ideas. Then, when you are satisfied with your shots you can transfer them to your storyboard in the correct order.

Storyboards can be sketched, like Figure 3.22, or if you have the time you could use a digital camera, although for a music video this can be quite time consuming. This shot list can then be used as planning evidence in your Production log.

▲ *Figure 3.22: Hand-drawn storyboard*

Brief 6

An extract from a new television programme, in any genre or mix of genres chosen by the centre, such as a sitcom, a crime drama, or a new children's television programme, together with a storyboard. The sequence may include titles. The maximum length is three minutes.

- All material must be original, produced by you, with the exception of the music or audio effects. This means that you cannot take clips or extracts from a real television programme or from a project created by other students and put it into your sequence.
- If you are working as a group, each group member is expected to take on a specific role, such as director, camera operator or editor. This is to ensure that everyone gets the opportunity to have input in the project.

Creative choices

This is quite a broad brief that gives you the opportunity to be really creative with the camera. The opportunity to make an extract from a programme in any genre or mix of genres can be a really exciting prospect. You may be lucky enough to have a choice of genre, in which case you should bear in mind the props, locations and actors available to you for filming. Be creative with the resources at your fingertips!

- If your school is in a large town or city, you could produce an interesting crime drama set in the local streets and buildings.
- If there is a primary school connected to your school you could ask if it is possible to use one of their Year 1 classrooms as a backdrop for filming a new children's television programme.
- You could choose to make a new soap opera based in a school or college, or even a new sit-com based in a school or college.

Continuity

Ever noticed your favourite character on *EastEnders* opening the door to the Queen Vic wearing a red coat and arriving at the bar four seconds later wearing a black coat? It's unlikely (although not impossible!) because soap operas employ people specifically to make sure that continuity errors like this don't happen. Continuity is also an important factor for you to remember when filming Briefs 6 or 7. If you are shooting out of sequence, and particularly if you are using props, you will need to make sure that you keep a clear record of what is used in each shot.

Let's research – Ratings

- Research audience ratings (viewing figures) on http://www.barb.co.uk/, the website of the Broadcasters' Audience Research Board (BARB).
- Which are the most popular television channels?
- Which are the top ten programmes on these channels?
- Look at the schedules for the BBC for a week and make a tally of the different genres of programmes that they screen.
- Compare that with the output on Channel 5.
- What differences and similarities are there in the content of their schedules?

Let's research – Audiences

You will need to make sure that your television extract is going to appeal to your target audience.

- Go to www.bbc.co.uk/commissioning/marketresearch.
- Examine the audience profile for 16–24-year-olds.
- Compare that to the profile for 25–34-year-olds.

16–24-year-olds watch an average of 15 hours of television a week, which is just over two hours a day. This age range now spends more time gaming and online. In contrast, 25–34-year-olds watch an average of 25 hours of television a week. This sort of information will be important when you come to choose your genre, as it is essential for there to be a market for your show.

Let's analyse

This activity is based on soap operas, but can also work well with other television genres.

- Watch an episode of a soap opera.
    - Make a list of all the storylines and label them in order of importance; for example the main story would be 'A', and the second 'B', etc.
    - Make a list of all the characters in your chosen soap opera and try to link as many of them together as you can, using a diagram.
    - Note down all of the different sets that are used in this episode.
    - Identify the themes that are being touched on in this episode.
    - What observations are you able to make about the number of storylines and characters in soap operas, and what might this tell you about the target audience? How many different sets are used and how do they link with the storylines?

Let's discuss – Title sequences

Watch three or four soap operas (including at least one Australian soap opera) and brainstorm the following areas:

- **Music** – Describe the type of music used – is it orchestral? Rock? Does the song have lyrics?
- **Titles** – What style of font is used? What information is given about characters' or actors' names? What colour are the fonts?
- **Characters** – Do we see characters in the title sequence? If so, describe what they are doing and how many characters we see.
- **Location** – Is the geographical location clear from the title sequence? How many different locations are we shown? Describe any sets that you see.
- **Camerawork** – Is there any camera movement? Describe the shot types that are used to show the location.
- **Special effects** – Are any special effects used in the title sequence, such as interesting edits, shots within shot, etc.

■ Planning

You need to make sure that the genre of your sequence is clear to your audience through your use of codes and conventions.

Whichever genre you choose, brainstorming characters, locations and storylines is a good starting place. Your choice of characters and locations must appeal to your target audience: if you are producing the opening title sequence to a new BBC1 soap opera that will be screened at 9 pm on Wednesdays and Fridays, you will be directly appealing to the mass audience that makes up BBC1's viewers on Friday evenings. Therefore, your soap should contain a range of different types of character to appeal to the wide range of different audience members. Producing a soap aimed at teenagers, like *Hollyoaks*, and screening it at 9 pm on a Wednesday evening on BBC1 would not appeal to this target audience.

■ Planning a soap opening sequence
OPTION 1:

You could choose to follow the style of Australian soaps such as *Neighbours* and *Home and Away* by beginning with some action from the previous episode, known as 'pre-sequence' action. This can then be followed by a short title sequence, including captions to introduce characters.

OPTION 2:

You could choose to start with a more conventional title sequence, where you introduce your characters and the location of the soap (including captions), and show a little bit of the 'everyday' lives of your characters going about their business. This could then be followed by the opening part of the action.

■ What is pre-sequence action?

Pre-sequence action is a short reminder for the audience about what happened in the previous episode. It often starts with the caption 'Previously on *Home and Away/Neighbours*', for example, and comes before the title sequence. It is usually something fairly dramatic that resulted in the conventional cliffhanger ending.

■ What could be included in pre-sequence action?

The important thing to remember is to keep it very simple – don't try to tell a complex story as you have very little time in which to do this. A few very simple shots of your main characters, involved in some basic action, is all you need. Some examples of possible pre-sequence action are provided on the next page to get you thinking about possible scenarios.

■ What should be included in a title sequence?

- ■ In your title sequence you will need to introduce your audience to the location that the soap is set in, plus the main characters. Think about how you could effectively do this.
- ■ You will also need to think about the sort of music that will suit your opening. Think about your target audience when deciding on music – you may not use a recent hip hop track on a prime-time BBC1 soap, for example.
- ■ Think carefully about the colour and position of the titles (captions) themselves. Watch some soaps and make notes on the style of their titles. Try to avoid using red font as this does not show up clearly.

■ Which option should we choose?

It is very important to think about your acting skills as Option 1 requires more acting. If you are uncomfortable about spending lots of time in front of the camera then Option 2 may be a more suitable choice. If you dream of one day being an actor or actress then Option 1 may be more appealing!

Possible soap locations/situations could be your school or college (very good mise-en-scène), the local market or a local estate, with surrounding shops.

 Let's discuss

Examples of possible pre-sequence action

This list is to stimulate discussion in your group about possible scenarios that could make good pre-sequence action. Obviously, your pre-sequence action will need to relate carefully to the concept of your soap and the expectations of your target audience.

Scenario 1
Character 1 waits nervously in line to collect his GCSE results. He shuffles forwards slowly, biting his nails, clearly very anxious. He wipes nervous sweat from his forehead. He reaches the front of the queue and is given an envelope with his name on it. He opens the envelope and lifts the letter out – the camera focuses on his face and the look of shock. The camera then cuts away (a nice cliffhanger).

Scenario 2
Character 2 is late. She wakes, glances at the clock and panics when she realises it is 9.15 am. She jumps up, dresses quickly (we don't need to see this bit!), grabs a piece of toast and runs for the bus. She misses the bus by two seconds, so decides to run. Next, we see her arrive at her destination (could be college or workplace), but she is stopped from entering because she's so late. She slumps down on the steps with her head in her hands.

Scenario 3
Character 3 is walking in the market, looking at the stalls, chatting to the traders. She is unaware that she is being watched, but the viewers know, as we see the back of someone following her. The stalker gets closer and closer. The woman is still totally unaware. The sequence ends with the woman being grabbed by the shoulder and turning to face the camera – there is a look of shock on her face. The sequence ends.

Scenario 4
Character 4 arrives at a café, orders a coffee and sits down. A guy sitting across the café catches her eye. She smiles and starts to read a newspaper. On his way out of the café the guy drops a note onto Character 4's table and walks out. Character 4 unfolds the note, reads it and smiles. The sequence ends.

Storyboarding

If you can, have a go at producing a digital storyboard for this brief. The digital storyboard in Figure 3.17 (see page 247) is an example that was produced by a group of GCSE students for the soap opera genre. Figure 3.23 is a screengrab from the same student project, showing a shot from the video. The storyboard is a vital part of your planning and must be submitted along with your finished product.

▲ *Figure 3.23: Example from student project*

Brief 7

Opening sequence from a new film, including titles, in any genre or mix of genres chosen by the centre, such as a comedy or a thriller, together with a storyboard. The maximum length is three minutes.

- All video and audio material must be original, produced by the candidate(s), with the exception of music or audio effects.
- If candidates are working as a group, each group member is expected to take on a specific role, such as director, camera operator, or editor.

As with Brief 6, Brief 7 is a broad brief that will allow you to be creative by either choosing one film genre or by experimenting with a mix of genres.

Genre

A good film opening should signal to the audience what the genre is, perhaps by establish setting or location, and possibly character. You need to demonstrate that you understand how the codes and conventions of your chosen genre work to communicate messages and meaning to your audience.

It is essential, however, that the opening doesn't give away too much information as it could turn off the audience – have you ever guessed the ending of a film right from the start? It is an anti-climax when the ending finally comes and the narrative can sometimes drag on. Equally, the opening must supply *some* information or else the audience could become confused or frustrated. Finding the right balance of information is one of the keys to success with this brief. One of the commonest mistakes that can be made with this brief is trying to tell the whole story in the opening. An opening doesn't need an 'ending', although when you are planning your narrative it is useful to envisage how the narrative would develop and end if you were making the entire film.

■ Which genre should you choose?

As with television Brief 6, you could base your choice of film genre around the resources that are available to you. How easy would you find it to produce the opening to a science fiction film? It might be that you have access to an electronics lab in school or college that could form a great backdrop for this genre! The thriller genre is very broad and so offers you a variety of different directions to take, such as a political espionage, a spy thriller, a psychological thriller or romantic thriller. Each of these subgenres of thriller shares similar conventions in terms of creation of suspense and tension through sound, camerawork and lighting, but each could look significantly different on screen.

 Let's research

- Watch the first five minutes of several film openings, preferably including one or two that you have not seen before. Think about the ways in which genre and narrative are established for the audience. Ask yourself:
  - How much narrative information, if any, is given?
  - What do we learn about the characters and their relationships with each other/ their surroundings?
  - What mood or tone is established, and how do the technical codes of lighting and sound help?
  - What narrative predictions can we make about the rest of the film, based on this opening?
- Use a grid to record what you notice about sound, mise-en-scène, camerawork, editing and titles. What do you think is effective and works well?

Production Portfolio in Media Studies

UNIT 3

■ Institutions

Ever wondered where all the money to fund the film industry comes from? As part of your pitch you will need to decide who you would approach for funding to make your film. If you have chosen a popular genre and your target audience is a mainstream one then you could approach one of the large American production companies, such as Universal, to put up the money. Or if your film's appeal is likely to be more niche, then you may want to approach a company such as Warp Films.

■ Audience research

Who goes to the cinema? If you were working on a real film production you would want to make as much money as possible from ticket sales, so you would have to be sure that the audience is out there. Do the 'audience bag' activity on page 222 to help you make sure you know who your audience is.

■ Planning checklist

- ■ Choose your genre.
- ■ Brainstorm possible narrative ideas on a large piece of paper with your group. If you can't decide which idea to work with you may want to weave together several ideas.
- ■ Scout for locations, taking a digital camera or using your mobile phone to take some location shots. These can be used in your Production log or appendix.
- ■ Develop ideas for your shot list.
- ■ Create a storyboard.
- ■ Pitch your ideas to your teacher and class.

▲ *Figure 3.24: Location stills and storyboard*

Let's pitch

Once a writer has developed an idea for a new film they will present this idea to film producers in the hope that they will be given the money to make the film. This is called making a pitch.

The writer will bring the script, and will talk through all aspects of their idea for the film. They will aim to make their film sound new and exciting. A script is sold on the first 15 pages alone – if it is successful it is referred to as a 'grabber'.

You could pitch your idea for the opening sequence to your class and teacher. Imagine they are representatives from a big production company that you desperately want to fund your project. This 10-minute pitch can be used as evidence in your Production log.

You need to cover the following key areas:
- Describe the key images or icons used within your opening sequence.
- Describe the kinds of setting and locations that you are going to be filming around. What aspects of the setting will be used (front of building, under stairs, etc.)?
- How are you going to use lighting in your opening sequence? Describe how individual shots are going to be lit, and what effect you hope to create with this use of lighting.
- Camerawork – the choice of shot distance and angle, and movement of the camera, is crucial when constructing film openings, as so much can be communicated to the audience through this. Describe a sequence of shots from your opening, and the effect that you hope to create through this choice.
- Music is another crucial aspect of a film opening. It must create the right kind of mood for the audience. Describe your choice of music (bring it in and play it to your pitch audience). What kind of atmosphere are you hoping to create through use of this music?
- Audience – who is the film aimed at? Be very specific about your target audience.
- Storyboard – you must show a completed storyboard for your opening title sequence.
- Production schedule – you must have a completed production schedule.

The next steps

Allocate tasks to each group member. Using the appropriate pages in the log book, each group member must prepare a short presentation on their designated tasks.
- You may use music, visual aids, demonstrations or even audience participation!

Topic 3: Audio Briefs

■ Overview

Radio is a popular source of entertainment and has been around for quite some time. People listen to the radio in their cars and in their kitchens, through their mobile phones on the bus and even online at work during the day (see Topic 5 on page 54). The development of podcasting allows listeners to download excerpts from their favourite radio shows and listen to them over and over. There is a very strong market for popular radio programmes. Radio is a source of news, entertainment, information and education. As part of your initial research, it might be interesting for you to consider what the lasting appeal of radio is.

Creating an audio production can be really good fun and gives you the opportunity to test out your writing and practical production skills as you will need to script either of the briefs on offer carefully.

There are two briefs (Briefs 8 and 9) to choose from for audio work:

■ An extract from a magazine-style radio programme, with a specified audience. The extract should demonstrate a mixture of sound elements, such as title music, presenter, outside broadcasts, vox pop, recorded interviews and appropriate sound effects. A sound script should be included. The maximum length is four minutes.

■ An extract from a radio drama, scripted from new material or an adaptation of a novel or short story, together with a sound script. The maximum length is four minutes.

This unit concentrates specifically on Brief 8, but much of the guidance on research, planning and production processes is exactly what you would need to do if you chose Brief 9, so the activities can be adapted.

■ What is being assessed?

The audio briefs will test your skills in:

■ recording appropriate sound
■ recording sound at the right level
■ recording sound in the right environment
■ editing and mixing
■ using generic conventions effectively.

■ Equipment checklist

Although it is possible to make radio programmes with little in the way of specialist equipment, it is probably best not to embark on a radio brief without access to:

- ■ a digital recording programme such as Adobe Audition (a multi-track recording package)
- ■ a digital voice recorder so that you can record your outside broadcasts or vox pops, if you are choosing Brief 8. Most mobile phones also have pretty sophisticated voice recorders within them, so check with your teacher if it is possible for you to use your mobile phone and then either bluetooth the file or upload the file to your audio package
- ■ access to good microphones – this can make a world of difference in terms of the quality of the sound recording
- ■ proper headphones, as this is the only way that you will be able to really hear what your audience will hear – wearing headphones will make you look like a professional radio presenter and help you feel the part too!

■ The Production log

Items to include:

- ■ outline of the script
- ■ cue sheets
- ■ drafts of scripts
- ■ your production schedule, detailing key dates, deadlines and decisions
- ■ your contribution to the project if you are working in a group.

■ Brief 8 or Brief 9?

Although both briefs require sound scripts and a certain technical skill level, they do differ in terms of demands:

Brief 8: magazine-style programme	Brief 9: radio drama
■ Wider mix of sound ■ Title music ■ Outside broadcasts ■ Vox pops	■ Good acting skills ■ Good scriptwriting ■ Coherent narrative

■ Sound template

You will need to produce a sound template and submit it as part of your portfolio. Figure 3.25 is an example of what a sound template can look like. This sound template is used to achieve the effective timing of a bulletin or report – you can see that it calculates roughly how long it takes to speak.

Script Write one word in each box.			Word count/ time in secs
			3 words 1 sec
			6 words 2 sec
			9 words 3 sec
			12 words 4 sec
			15 words 5 sec
			18 words 6 sec
			21 words 7 sec
			24 words 8 sec
			27 words 9 sec
			30 words 10 sec
			33 words 11 sec
			36 words 12 sec
			39 words 13 sec
			42 words 14 sec
			45 words 15 sec

▲ Figure 3.25: Sound template

■ Production process

Once you have pitched your ideas, scripted your radio broadcast, drawn up your cue sheets and had several run-throughs to check for timing and flow of dialogue, you can begin to create your product. This section of the unit will not teach you how to use audio production equipment and software as not everyone will be using the same packages. There are however some general points to make about the production of audio broadcasts that you should bear in mind when creating your product.

■ When you record your OBs (outside broadcasts) or vox pops for Brief 8, you must pay really close attention to the sound levels that the microphones pick up, so make sure you are wearing your headphones. Keep an eye on the sound meter (if you are using one) to check that the levels do not go out of range.

- It is essential that OBs and vox pops are recorded in the right environment – they should sound like they are real and have been recorded in the street/on location.
- You must ensure that the voice of your presenter sounds like he/she is in a studio, so that it sounds like a real radio broadcast.
- With radio drama, think about the background noises you will need to add realism to your piece – if your character is meant to be waiting in a doctor's surgery then you must ensure that you have appropriate sounds of telephones ringing, voices, the receptionist answering the phone, etc.
- Master the smooth mixing or editing of your sound, ensuring that all the recorded and 'real sounds' are at the right pitch and level – try to avoid the volume of the different sound sources changing between segments of your show.
- Avoid inappropriate silences by following your script closely and making sure you know what is coming up from your cue sheets.

■ Activity

Visit the BBC online training page (www.bbctraining.com), where you can take a short online course in audio production, including 'Interviewing for Radio', and 'Microphones and sound for Radio'.

■ Brief 8

An extract from a magazine-style radio programme (see page 266).

Key terms

Jingle: short piece of music played between segments of a magazine radio programme, often including 'lyrics' of the radio station name. Listen to *Steve Wright in the Afternoon* for a good example of a jingle

Outside broadcasts (OBs): reports recorded/reported from elsewhere (often 'outside'!) – usually at places that are relevant to the story being reported

Recorded sound: sound used in a radio production that is recorded at another time and played back during the show

Sound bridge: sound used to link different elements of a radio broadcast together

Vox pops: recorded unrehearsed excerpts of interviews with the general public, often edited together to show many responses to the same question to illustrate public opinion on a hot topic

■ Research and planning

Listen to the radio to establish exactly what a magazine-style radio programme is, and how it differs in form and style to news or drama.

■ Find out what radio programmes are on and when by looking in either a radio listings magazine, in a newspaper or online.
■ Choose a range of programmes from different channels.
■ Carry out your own primary research through textual analysis. Identify:
  ■ the kinds of reports there are
  ■ the variety of different elements that make up the programme
  ■ the role of the main presenter(s)
  ■ the use of music in the programme
  ■ the length of the programme.
■ Record all of this information on a grid that you can use in your Production log as evidence of your initial research into the brief.

You can then begin to develop your own ideas for your programme from this research.

■ Target audience and institution

Which station would your programme be broadcast on? The BBC has 10 main radio stations, plus many more local and regional channels. Some are only available as digital broadcasts. Visit www.bbc.co.uk/radio and have a look at the listings.

You will need to make sure that the contents of your show will appeal directly to your target market, by including:

■ interviews about topics that will interest them
■ vox pops on subjects that will appeal to them
■ a presenter addressing them in a way that they understand and appreciate.

Let's research

The brief states that you must clearly specify your audience, so you should make a point of collecting data on who listens to magazine-style radio programmes, why and when.
■ Visit http://www.rajar.co.uk/, the website of the Radio Joint Audience Research (RAJAR).
■ Identify which radio stations carry the largest market share and examine their schedules to see what percentage is given over to magazine-style programmes.

Cue sheets

Using a cue sheet such as Figure 3.26 during the recording process will help you tremendously with the construction of your radio broadcast, and can be submitted as part of your Production log. It will ensure that you and your team are properly organised, and know what is coming up next and the duration of each segment of the show.

Programme	*Candi magazine programme*
Title of report	New student union president elected
Name of presenter	Aoife
Duration of report in minutes	Two minutes
Cue	'Hi, everyone, I'm here in the SU with the newly elected president... Thank you for taking the time out to talk to us. Let's go back to the studio and Nick' In: music fades out/background noise of SU Out: background noise of SU fades to music

▲ *Figure 3.26: Cue sheet*

Brief 9

An extract from a radio drama, scripted from new material or an adaptation of a novel or short story, together with a sound script. The maximum length is four minutes.

Radio drama relies solely on dialogue and added sound/music to convey the narrative information to the audience, unlike television drama that has the luxury of moving image to help. This may sound like a very obvious comment to make, but it should help you to understand how important scripting is to this brief. Your audience will be hanging on every word or sound that they hear, so it is essential to get the tone, level and mix of sounds just right. Equally, you must make sure that the scenes are edited together seamlessly to create continuity and meaning for the audience.

Let's research

- Listen to as many different radio dramas as you can to get a feel for the style and format of them.
- Listen to *The Archers*, the long-running BBC Radio 4 drama (see Topic 5 on page 54). It may not necessarily appeal to your taste, but as it is so successful it is good research.
- Check the radio schedule for one-off dramas or radio plays, and compare these to *The Archers*.
  - How do the conventions differ?
  - Is narrative information conveyed in the same way?
  - How are sound effects used?
  - How are the scenes edited together?

The option to adapt a novel or short story into your drama script gives you a world of opportunities to create something really exciting. This is a great place to start your planning too – by bringing in favourite excerpts from stories and reading them aloud to your group. You could choose to adapt a short story that you or a group member has created during your English lessons.

■ Scriptwriting support

- Visit the BBC website http://www.bbc.co.uk/writersroom/insight/radio_drama.shtml and have a look at some of the scripts that new writers have submitted to BBC Radio in the hope that they will be made into real radio productions.
- Read through the first couple of pages of one or two of the scripts and observe how they are set out. If you are working in a group, read a few pages from one of these scripts aloud. Is there a lot of dialogue in a very short space of time?

Topic 4: Website Briefs

■ Briefs 10 and 11

■ Overview

Web design is a really exciting part of practical production work for GCSE Media Studies. As ideally the website should be accessible online, it is one of the easiest ways of becoming a real media producer – getting your product out to a real audience through the internet. However, it is not one of the most popular choices for production, which could be partly due to the technical demands, and so this section gives an overview of website production rather than covering each brief in detail. The two briefs (Briefs 10 and 11) on offer are:

- A minimum of four linked pages, including the homepage, of a new TV channel, including some original photography (if you are working in a group then you must produce at least two pages individually).
- A minimum of four linked webpages, including the homepage, for a new entertainment website with a specified audience, including some original photography (if you are working in a group then you must produce at least two pages individually).

Things to consider

You should be familiar with the basics of making a webpage from your ICT lessons, but you could ask for further guidance if you do not feel confident. However, if you are a dab-hand with web design packages, then both briefs offer the opportunity to be really creative.

■ What is being assessed?

Website briefs will test:

- your understanding of the conventions of websites through construction and design
- your ability to manipulate images effectively
- your ability to use images and text together to communicate with the web user.

Production Portfolio in Media Studies

UNIT 3

■ Equipment checklist

For either of these briefs you will need good regular access to either a PC or a Mac, as well as the right software for the job. Remember that because of the controlled assessment requirements of this GCSE you will be unable to make your website at home – the construction of your product will have to be under the supervision of your teacher. It is therefore important that you have the necessary equipment in school. You may be lucky enough to have a choice of packages to use: PC-based web design packages include Dreamweaver or Fireworks, or if you are using an AppleMac you may have access to either iWeb, QuarkXPress or RapidWeaver. Any one of these packages will give you the ability to produce a very professional looking webpage.

Key terms

Address bar: box that displays the web address in full; can also be typed into directly if the user knows the site address
Links: text (often signified by being <u>underlined</u>), or an object that forms a 'hyperlink' to another site or page
Menu: series of buttons or links to the main webpage, either situated along the top or down the side of the webpage
Status bar: bar at the bottom of the webpage that indicates the status of components of the page – hover the mouse over any aspect of the webpage and its status will be revealed in this bar

■ The Production log

Items to include:

- outlines for initial ideas
- test shots for images
- sketches or mock-ups of webpages
- screenshots of test pages
- production schedule, detailing key dates involved in the production process and decisions made
- a record of your contribution, which is particularly important if you have worked in a group.

Material that you did not use to plan and construct your final website, such as early ideas or sketches, can be included in an appendix.

Did you know that 35–45-year-olds represented 41% of the online population in 2005? This age range uses the internet for a variety of reasons, including shopping, finance, search engines and news (source www.bbc.co.uk/commissioning/marketresearch). The percentage of this age range could seem quite large to you, particularly as this age range did not grow up in the era of the internet. Finding out who uses the internet and for what purpose will be an essential part of your research, as it will help to ensure that your webpages are pitched at the right market.

- Visit the BBC market research webpage, www.bbc.co.uk/commissioning/marketresearch.
- Examine the audience profiling research that has been conducted.

You will see that the audience has been split into age categories and each category is examined in close detail, looking at the kinds of media that the group consumes. Here you will see what each category uses the internet for. This could form the basis for your production. Once you have identified who your target audience is, you should move onto looking at existing sites from the same genre.

- Take a look at the websites for CBBC (http://www.bbc.co.uk/cbbc) or any of the UKTV channels, including Watch and G.O.L.D. (www.uktv.co.uk), if you are thinking of tackling Brief 10.
- Log on to the Channel 4 T4 website (www.channel4.com/t4) if you are thinking of tackling Brief 11.

▲ *Figure 3.27: T4 website*

Let's analyse

- Using an A3 sheet of paper, sketch out the rough layout of three different websites from the genre chosen. Make a note of:
  - where the links go
  - whether there is any video or audio content, and the placing of it on the page
  - the use of colours
  - the use of fonts
  - the position of the navigation tools.

Although this may seem like a very old-fashioned approach (using a pencil and paper), it is a really useful piece of research to do as it will help you with your layout ideas.

Questions to think about:
- Who is the target audience for the three websites?
- What conventions do the three websites share?
- How do they differ?
- How does the content of the sites attract the target audience?

■ Planning

Allowing yourself plenty of time to plan your website is essential, as there are several important factors to consider. Once you are clear on your target audience you will then need to plan the layout and tone of your site. Font size, positioning of navigation tools, colour, layout of text and images, and overall tone are just some of the important components to a webpage. For example, font size should be large enough for people to be able to scan through the text quickly, but without being so large that it overpowers the rest of the page.

Let's compare

Website visitors rarely read every word on the homepage – they scan the text for the links and important content – so you will need to ensure that you know exactly what your target audience is looking for. The colour of the font should also be thought through, and this will depend on your target audience.

- Look at the colours used on the CBBC website (www.bbc.co.uk/cbbc) and compare them with the colours used on the G.O.L.D. site (www.uktv.co.uk).

Bright colours and a very clear theme compared with subtle grey and white colours help to illustrate the very different target audiences for these two websites. Red is a very bright colour and will draw the eye of the user quickly, so could be used for links. However, colouring all the fonts red could make it hard on the eye, as it could be too bright. Therefore, try to choose a colour that will make your page both inviting and ordered, while appealing to your target audience at the same time.

■ Positioning

The positioning of the navigation tools must be correct: we read from left to right, so our eye is naturally drawn to the top left-hand side of the computer screen first. This is why putting your links in a list down the left-hand side, or across the top of the page starting on the left, is conventional. It is also essential to put all the important content of each page near the top, and not at the bottom, as this would rely on your user scrolling down to find it, and so could be easily missed.

How will you lay out the content of your site? You could choose to arrange your site in columns, or you could keep your content in a central position on the page. Getting the tone of your website correct is crucial, and this can be achieved through pitching the language at the right level. Remember who will be reading your site and write your content in a style that they will recognise and understand. Getting this wrong can be one way of missing your target audience.

■ Web design support

The website www.webmonkey.com is a useful online resource for help and guidance with web design. It can look a bit 'techy' on first glance but it has a series of useful tutorials to help you through the production of your site.

Topic 5: Cross-Media Briefs
■ Brief 12
■ Overview

This section of the unit includes a basic overview of Brief 12, as each part of it is covered in some way in another section. The cross-media package, as its title suggests, is a production that includes material from more than one medium. It is a great choice for anyone who cannot decide between which brief to pick and it allows you to experiment with several different media at the same time. The brief outline is:

A promotional package for the release of a new album to include material from more than one medium (e.g. website, CD cover, extract from a music promo video, radio interview, television advertisement, magazine advertisement/article). The package should include some original photography.

At first glance this brief can seem quite overwhelming, until you notice that each part of the promotional package is not required to be in the same depth as the corresponding brief in this unit. You are also not being asked to produce every item – just items in more than one medium. For example, if you choose to make a website and a magazine advertisement, you are only being asked to make one of each, rather than a series of linked pages and three advertisements.

The important thing to consider when tackling this brief is that each part of the promotional package clearly links together, through the visual style. For example, stills from the video could be used on the website or magazine advertisement; an excerpt from the video could be included in part of the television advertisement; and the CD cover could appear on the webpages. This is important, so that your audience can make a connection between what they read, see or hear. How you choose which media to use can depend on your enjoyment or knowledge and technical skills.

▲ Figure 3.28: Student's CD cover example

 Let's research

Choose a new release from a popular artist and collect information on the marketing and promotion of the song. Aim to include:
- magazine or newspaper articles covering the release, including reviews
- magazine or other print advertisements
- the press release
- background information on the record label
- a record of any television coverage, including airplay on music channels and promotional appearances on television programmes
- information on how the record label or artist is using the internet in the promotion of the release, such as MySpace, YouTube or a dedicated website for the artist.

Collate the information and give an informal presentation to your class. You could choose to mount the work on sugar paper.

Evaluating Your Production

Let's evaluate

The evaluation section of your production is as important as the planning and research and will count for a quarter of the overall marks, and for that reason you should set aside plenty of time to complete this task well. It is an individual task and is a great opportunity for you to take a step back from your finished project and think about what you have learnt and how successful you think your finished product is.

You need to have kept a log book or diary throughout this unit, as the records you've kept in it will be invaluable. It will give you the opportunity to reflect on what you have learnt since the start of the unit, and will also act as a memory-jogger for all the technical decisions you took, revisions you made to your initial plans and new skills you have learnt.

■ Presentation

The presentation of the evaluation can take the form of any one, or combination of, the following:
- a written commentary of 500–800 words
- a PowerPoint presentation of 5–10 slides (which can be videoed)
- an audio podcast or audio presentation of 3–5 minutes in length
- a DVD with extras of 3–5 minutes in length.

If you have the opportunity to choose your own method of evaluating your production then the following details should help you decide.

■ Written commentary

This is a traditional essay-based evaluation of your finished piece. If you enjoy writing and find expressing yourself on paper enjoyable then this could be the choice for you. You might want to subhead the different aspects of the project and tackle each one individually, which is fine. The word count is a guideline.

■ PowerPoint

The rule with PowerPoint is not to write absolutely every word on the slide. PowerPoint is a presentation package and the slides should act as a tool to aid your presentation of your work. Summarise your main points under headings, and use the animation facility to reveal each point as you go, which will prevent your audience from 'reading ahead'. Not writing every word on the slide should also ensure that your audience listens carefully to what you are saying, as you should be elaborating on your main points orally.

It is possible that your teacher will want to video you giving your presentation as evidence for the exam board. In any case, you should practise your presentation beforehand, perhaps to a family member or friend, so that you get used to an audience and get your timings right.

Audio podcast or audio presentation

If you have produced one of the audio briefs, then you should find producing an audio podcast or audio presentation relatively easy. It could be more interesting, however, to challenge yourself by producing your evaluation using a different form, in order to broaden your skills. This will need proper planning and scripting before you record, just as you would plan an essay before you write it. Running through before you record to get your timings right is useful, and should remove the need for rerecording because of overrun.

DVD with extras

If you have chosen a video brief, then it is possible that you have access to iDVD, which is a DVD extra package on most AppleMacs. Producing a DVD with extras will require some technical know-how, but is great fun.

You may want to combine two of the options; for example, a PowerPoint presentation during which you pause to screen the extras from your DVD.

Feedback

Before you begin tackling the evaluation, you need to analyse your own finished product and show it to a test audience (ideally, your target audience) to get some honest feedback. You might find it useful to draw up a questionnaire, asking:
- How well does the product fit the codes and conventions of the genre?
- How well does the product meet your needs?
- What does the product communicate to you?
- Which parts were most successful?
- Which parts were least successful?

■ Evaluation

Use the questions below to help your evaluation:

1 What were some of the main decisions and choices that you had to make during the planning and construction process?
   Where did your final idea come from? What influenced your choices? Did you discard any initial ideas, and if so, why?

2 How closely were you able to stick to your original plan?
   Did you find yourself deviating from your initial mock-up or storyboard? Was there a technical reason behind this?

3 How successfully do you feel your finished product matches the original brief?
   Is it reminiscent of other similar, real media products?

4 How does your finished product use the codes and conventions of the genre?
   Make specific reference to one or two examples of effective use of codes and conventions.

5 How did your target audience receive your finished product?
   What comments did you receive? Did they like/enjoy your product? Did they make any suggestions for improvements?

6 How has the feedback you received from your audience helped you in judging the success of your product?

7 Would you change anything if you had the opportunity to do this project again?

Glossary of key terms

acoustic: music played through non-electrical means

address bar: box that displays web address in full

advertising agency: the company that organises the advertising campaign for a client

advertorial: looks like an article but is actually a paid-for advertisement

anchorage: the fixing of a particular set of meanings to an image, usually through a caption

arc plot: a long-running storyline that is increasingly used in TV drama series

arcade game: a pay per play game played in a public locations

banner: text that stretches the width of a newspaper or magazine front cover

brand image: a set of values such as power, success, sexual appeal, that are associated with the brand through advertising

byline: a line at the top of an article or newspaper giving the author's name

caption: written text that anchors, or fixes, the meaning of an image

channel idents: logos, short films or animations that help to establish a channel's identity

ciné-vérité: hand-held footage with minimal editing

citizen journalism: where news providers use images, articles and blogs provided by the public

cliché: an image, phrase or storyline repeated so often it has become predictable

cliffhanger: an incomplete storyline at the end of a TV or radio episode

column: the narrow blocks of print that are part of the layout of a newspaper or magazine, making the articles easier to read

conglomerate: a large business organisation that is made up of a number of different companies

convergence: merger of two or more businesses or media products to create something new

crossover: describes a movement from one medium, genre or market into another

demographics: information on the characteristics of an audience, such as age, salary, gender

diegetic sound: sound within the world of the programme or film

dissolve: a cross-fade between two shots

docusoap: a reality TV series that mixes documentary with TV soap

dolly: a wheeled platform that the tripod sits on – used for tracking shots

downmarket audiences: low-income or less "serious" audiences

ensemble cast: a large cast where all characters have an equal level of importance

fade in/out: transition used in editing, where a shot gradually appears or disappears on screen

flagship programme: a programme that is used by a channel to promote itself

FMV: full motion video – a term used in video games

format: the particular style and structure of a TV programme or radio station or programme

globalisation: the coming together of countries around the world

graphics: drawn illustrations in any media text

headline: the title of any article in a newspaper, magazine or on the internet or the main stories in broadcast news

hierarchy: order according to how powerful a person or institution is

high angle: camera shoots from high up, looking down, often to emphasize weakness

iconography: a set of visual elements that indicate the genre of a media text

institution: any organisation that produces media texts or controls the media (such as OFCOM)

jingle: a short piece of music played between segments of a radio programme to reinforce brand identity; a short piece of music, sometimes with words, used to advertise a product on TV, radio or the internet

juxtaposition: the placing of written texts, still or moving image sequences next to each other to create a particular effect

layout: the positioning of words, images and graphics on a printed or webpage

lip-synch: when an artist mouths along or mimes to the lyrics of the song

low angle: camera shoots from low down, looking up, often to emphasize power

mainstream: appealing to a mass audience

marketing: the process of selling a media product

mass audience: a large, broad audience group

masthead: large title at top of front cover of magazine or newspaper

menu: series of buttons or links of importance on the homepage

metrosexual: a heterosexual man who works hard on his appearance

mixed schedule: when a channel broadcasts a range of different types of programmes

MMORGP: massively multiplayer online role playing game

mode of address: the way in which a media text speaks to its audience

multichannel television: many television channels competing for audiences

multiplayer: a game that allows more than one player

narrative: the way in which the story is told to the audience

'new' man: a 'new' man is seen as more in touch with his emotions

news agency: organisation that gathers and distributes news stories

news agenda: the selection, rejection and ordering of news stories

niche audience: a closely defined audience with a particular special interest

non-diegetic sound: sound not produced by a source within the world of the programme or film

outside broadcasts: reports recorded/reported from outside the studio

pan: movement of camera from side to side on its own axis

paparazzi: photographers of celebrities

parody: a copy of a narrative or genre for comic effect

pastiche: a copy of a narrative or genre, which can be light-hearted but is also respectful

pay per view: where the viewer pays for the individual programme they wish to watch

primetime: the most popular timeslot on television in the early evening

product placement: a branded product used in a TV programme or film

psychographics: defining an audience according to lifestyle, attitudes and interests

public service broadcasting: broadcasting in the public interest, designed to educate, inform and entertain

RAJAR: Radio Joint Audience Research – the organisation that measures radio audience figures

reality TV: focuses on the 'real lives' of individuals or groups

recorded sound: sound recorded at another time and played back during a show

remit: the terms that set out what a radio station must deliver

role model: a person that members of the audience can look up to and relate to

scheduling: placing a programme into a particular time slot

simulcast: programmes that are broadcast across more than one medium or wavelength at the same time

slogan: a memorable line or phrase that sums up the message of the advertising campaign

social class: a hierarchy (layering) in society based on education, occupation, income, etc.

social networking site: a website designed to act as a social environment for a group of people who share interests or activities

social realism: a gritty representation of social injustice or poverty, often with working class 'heroes'

soundbite: a short, quotable statement taken from a longer interview or speech

sound bridge: an editing technique where sound from the following sequence begins before the shot has changed location or vice versa

specialist schedule: when a channel broadcasts only one or two types of programme

spectatorship: a media concept that focuses on the ways in which audiences respond to texts

sponsorship: the method of a company investing money in return for the company's name to appear on the programme, event or product as a form of advertising

status bar: bar at the foot of a webpage that gives information about the page/site; bar that gives details about a player in a videogame

stripped schedule: when a channel has the same programmes on at the same time every day

tabloidisation: an increase in tabloid news values, with a greater focus on celebrity and human interest stories

target audience: the audience group that the media text is aimed at

terrestrial television: television from a non-satellite or cable source, available to everyone with access to a TV

theme: a central issue or idea contained within a text

tilt: movement of camera up or down while on its own axis

track: the camera moves with the action on a dolly or track

type casting: when an actor is constantly cast in the same sort of role

upmarket audiences: audiences with higher incomes

video game console: a machine devised specifically for playing videogames

visual imperative: when the demand for pictures dominates the news agenda

'Voice of God': the technique of using an authoritative voice-over that interprets the subject matter for the audience

vox pop: unrehearsed interviews with members of the public, usually in public places

watershed: 9 pm: the time after which progressively more adult material may be broadcast on television

zoom: the camera is fixed while the zoom lens moves closer to or further away from the subject

Glossary

Resources

Books

Teaching TV Sitcom by J Baker, 2003, BFI
Teaching Film at GCSE by J Baker and P Toland, 2007, BFI
Complete A-Z Media and Film Studies Handbook by V Clark et al, 2007, Hodder
GCSE Media Studies by V Clark, and R Harvey (eds), 2001, Longman
The Cinema Book by P Cook and M Bernink, 2008, BFI
Women and Soap Opera by C Geraghty, 1991, Polity
Teaching TV Advertising by W Helsby, 2004, Auteur
Teaching Television at GCSE by E Lewis, 2008, BFI
Action Adventure Films by R McInnes, 2003, Auteur
Studying the Media by T O'Sullivan, B Dutton and P Rayner, 2003, Arnold
100 Greatest TV Ads by M Robinson, 2000, Harper Collins
The Grammar of The Edit by R Thompson, 1997, Focal Press
Dictionary of Media & Communication Studies by J Watson and A Hill, 2003, Arnold
Teaching Digital Video Production at GCSE by M L White, 2007, BFI
Documentaries: A Teacher's Guide by J Wilcock, 2000, Auteur

Websites

www.advertisingarchives.co.uk: advertisements from the past
www.asa.org.uk: Advertising Standards Authority website
www.auteur.co.uk – publishes a range of classroom resources for teachers
www.barb.co.uk: Broadcasters' Audience Research Board (BARB)
www.bbc.co.uk: useful for articles as well as websites for BBC programmes
www.bfi.org.uk: informative articles on television
www.britishpathe.com: useful clips from Pathé News
www.cap.org.uk: the advertisers' code of practice
www.clearcast.co.uk: the organisation that clears TV advertisements for broadcast
www.eu.levi.com (Europe): Levi's website with advertisements
www.gamespot.com: a gaming website providing reviews and news on video games
www.holdthefrontpage.co.uk: useful site for journalists
www.imdb.com: very useful database on films
www.lbc.co.uk: website of LBC news radio
www.mediaedassociation.org.uk: Media education association
www.mediaguardian.co.uk: *The Guardian*'s media website
www.mediaknowall.com: useful site for Media students

www.mediauk.com: directory of UK media organisations
www.mtv.co.uk: news and videos from a variety of bands old and new
www.nme.com: webpage of NME (New Musical Express)
www.nmpft.org.uk: National Museum of Photography, Film and Television, Bradford
www.nrs.co.uk: the National Readership Survey site
www.oaa.org.uk: useful site for advertising
www.ocr.org.uk/Data/publications/support_materials/GCSE_Media_Studies_SM_CA_Guide.pdf: OCR resources
www.ofcom.org.uk: organisation that regulates broadcasting in the UK
www.pcc.org.uk: Press Complaints Commission
www.radiocentre.org: commercial radio website
www.screenonline.org.uk: articles and access clips from archive TV programmes
www.tellyads.com: range of TV advertisements past and present
www.theory.org.uk: David Gauntlett's site at University of Westminster
www.thesoapshow.com: a website on British, Australian and American soaps
www.tvark.co.uk: site with archive footage, particularly useful for title sequences and channel idents
www.tvhistory.btinternet.co.uk: some useful pages on British television history

Packs and publications

Doing News – Approaches to the 21st century (English and Media Centre)
The Media Pack – Units for GCSE English and Media (English and Media Centre)
Sight & Sound magazine – excellent resource on film and TV (BFI)
Media Magazine: a quarterly for Media students (English and Media Centre)

Useful contacts

British Film Institute Education, Belvedere Rd, South Bank, Waterloo, London SE1 8XT. Tel: 020 7957 4787, www.bfi.org.uk
The English & Media Centre, 18 Compton Terrace, Islington, London N1 2UN. Tel: 020 7359 8080, www.englishandmedia.co.uk
Film Education, 9 Berwick St, London, W1F 0BP. Tel: 020 7292 7330, www.filmeducation.org
The Video Studio, Richmond upon Thames College, Egerton Rd, Twickenham, Middlesex, TW2 7SJ. Tel: 020 8607 8423, email: video@rutc.ac.uk